The DevelopMentor Series

Don Box, Editor

Addison-Wesley has joined forces with DevelopMentor, a premiere developer resources company, to produce a series of technical books written by developers for developers. DevelopMentor boasts a prestigious technical staff that includes some of the world's best-known computer science professionals.

*"Works in **The DevelopMentor Series** will be practical and informative sources on the tools and techniques for applying component-based technologies to real-world, large-scale distributed systems."*
—Don Box

Titles in the Series:

Essential COM
Don Box
0-201-63446-5

Essential XML
Beyond Markup
Don Box, Aaron Skonnard, and John Lam
0-201-70914-7

Programming Windows Security
Keith Brown
0-201-60442-6

Advanced Visual Basic 6
Power Techniques for Everyday Programs
Matthew Curland
0-201-70712-8

Transactional COM+
Building Scalable Applications
Tim Ewald
0-201-61594-0

ASP Internals
Jon Flanders
0-201-61618-1

Essential IDL
Interface Design for COM
Martin Gudgin
0-201-61595-9

Debugging Windows Programs
Strategies, Tools, and Techniques for Visual C++ Programmers
Everett N. McKay and Mike Woodring
0-201-70238-X

Watch for future titles in The DevelopMentor Series.

Essential IDL

Interface Design for COM

Martin Gudgin

Addison-Wesley

Boston • San Francisco • New York • Toronto • Montreal
London • Munich • Paris • Madrid
Capetown • Sydney • Tokyo • Singapore • Mexico City

The publisher offers discounts on this book when ordered in quantity for special sales. For more information, please contact:

Pearson Education Corporate Sales Division
One Lake Street
Upper Saddle River, NJ 07458
(800) 382-3419
corpsales@pearsontechgroup.com

Visit us on the Web at www.awl.com/cseng/

Library of Congress Cataloging-in-Publication Data

Gudgin, Martin
    Essential IDL : interface design for COM / Martin Gudgin.
      p. cm. – (DevelopMentor series)
    Includes index.
    ISBN 0-201-61595-9
    1. IDL (Computer program language)   2. Application software–Development 3.
    Computer interfaces. I. Title. II. Series.

    QA76.73.I194 G83 2000
    005.13'3–dc21
                                                                    00-050427

ISBN 0-201-61595-9

Text printed on recycled paper.
1 2 3 4 5 6 7 8 9 10—CRS—0403020100
First printing, December, 2000

To Hayley, for being there

Contents

Figures

Chapter 5

Chapter 6

Tables

Listings

Foreword

Type is everything.

This book describes the type system of the Component Object Model in greater detail than any other source I have encountered. More importantly, it details the current state of the Microsoft IDL compiler (MIDL.EXE), the tool used by COM developers to define new application-specific types for use in COM. In a perfect world, MIDL.EXE would perform exactly as expected. Unfortunately, we don't live in such a world. Fortunately, Martin has taken the time to document the darker corners of MIDL.EXE so that we all might avoid the more hazardous neighborhoods of [oleautomation] and /Oicf.

It is easy to dismiss a book on IDL at this stage in COM's evolution. With the Common Language Runtime about to revolutionize component development by replacing IUnknown and IDL with System.Object and integrated metadata, one could reasonably question the role of IDL in modern component development. However, given that type information is the key to integrating managed and native code in the Common Language Runtime, proper use of IDL today ensures that your COM components have a future in the forthcoming .NET world. Moreover, as long as key operating system components continue to be written in native (that is, unmanaged) code, using IDL and TLBs to access those components will be critical even after every application moves to C#.

While the Common Language Runtime may eliminate the need for a distinct interface definition language, the value of defining typed interfaces independent from the components they apply to remains equally relevant in the new world. In that sense, the spirit of IDL will live on long after the world has seen its last IUnknown-based interface. Until that day comes, we are fortunate to have this book to guide us through the syntax and semantics of COM IDL.

Don Box
Manhattan Beach, California
September, 2000

Preface

All developers targeting the Component Object Model (COM) need a working knowledge of the COM Interface Definition Language (IDL). IDL is a reasonably complex language and can be quite arcane, and acquiring a knowledge of it has been an uphill struggle. This book provides a comprehensive description of IDL and how to use it, making it accessible and understandable. It takes an example-based, top-down approach, laying out the various IDL constructs, why they exist, what they are for, and how and when to use them in interface definitions. In each case, example IDL is provided and, where applicable, source code is provided for client and object in C++ and Visual Basic. The source code examples are not intended to be cut and pasted into existing applications; rather, they illustrate particular points about IDL and its relationship to client and object implementations.

This is a book about COM IDL and hence does not cover IDL keywords, attributes, or other constructs that are usable only from standard Remote Procedure Call (RPC). In addition, the most important parts of IDL are concerned with efficient marshaling of data as performed by the COM interception layer, and the majority of the discussion is based on the IDL constructs that affect the behavior of that interception layer. IDL attributes that have no effect on the interception layer will for the most part be ignored.

This book represents a significant amount of research on and testing of the various facilities that IDL provides. In some cases, the information presented may be at variance with the official documentation. The author encourages readers to test the assertions in this book for themselves and confirm that they are correct. All testing performed by the author was done using Microsoft IDL (MIDL) compiler Version 5.03.0280. Earlier versions may not support some of the features detailed in this book.

New versions of the MIDL compiler will emerge, and IDL itself will evolve. One day, IDL per se may disappear completely, but developers will still need to deal with the things that IDL allows them to describe. Given its popularity and general applicability, eXtensible Markup Language (XML) seems to be an obvious choice as a basis for a description language. To get a head start on the future of IDL (or the IDL of the future), the reader is encouraged to read the W3C Working Draft on XML Schema and the W3C note describing the Simple Object Access Protocol:

http://www.w3.org/TR/xmlschema-0
http://www.w3.org/TR/xmlschema-1
http://www.w3.org/TR/xmlschema-2
http://www.w3.org/TR/soap.html

The author welcomes feedback; any and all questions, observations, and corrections should be sent by e-mail to *marting@develop.com.* A Web site for this book is maintained by the author at *http://www.develop.com/marting/essentialidl* and includes an errata page and samples.

Intended Audience

This book is aimed at developers and interface designers using COM, Microsoft Transaction Server (MTS), or COM+ from C++ or Visual Basic. It assumes that the reader has a working knowledge of COM, such as can be found in *Essential COM* by Don Box or in *Programming Distributed Applications with COM+ and Microsoft Visual Basic 6.0* by Ted Pattison.

What to Expect

This book is divided into two parts. The first six chapters describe the various constructs available in IDL using fully formed sentences with subjects, verbs, and adjectives. The IDL constructs are shown along with the client-side call sequences and method implementations. Each chapter other than the first concludes with a list of guidelines for using the IDL constructs discussed. The last four chapters provide a tabular reference for IDL types, modifiers, keywords, and attributes.

Chapter 1: Hello, IDL

Many COM developers are either unaware of the existence of IDL or unsure as to why it exists. Chapter 1 describes the fundamentals of IDL and the reasons for its existence along with the basics of defining interfaces.

Chapter 2: Structure of an IDL file

The MIDL compiler can output two forms of type information. Which one is generated often depends on the position of a given IDL construct within the IDL file. Chapter 2 covers the details of generating type information and building proxy-stub DLLs, local and remote interfaces, and the various file management constructs.

Chapter 3: Data types and interface issues

Using the proper data types is critical to interface design and component integration. Chapter 3 deals with the details of the primitive IDL types and also covers object references; user-defined types; and enums, structures, and unions. Information about how to ensure that the correct information is present in any generated type library is also presented. This chapter also provides a discussion of interface inheritance.

Chapter 4: Pointers and arrays

Many interfaces need to support output parameters, while others need support for arrays of data. Chapter 4 deals with the details of pointers in IDL, including the different ways that IDL and the COM interception layer treat top-level and embedded pointers. It also covers various array types, including fixed arrays, conformant arrays, and SAFEARRAYs.

Chapter 5: Aliasing

IDL provides support for method and type aliasing, both of which allow interface designers to inject arbitrary code into the COM interception layer. Chapter 5 details how to use both types of aliasing, including two approaches to type aliasing: [transmit_as] and [wire_marshal].

Chapter 6: Asynchronous COM

Windows 2000 provides support for asynchronous COM calls from both client and server perspectives. Chapter 6 describes the IDL attribute that makes this possible, along with the details of writing the client-side and server-side code.

Chapter 7: IDL Types

IDL provides certain built-in, primitive types, and the system IDL files provide several constructed types. Chapter 7 is a reference for all the primitive IDL types plus the constructed types `BSTR`, `SAFEARRAY`, `VARIANT`, and `VARIANT _BOOL`. It provides information such as the size of each type, the type library and Oicf mappings for each type, and the C++ and Visual Basic mappings.

Chapter 8: IDL Type Modifiers

IDL allows types to be qualified with certain type modifiers, including `const`, `signed`, and `unsigned`. Chapter 8 is a reference to all the modifiers supported by IDL and includes information such as whether a given modifier is represented in a type library and the data types to which the modifier can be applied.

Chapter 9: IDL Keywords

IDL provides a large number of keywords with various uses from defining interfaces and structures to importing other IDL files. Chapter 9 is a reference for all the IDL keywords from `coclass` to `union`. The information presented includes the forms of type information that represent the keyword, which attributes are mandatory, and which are optional.

Chapter 10: IDL Attributes

The keywords and other constructs in IDL can be annotated with various attributes. Chapter 10 is a reference for all the IDL attributes related to marshaling, plus some others, and includes information about whether a given attribute is present in the type library along with the keywords and constructs to which the attribute is applicable.

Acknowledgments

Although this book has but a single author, many people contributed to its content in many different ways. The major contribution was made by my family, and I would like to thank my wife, Hayley, and my two sons, Matthew and Samuel, for giving me the time and space to write this book. I know that at times it was hard, and I really appreciate all their help and understanding.

A host of reviewers provided useful, insightful, and comprehensive feedback during the writing process. Members of the host include Daniel Sinclair, Dan Sullivan, Simon Horrell, Paul Hollingsworth, Steve Johnson, Naveen Thakur, Tim Ewald, Chris Sells, Don Box, Steve Rodgers, and Bob Beauchemin.

Special thanks go to Don Box, Tim Ewald, Simon Horrell, and Keith Brown for putting up with numerous lengthy telephone, e-mail, and face-to-face conversations about knotty IDL problems.

Thanks also to the numerous people on the DCOM and ATL lists at *http://discuss.microsoft.com* for the various discussions on IDL-related minutiae.

Thanks to all the staffers and instructors at DevelopMentor for making it such a fun place to work and for covering for me when I disappeared for large chunks of time in order to write.

I would like to thank Kristin Erickson, my editor at Addison-Wesley, for all her help with the writing process and for knowing exactly when to badger me and when to leave me be. Thanks especially for putting up with my complete inability to stick to deadlines! Thanks also to all the production staff at Addison-Wesley who turned my electronic musings into a physical entity: Kristin Erickson, Marcy Barnes, and Jacquelyn Doucette.

For me, writing a book is a strange mixture of pleasure and pain. I hope that this volume brings the reader much of the former and none of the latter.

Martin Gudgin
Ashton Keynes, England
August 2000
http://www.develop.com/marting

Chapter 1

Hello, IDL

What Is IDL?

COM interfaces represent the boundaries between components. These boundaries may be programming language boundaries or they may be thread, process, or machine boundaries. COM Interface Definition Language (IDL) is used to describe COM interfaces unambiguously. Defining interfaces is the primary purpose of IDL and should be the first task in any COM project.

Defining an interface means defining a set of abstract methods that a class will implement and a client will call on an object that is an instance of that class. This effectively specifies a contract to which the various parties must adhere. The client and the class/object[1] are party to the contract as is the COM runtime. In order to cross an interface boundary successfully, three things must be specified unambiguously to the satisfaction of all parties.

First, because COM provides an in-memory interoperability model, allowing the client and object to be directly connected, the physical stack frame for each method must be defined—how many parameters the method takes, which order they are in, and what their types are. All types in IDL are of known size, and consequently no ambiguities exist in IDL with respect to the size of a given data type.

The client cares about the stack layout because it has to construct the correct stack frame in order to make the method call. Any mismatch between what the object expects and what the client passes—be it type, order, or number of parameters—will result in an error. The object cares about the stack layout because it has to use the parameters passed in by the client to perform its work.

---

[1] The term "client" is used to refer to any consumer of a COM object. Occasionally, for reasons of consistency, the author will use the term "object" where the term "class" would otherwise be more appropriate.

It may also have to return information to the client. Again, any mismatch between what the contract specifies and what the object passes back will result in an error.

Second, the order of the methods in the interface is specified. The methods are laid out in a table, sometimes called a virtual function table or v-table. Each method in the interface has its own entry in the v-table. Because interface definitions are abstract, the v-table entries are initially just placeholders. When a class implements an interface, the compiler or interpreter fills in each placeholder with the address of the corresponding method implementation, as shown in Figure 1.1.

The ordering of methods within an interface is important, because method calls are made using an offset into the v-table. This provides a layer of indirection, as the client does not need to know the actual memory address of the method it is calling. The table is also important to the object, because the object needs to make sure that the correct method implementations are present at the correct offsets.

In a world where clients make direct calls into objects, the story would end here. A client would construct a stack frame and make a call through the v-table. The object would access the parameters on the stack and service the method call, placing any output parameters on the stack to return them to

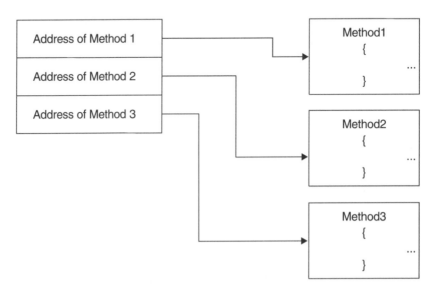

Figure 1.1 Layout of interface methods in a v-table

ESSENTIAL IDL

the client. This is the scenario shown in Figure 1.2, where the client has a direct reference, r, to an interface on the object.

However, more often then not, clients and objects are not directly connected. Every object in COM lives in a context, a runtime environment that satisfies the needs of the object. All methods on the object must execute within its context. Similarly, clients also live in a context. If the client and the object are in different contexts, they cannot communicate directly but must communicate through an interceptor. An interceptor is a piece of code supplied by the COM runtime that is used to cross a context boundary. The interceptor may provide runtime services such as object synchronization and transaction support.

When a client and an object are in different contexts, they do not share a call stack, and the object cannot directly access the input parameters placed on the stack by the client. Similarly, the client cannot directly access output parameters placed on the stack by the object. In such cases, the call stack must be copied from one context to another, and the interceptor is responsible for performing the copy. This involves serializing and deserializing the parameters, a process known as marshaling.

To ensure that serialization and deserialization work correctly, the interface definition specifies a third constraint—the serialization format, also known as the wire representation, for a given method. This wire representation is the third thing specified by the interface definition and can be thought of as a logical stack frame that defines the order and size of the serialized parameters.

A cross-context call may in fact be cross-host. Different platforms may define different physical stack frames and may also encode data differently—

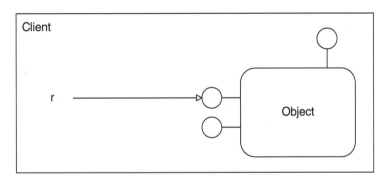

Figure 1.2   Direct connection between client and object

with respect to byte ordering, for example. The wire representation is also able to deal with any mismatch in these two areas. Any potential difference in physical stack frame is dealt with by mapping to and from the wire representation during marshaling. Differences in data encoding are dealt with using a "reader-makes-right" technique in which the marshaling process writes out the data and a bit field that specifies the encoding format used. This bit field specifies three things: ASCII or EBCDIC character encoding; IEEE, VAX, or IBM floating point format; and little- or big-endian byte ordering. When the data is unmarshaled, the interceptor checks the bit field and performs any necessary conversion. Hence, the "reader," the unmarshaling interceptor, "makes" the data "right" for the platform on which it is running.

The interception code is created dynamically by the COM runtime based on the v-table layout and the physical and logical stack frames described in the IDL. Without an interface definition, the runtime would be unable to build interception code correctly. The COM runtime needs to know the physical stack frame and the wire representation for a method in order to provide marshaling support. It also needs to know the order of methods in the v-table in order to build a v-table inside the interceptor for the client to call.

An interceptor consists of two portions: the proxy and the stub. The proxy lives in the client's context, and the stub lives in the same context as the object. The two are connected by a piece of plumbing called the channel, as shown in Figure 1.3.

As far as the client is concerned, the proxy is the object and implements the set of interfaces in which the client is interested. However, when the client makes a method call, it does not execute directly. Rather, the proxy examines the input parameters on the stack and serializes them according to the wire representation into a request packet. The method id, the index of the called method in the v-table, is also serialized. The request packet is then passed to the channel.

The channel is an abstraction of the underlying communication channel between the proxy and the stub. It is responsible for transmitting the request packet across the context boundary and delivering it to the stub. The stub extracts the method id and deserializes the parameters from the request packet, constructing a stack frame. This stack frame is logically equivalent to the stack

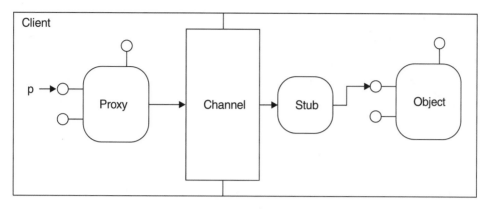

Figure 1.3   Client and Object in separate contexts

frame constructed by the client even though the physical layout may be different. The stub then calls the object, which executes the method. When the
method ends, the stub serializes any output parameters and the value returned
by the method into a response packet. The channel then transmits the response
packet back to the proxy, which deserializes the output parameters and the
return value and returns control to the client. The request and response are
shown in Figure 1.4.

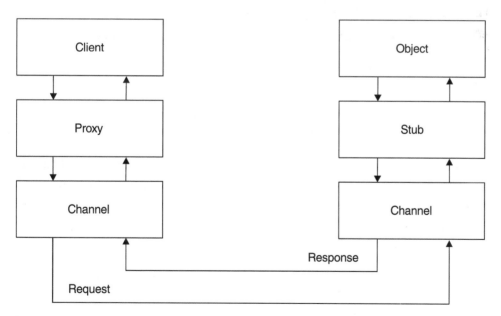

Figure 1.4   Request and response

The proxy, the stub, and the channel, together, make up the interception code, and whenever a context boundary is crossed, interception code must be present. As mentioned earlier, the more obvious context boundaries include thread, process, and host boundaries. Other, more subtle boundaries include different security contexts, different transactional contexts, and different synchronization contexts.

Defining Interfaces

IDL has a syntax based on the C programming language, but it is not an implementation language. Rather, it is a declarative language, allowing developers to describe COM interfaces and other types, such as structures, in a language-neutral fashion. This makes IDL the "lingua franca" for COM developers, a standard language that can be used to communicate the syntax of a particular interface contract. The syntax of the interface defines everything needed by the three parties mentioned earlier: the client, the object, and the runtime. The syntax defines the inputs and outputs for a given set of methods but does not provide any information about the meanings of those inputs and outputs or how they are related. The semantics of an interface have to be communicated through documentation.[2]

Interfaces are defined in IDL using the interface keyword, which is followed by a colon and the name of a base interface. The interface inherits all the methods of the base interface, which either is, or ultimately derives from, IUnknown. An attribute block precedes the interface keyword. Attribute blocks appear in a variety of places in IDL and consist of various IDL attributes enclosed in square brackets. In all cases, the attributes apply to the IDL construct they precede, specifying certain characteristics or properties of that construct. Attributes are effectively metadata about the construct to which they are attached. For example, consider the following interface definition.

```
[
  uuid(1FC63996-A9D7-4a72-8F10-B1A1F6907291),
  object
]
```

---

[2] Some semantics about parameters, specifically pointer types, can be specified in IDL, as shown in Chapter 4.

```
interface IHelloIDL : IUnknown {
  HRESULT Hello();
}
```

The attribute block in this case contains two attributes. The [uuid] attribute defines the 128-bit unique identifier for this particular interface. The symbolic name of the interface, IHelloIDL, is not guaranteed to be unique, and therefore a separate identifier that is unique is needed. COM interfaces are immutable; once an interface has been published it cannot be changed. If modifications need to be made after publication, a new interface with a new UUID must be defined. The [object] attribute marks the interface as being a COM interface rather than an RPC interface.[3]

Given that the interface above has but a single method and that the method takes no parameters, it may seem somewhat redundant to have IDL describe a stack frame for the method and an order for the methods in the interface. However, even in this simple case a stack frame must be constructed and an offset used to make the call. For example, consider the following Visual Basic call sequence.

```
Public Sub MakeCalls ( obj1 As IHelloIDL,
                       obj2 As IHelloIDL )
obj1.Hello
MsgBox "Made first call through obj1"
obj2.Hello
MsgBox "Made second call through obj2"
End Sub
```

There are two calls to the Hello method in the example above: one made through object reference obj1 and the other through obj2. Even though no explicit parameters are placed on the stack, two implicit parameters are needed: the object reference through which the call is being made and the return address. The object reference must be placed on the stack, because every COM method has an implicit first parameter, often referred to as the "this" or "me" pointer, which is used to locate a particular object instance. The

---

[3] The object attribute used to be mandatory, but more recent MIDL compilers use the presence of a base interface to deduce that an interface is a COM interface, because interface inheritance is not supported in RPC.

"this" pointer provides the identity of the object, which binds together its state and behavior. If the object reference were not present on the stack, the method implementation would have no way to determine which object instance to work with.

Whenever any method call is made, whether it is to a local subroutine or to a COM object, the called function needs to know where to return to after it has executed. So whenever a method call is about to be made, the return address is placed on the stack. Figure 1.5 shows the return address and the "this" pointer on the stack.

The "this" pointer is placed on the stack by the machine instruction at address 0x00401760. The method call happens at address 0x00401761. The

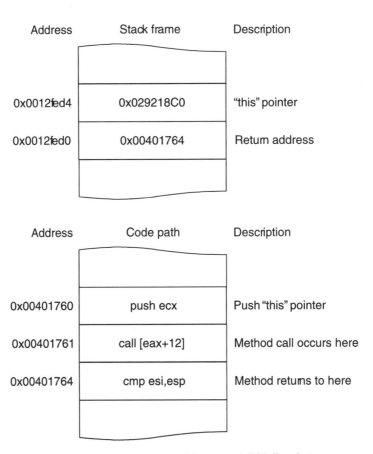

Figure 1.5   Stack frame showing return address and "this" pointer

return address is the address of the next line of code, 0x00401764 in this case. The value 0x00401764 is placed on the stack after the "this" pointer. Note that for the second call through `obj2`, the value of the "this" pointer and the return address are different.

When interception code exists between the client and the object, the client-side calling code looks the same, at both the source code and the machine code level. However, the "this" pointer the client holds identifies the proxy, and the method call enters the proxy instead of the object. Because the client and the target object may be in different address spaces, the proxy cannot hold a "this" pointer to the target object. Instead, the proxy contains a token that represents the target object. This token is a network-wide identifier for a particular interface on a particular object instance. The proxy passes the method id and the token to the stub, and the stub uses this information to execute the required method on the object. While the stub and the object are executing code, the proxy is blocked waiting for the method to return. When the stub returns control to the proxy, the proxy then returns control to the client.

Adding Parameters

In the example above, the interception code did not have to marshal any explicit parameters, because there were none. Only the method id and the token representing the target object were present in the request packet. Typically, interface methods have parameters. They may take input parameters and may also have output parameters. For efficiency reasons, IDL distinguishes between input and output parameters by requiring that all method parameters be annotated with a directionality attribute. Consider the following interface.

```
[
  uuid(AFCEF672-4482-465a-AF99-A3F22F42E707),
  object
]
interface ISimpleCalls : IUnknown {
  HRESULT TakeAShort ( [in] short s );
  HRESULT ReturnAShort ( [out] short* ps );
}
```

Parameters marked with the `[in]` attribute are input parameters and are present only in the request packet.[4] Calling TakeAShort in C++ would look like this:

```
short s = 50;
HR(pObj->TakeAShort ( s ));[5]
```

and the Visual Basic equivalent would be:

```
Dim s As Integer
s = 50
pObj.TakeAShort s
```

A local variable is passed into the method, the value of the variable is placed on the stack, and the proxy serializes it into the request packet. The stub recreates the stack on the object side using the value in the request packet. The return value, the HRESULT, is passed back in the response packet, and the proxy stores it in the `hr` variable in the C++ case. The Visual Basic runtime will convert failure HRESULTs into language-level exceptions. The stack frame for the call is shown in Figure 1.6. Note that the information in the stack frame is the same for the client call into the proxy and for the stub call into the object. The stub will create a local variable and initialize it with the value from the request packet. The actual value of the return address will be different, but both it and the parameter value 50 will be present.

Parameters marked with the `[out]` attribute are present only in the response packet. All `[out]` parameters must be passed by reference and so must use the pointer syntax in IDL. This translates to the same pointer syntax in C++ and to `ByRef` in Visual Basic. The parameter needs to be passed by reference so that the proxy can store the value returned by the object in a location

---

[4] The MIDL compiler assumes that parameters that do not have a directionality attribute are marked `[in]`. However, it is considered bad style to have missing directionality attributes, because it implies that the interface designer has not thought sufficiently about the interface contract.

[5] The HR macro used here and elsewhere in this book is defined as `#define HR(ex) { HRESULT _hr = ex; if(FAILED(_hr)) return _hr; },`

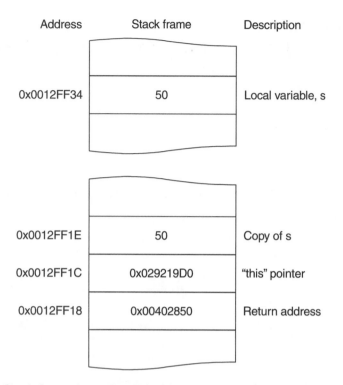

Address	Stack frame	Description
0x0012FF34	50	Local variable, s
0x0012FF1E	50	Copy of s
0x0012FF1C	0x029219D0	"this" pointer
0x0012FF18	0x00402850	Return address

Figure 1.6   Stack frame for call to TakeAShort

accessible to the client. The call to `ReturnAShort` would look like this in C++:

```
short s = 0;
HR(pObj->ReturnAShort ( &s ));
```

and like this in Visual Basic:

```
Dim s As Integer
s=0
pObj.ReturnAShort s
```

The client passes the address of the local variable `s` into the proxy. However, the proxy passes only the method id into the request packet. The stub allocates storage for the output parameter and passes the address of this storage to the object. The object executes the method and returns some value, say 42, to the stub. The stub serializes the value into the response packet and returns to the proxy. The proxy then deserializes the value from the response packet and writes the value to the address passed in by the client. Because this was the address of the local variable s, the value 42 is stored in s. The stack frame before the call is shown in Figure 1.7. Note that the location of the local variable s, rather than the content of the variable, is placed on the stack. As with the call to `TakeAShort`, this is the case both when the client calls the proxy and when the stub calls the object. After the call, the bottom of the stack is cleaned up and the returned value is placed into the local variable s, as shown in Figure 1.8.

The Visual Basic call sequence shown on page 11 is atypical. The usual call sequence has the local variable as the target of the assignment operator.

```
Dim s As Integer
s=pObj.ReturnAShort
```

This can be achieved in IDL by annotating the parameter with the `[retval]` attribute.

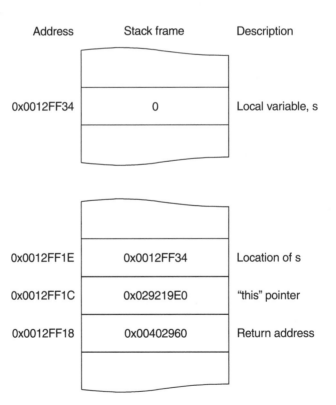

Address	Stack frame	Description
0x0012FF34	0	Local variable, s
0x0012FF1E	0x0012FF34	Location of s
0x0012FF1C	0x029219E0	"this" pointer
0x0012FF18	0x00402960	Return address

Figure 1.7 Stack frame before call to ReturnAShort

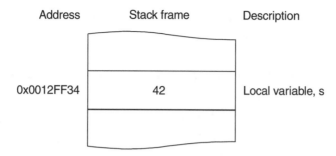

Address	Stack frame	Description
0x0012FF34	42	Local variable, s

Figure 1.8   Stack frame after call to ReturnAShort

```
HRESULT ReturnAShort ( [out,retval] short* ps );
```

This marks the parameter as the logical return value from the method. The Visual Basic runtime uses this information to allow the syntax above. The `[retval]` attribute can be applied only to the last parameter in a method, and the parameter must also be annotated with the `[out]` attribute. Note that `[retval]` has no effect on native C++ clients.

Parameters can be marked with both `[in]` and `[out]` attributes.

```
HRESULT TakeAShortModifyItAndReturn ( [in, out] short* ps );
```

Note that the parameter is a reference parameter, as in the pure `[out]` case. Parameters thus marked will be present in both request and response packets, possibly with different values in each case. Marking simple types with both directionality attributes in this fashion poses no problems, but annotating more complex types as `[in,out]` is dangerous. For a discussion of why this is the case, see *Effective COM* (Box, et al., Addison-Wesley, 1999), Item 15.

More on Directionality

Directionality attributes provide information that cannot be described in a programming language such as C++ or Visual Basic. They allow IDL to be specific where programming languages are ambiguous. Given the following C++ method signature:

```
HRESULT M1 ( short* ps );
```

and the corresponding Visual Basic method signature:

```
Private Sub M1 ( ByRef ps As Integer )
```

there is no way to tell whether the parameter, ps, is used for input, output, or both. Because programming languages tend to assume that caller and callee share an address space and a stack frame, all reference parameters are inherently bidirectional, and there is no way to specify otherwise.[6]

As mentioned earlier, in COM there are many occasions in which the client and object do not share a stack frame and other occasions in which they do not share an address space, either. In these cases, the interception code needs to know whether parameters are used for input or output. This is partly for efficiency reasons: there is no point in marshaling data from the client to the server if the server will not use that data. In some cases, the interceptor needs to know about directionality in order to avoid errors.

Consider the case of returning a linked list from a C++ function, with the structure definition and function prototype

```
struct Node {
   long data;
   struct Node*pNext;
}
void Fn ( struct Node* pHead );
```

and the call sequence

```
Node head;
Fn ( &head );
```

Because of the shared address space, the address of the local variable, head, will be passed to the method. The method will then fill in the parameter with the list content and return to the caller. In IDL terms, the parameter is an [out] parameter.

Consider what would happen if directionality attributes did not exist in IDL and the call was a COM method call. The interceptor would have to marshal all method parameters into both the request and response packets. In the example

---

[6] The const keyword could be used in C++, but a determined developer could override it using const_cast.

above, the local variable, `head`, contains random data on the stack. Marshaling the variable into the request packet would at best result in an access violation. At worst, a random number of list nodes containing random data would be passed to the server.

Directionality also has an impact on memory management in COM, and this will be discussed in detail, along with a more in-depth treatment of pointers, in Chapter 4.

Conclusions

IDL provides a programming-language-neutral way of defining COM interfaces, thus avoiding assumptions typically made by programming languages and allowing precise, unambiguous definitions. The IDL definition of an interface forms a contract among the client, the object, and the COM runtime with respect to the number of methods, their order within the interface, and the number, order, type, and directionality of the method parameters. The interface definition also defines a serialization format for each method in the interface. The COM runtime uses this information to build interception code dynamically at runtime.

Chapter 2

Structure of an IDL File

Interfaces and Type Information

Interface definitions located in IDL files are compiled using the MIDL compiler, MIDL.EXE, which generates various forms of type information as output. This type information provides a representation of the interfaces and other types described in the IDL that are typically parsed by compilers, development tools, and the COM runtime. Some of this type information is textual in nature and language-specific, and some is binary in nature and language-neutral.

Type information in COM actually takes various forms, describes several different kinds of information, is generated from many different sources, and is stored in a multitude of different locations and file formats. For example, component categories are used to group classes by capability and are primarily of interest to clients. This information is stored in the registry.[1] Type information regarding an object's runtime requirements, such as transaction support, synchronization, or object pooling, is stored in the COM+ catalog. This type information has an effect on how interceptors get constructed but has no bearing on the IDL or marshaling discussions in this book.[2] All MIDL-generated type information is concerned with either providing marshaling information to the COM remoting architecture or providing information about component capabilities to development tools or the COM+ runtime. This chapter and indeed the majority of this book generally focus on the former.

---

[1] For more information about component categories, see Chapter 3 of *Essential COM* by Don Box (Addison-Wesley, 1998).

[2] For a complete treatment of the COM+ catalog and the interception services the COM+ runtime supports, see *Transactional COM+* by Tim Ewald (Addison-Wesley, 2000).

The three parties to the interface contract discussed in Chapter 1 use type information generated from IDL files. Clients use type information to generate code to call methods on the interface. Objects use type information to populate v-tables with correctly formed entry points. Interceptors are dynamically generated from type information and loaded as needed by the COM runtime to provide services such as marshaling and transaction support. At the point at which an interceptor is needed for an interface, the COM runtime uses the interface identifier, the uuid, to locate a class that is able to build an interceptor for the interface from its type information. For historical reasons, this type information will be in one of two forms: either standard type information or a form known as Oicf type information.[3] Standard type information grew out of the needs of development environments such as Visual Basic, while Oicf type information grew out of the needs of the COM runtime.

An IDL file is, broadly speaking, divided into two parts: definitions inside the library block and definitions outside the library block. The presence or absence of each of these sections controls which output files, and, therefore, which kinds of type information, the MIDL compiler will generate by default.

Inside the Library Block

A type library is a binary file containing standard type information about the types described in the IDL. Type libraries can be examined by any party through the system-provided implementations of the `ITypeLib` and `ITypeInfo` interfaces returned by the `LoadTypeLib` and `LoadRegTypeLib` API functions. If a library block is present in the IDL file, the MIDL compiler will generate a type library. For example, given the file `atom.idl` shown in Listing 2.1, the MIDL compiler will generate a type library, `atom.tlb`.

Listing 2.1 Initial atom.idl file

```
// atom.idl
[
    uuid(48705370-DE6A-4347-9C51-A8F2D1947C0B)
]
```

---

[3] The origins behind this name shall remain shrouded in mystery until later in this chapter.

```
library AtomLib {
  [
    uuid(FAC852FF-35FE-48D3-B3FC-89D1364839AB),
    object
  ]
  interface IAtom : IUnknown {
    HRESULT Collide ( [in] IAtom* pOtherAtom );
  }
}
```

In general, the generated type library should be registered with the system using the `RegisterTypeLib` API function or a tool that calls this function.[4] Registering the type library is an optional step that allows development tools and type browsers to know about the type library. `RegisterTypeLib` writes the registry entries COM needs to locate the type library at runtime. The following information would be present under `HKEY_CLASSES_ROOT\Typelib` for the example shown above.

```
[HKCR\TypeLib\
  {48705370-DE6A-4347-9C51-A8F2D1947C0B}]
[HKCR\TypeLib\
  {48705370-DE6A-4347-9C51-A8F2D1947C0B}\0.0]
@="AtomLib"
[HKCR\TypeLib\
  {48705370-DE6A-4347-9C51-A8F2D1947C0B}\0.0\0]
[HKCR\TypeLib\
  {48705370-DE6A-4347-9C51-A8F2D1947C0B}\0.0\0\win32]
@="C:\\atom\\atom.tlb"
```

The `LoadRegTypeLib` API uses these registry keys to load the type library on the basis of its library ID and version number. The presence of these keys also informs COM-aware tools and type browsers of the existence and location of the `atom.tlb` file.

Currently, the type library file `atom.tlb` serves only one purpose; it provides type information for `IAtom` to development environments such as Visual Basic, enabling those environments to call and implement the interface. To enable the COM runtime to use the type information to build an interceptor for

---

[4] Stand-alone type libraries can be registered with the regtlib or oleview utilities. Type libraries embedded within component DLLs are normally registered automatically by registering the component.

`IAtom`, the interface definition must be annotated with the `[oleautomation]` attribute,[5] as shown in Listing 2.2.

Listing 2.2 IAtom annotated with [oleautomation] attribute

```
// atom.idl
[
  uuid(48705370-DE6A-4347-9C51-A8F2D1947C0B)
]
library AtomLib {
  [
    uuid(FAC852FF-35FE-48D3-B3FC-89D1364839AB),
    object,
    oleautomation
  ]
  interface IAtom : IUnknown {
    HRESULT Collide ( [in] IAtom* pOtherAtom );
  }
}
```

Now, registering the resulting type library with the system will generate extra registry entries under the `HKEY_CLASSES_ROOT\Interface` key. For example, shown below are the registry entries for `IAtom`.

```
[HKCR\Interface\
{FAC852FF-35FE-48D3-B3FC-89D1364839AB}]
@="IAtom"
[HKCR\Interface\
{FAC852FF-35FE-48D3-B3FC-89D1364839AB}\ProxyStubClsid]
@="{00020424-0000-0000-C000-000000000046}"
[HKCR\Interface\
{FAC852FF-35FE-48D3-B3FC-89D1364839AB}\
ProxyStubClsid32]
@="{00020424-0000-0000-C000-000000000046}"
[HKCR\Interface\
{FAC852FF-35FE-48D3-B3FC-89D1364839AB}\TypeLib]
@="{48705370-DE6A-4347-9C51-A8F2D1947C0B}"
"Version"="0.0"
```

When any interceptor for an interface is needed, the COM runtime looks under `HKEY_CLASSES_ROOT\Interface` for the interface's IID and uses the `ProxyStubClsid32` key to locate a class. That class implements a system

---

[5] The `[dual]` attribute implies the `[oleautomation]` attribute and, for the purposes of this discussion, would have the same effect.

interface, `IPSFactoryBuffer`, which has two methods, `CreateProxy` and `CreateStub`, whose signatures are shown below.

```
HRESULT CreateProxy ( [in] IUnknown *pUnkOuter,
                      [in] REFIID riid,
                      [out] IRpcProxyBuffer **ppProxy,
                      [out] void **ppv );
HRESULT CreateStub ( [in] REFIID riid,
                     [in, unique] IUnknown *pUnkServer,
                     [out] IRpcStubBuffer **ppStub );
```

The runtime calls these methods, passing in the IID of the required interface, and the class is able to construct an interceptor based on the type information for that interface.

In the case of `IAtom`, the class is provided by the system in `OLEAUT32.DLL` and is known by various names, including the universal marshaler or the type library marshaler. The universal marshaler can locate the type information for `IAtom` through the `Typelib` key under `HKEY_CLASSES_ROOT\Interface\ {FAC852FF-35FE-48D3-B3FC-89D1364839AB}`. The `TypeLib` key contains the UUID attached to the library block in the IDL, also known as the LIBID. The universal marshaler uses the LIBID to perform a lookup under `HKEY _CLASSES_ROOT\TypeLib` and retrieve the full path to the type library. Having loaded the type library, it locates the definition of `IAtom` and dynamically generates a proxy or stub as required.

Versioning Type Libraries

The only attribute that a library block requires is the `[uuid]`. Typically, a library block will also have a `[version]` attribute of the form `[version (x.y)]`, where x is the major version number and y is the minor version number. In fact, if a `[version]` attribute is not present, the MIDL compiler will use 0.0 as the version number, as in the previous example. Listing 2.3 shows `atom.idl` after adding a `[version]` attribute.

Listing 2.3   atom.idl with [version] attribute on library keyword

```
// atom.idl
[
  uuid(48705370-DE6A-4347-9C51-A8F2D1947C0B),
  version(1.0)
]
```

```
library AtomLib {
  [
    uuid(FAC852FF-35FE-48D3-B3FC-89D1364839AB),
    object,
    oleautomation
  ]
  interface IAtom : IUnknown {
    HRESULT Collide ( [in] IAtom* pOtherAtom );
  }
}
```

The version number allows for multiple versions of the type library to be present on a system at any one time, each version having the same UUID but a different version number. The version number of a type library should be changed whenever the content of the library block is changed and published. This usually coincides with a new version of a component.

The `LoadRegTypeLib` API takes the LIBID and the major and minor version numbers as parameters and uses them to load a type library with a matching LIBID. With regard to the version numbers, it first looks for an exact match of major and minor version numbers, and if such a library is registered, it is loaded. If no exact match is found, a type library with the same major version number but a higher minor version number is loaded. If multiple type libraries that fulfill these criteria are registered, the one with the highest minor version number is loaded.[6] If all the type libraries registered under the required LIBID have different major version numbers or have minor version numbers that are lower than that specified in the call to `LoadRegTypeLib`, no type library is loaded and the call fails.

The minor version number should be incremented whenever a forward-compatible change is made—for instance, if a new interface is added to the type library. The major version number should be incremented whenever a forward-incompatible change is made—for example, if a particular interface definition is removed.

---

[6] Note that the major and minor version numbers are unsigned short integers with a value space of 0–65535. The period is a separator, *not* a decimal point. Consequently, 1.20 has a higher minor version number than 1.2. If no minor version number is specified, zero is assumed.

Producing C++ Type Information

Although development environments such as Visual Basic can use type libraries to make calls on and implement interfaces, C++ developers and compilers usually prefer header files. In addition to the type library, the MIDL compiler will produce C++ type information if the `/header` or `/h` command line switch is used. The switch takes the form `/header <filename>`. For example:

```
midl /header atom.h atom.idl
```

With the command line above, three output files are generated, one being the type library as before. The other two files are the header file, `atom.h`, and another file, called the interface identifier file, `atom_i.c`. The header file contains C and C++ type definitions for `IAtom`. The C++ type definition for a COM interface takes the form of an abstract structure definition. The type definition for `IAtom` is shown below.[7]

```
EXTERN_C const IID IID_IAtom;
MIDL_INTERFACE("FAC852FF-35FE-48D3-B3FC-89D1364839AB")
IAtom : public IUnknown {
public:
   virtual HRESULT STDMETHODCALLTYPE Collide(
      /* [in] */ IAtom* pOtherAtom ) = 0;
};
```

A C++ compiler could use this definition of `IAtom` to produce client-side calling code or a correctly formed v-table for an object.

The interface identifier file contains C++ symbolic constant definitions for the UUIDs present in the source IDL, in this case the IID for `IAtom`, `IID_IAtom`, and the LIBID of the library block, `LIBID_AtomLib`. These constants can also be used in C++ code. For example, the following code fragment uses the interface identifier for `IAtom`.[8]

```
// pUnk initialized elsewhere
IAtom* pAtom= 0;
HR(pUnk->QueryInterface ( IID_IAtom, (void**)&pAtom ));
```

---

[7] Here and elsewhere, the `__RPC_FAR` symbol is not shown for reasons of clarity.

[8] Here and elsewhere in this book, the C-style cast is used merely for brevity. In production code, `reinterpret_cast` or `static_cast` should be used as appropriate.

For the linker to be able to locate the constant, `IID_IAtom`, the interface identifer file—`atom_i.c` in this case—must be included exactly once somewhere in the C++ project. A `#include` preprocessor directive could be used to bring in `atom_i.c`, or the file could be added to the project and compiled directly.[9]

Users of Visual C++ 5.0 or later have another option besides using the symbolic constants. The `MIDL_INTERFACE` macro in the header file expands to the `__declspec(uuid(..))` compiler extension. This attaches the relevant UUID to the C++ type definition. The UUID can then be retrieved inside a C++ source file by using the `__uuidof` keyword. For example:

```
// pUnk initialized elsewhere
IAtom* pAtom= 0;
HR(pUnk->QueryInterface ( __uuidof ( IAtom ),
                          (void**)&pAtom ));
```

Because of the way the `__uuidof` keyword works, the following is also legal.

```
// pUnk initialized elsewhere
IAtom* pAtom = 0;
HR(pUnk->QueryInterface ( __uuidof ( pAtom ),
                          (void**)&pAtom ));
```

This usage pattern is less prone to error, because the symbolic variable name, `pAtom`, is used rather than the symbolic interface name, `IAtom`, and therefore there is no possibility of a mismatch.

A convenient side effect of using `__uuidof` is that the interface identifier file is no longer needed by the C++ project.

Outside the Library Block

Using type libraries to produce interception code is reasonable for the majority of interfaces. However, because standard type information was originally designed for use by development tools, certain IDL attributes related to marshaling cannot be represented in a type library.[10] These attributes are important, but type libraries cannot be used to provide interception code for interfaces that use such attributes. However, such interfaces still require interception code in order to work

---

[9] Precompiled headers should be disabled for the interface identifier file.

[10] Examples of such attributes include `[iid_is]` and `[size_is]`. These attributes are discussed in detail in later chapters.

correctly in the face of cross-context calls. Oicf type information is able to express all of the IDL marshaling constructs, including those that standard type libraries cannot deal with, and is therefore higher in fidelity than standard type information with respect to marshaling information. The MIDL compiler will generate Oicf type information for any interface defined outside the library block when run with the /Oicf command line switch.[11] This Oicf type information can then be used by the COM runtime to produce interception code. Listing 2.4 shows an IDL file with an interface, INeutron, defined outside the library block. The import "unknwn.idl" statement will be explained later in this chapter.

Listing 2.4   atom.idl with interface definition outside the library block[12]

```
// atom.idl
import "unknwn.idl";
[
  uuid(380E3D07-A4D0-412A-9582-BE10547612BF),
  object
]
interface INeutron : IUnknown {
  HRESULT Split ( [out] long* pnParticles );
}
[
  uuid(48705370-DE6A-4347-9C51-A8F2D1947C0B),
  version(1.0)
]
library AtomLib {
  [
    uuid(FAC852FF-35FE-48D3-B3FC-89D1364839AB),
    object,
    oleautomation
  ]
  interface IAtom : IUnknown {
    HRESULT Collide ( [in] IAtom* pAtom );
  }
}
```

The MIDL compiler will output the Oicf type information for INeutron into a proxy file, atom_p.c. Because the definition of INeutron appears outside the library block, the MIDL compiler will also generate the header file and the interface identifier file, even in the absence of the /header command line

---

[11] The origin of the name "Oicf type information" should now be clear.

[12] The import "unknwn.idl" statement will be explained later in this chapter.

switch. In fact, these files are generated automatically whenever at least one IDL construct, be it an interface or any other type, appears outside the library block. The standard type information for IAtom appears in the type library as before.

The Oicf type information generated when the /Oicf switch is used is also known as Oicf strings or format strings. Unlike standard type information, the format of Oicf strings is not documented, nor is there a system-supplied parser. The generated format strings are highly self-referential; any complex data type will appear in the format string only once, irrespective of the number of times that data type appears as a parameter. Each occurrence of the type after the first will simply create a reference back to the first occurrence in the format string.

Occasionally, the MIDL compiler will be unable to build the format strings because the nesting level has grown too deep and it cannot generate the reference. This will result in the MIDL error "MIDL2002: compiler stack overflow". In this case, running the MIDL compiler with the /no_format_opt command line switch will result in format strings that do not use references. Each occurrence of a data type will result in the format string for that data type being output. This results in larger format strings, and consequently larger proxy-stub DLLs, but may be needed if the data structures defined in the IDL file are too complex for the optimized format string layout. It is worth noting that format strings are limited to 64K in size for a single IDL file. If this limit is exceeded, then MIDL error 'MIDL2379: The compiler reached a limit for a format string representation. See documentation for advice.' will be generated. One solution is to break the IDL file into two or more smaller files. Another is to run the MIDL compiler in 'mixed' mode by specifying the /Os command line switch in place of /Oicf. This causes the MIDL compiler to generate source code for the interface proxy and stub.[13] The resulting interceptor is typically larger than one built purely from Oicf type information but is also slightly faster at marshaling.[14]

---

[13] When run with the /Os command line switch, the MIDL compiler actually generates a mixture of source code and Oicf type information. Source code is generated for marshaling simple data types, and Oicf type information is generated for complex types.

[14] Note that the /Os solution is not applicable in an MTS environment, because MTS requires that the /Oicf switch be used.

Building a Proxy-Stub DLL

The universal marshaler understands only standard type information and so cannot be used to build interception code from Oicf type information. Instead, the interface designer must provide a class that can build such an interceptor as needed, a class that implements the methods of `IPSFactoryBuffer`. Fortunately, the MIDL compiler generates all the required code as part of its standard output when producing Oicf type information. The proxy file must be combined with other output files to create a proxy-stub DLL that contains the Oicf type information and also provides the class that implements `IPSFactoryBuffer`. This DLL will then be used by the COM runtime to build interception code. In order to build the DLL, the proxy file, the header file, the interface identifier file, and another output file, the dlldata file, are all needed. The dlldata file, by default called `dlldata.c`, consists almost entirely of macros defined in the system header file `rpcproxy.h`. These macros expand to produce the DLL entry point `DllMain` and the standard COM exports `DllCanUnloadNow`, `DllGetClassObject`, `DllRegisterServer`, and `DllUnregisterServer`. They also provide the class that implements `IPSFactoryBuffer`. The output files from the `atom.idl` in Listing 2.4 are shown in Figure 2.1.

The three C source files should be compiled with the following compiler flags.

```
/MD /c /Ox /DWIN32 /D_WIN32_WINNT=0x0500
/DREGISTER_PROXY_DLL15
```

The resulting object files should be linked with the following libraries.

```
kernel32.lib rpcndr.lib rpcns4.lib rpcrt4.lib
oleaut32.lib ole32.lib advapi32.lib uuid.lib16
```

Figure 2.2 shows the inputs and outputs from the build process.

Once the proxy-stub DLL is built, it must be registered just like any other COM object. Just as in the type library case, this writes the registry entries

---

[15] In building for Windows NT 4.0, the _WIN32_WINNT constant should be set to 0x0400.

[16] If the DLL is being built for use in an MTS environment, the library mtxih.lib must appear as the first library in the list. This builds the DLL in such a way that the MTS runtime can extract the Oicf type information and build interception code.

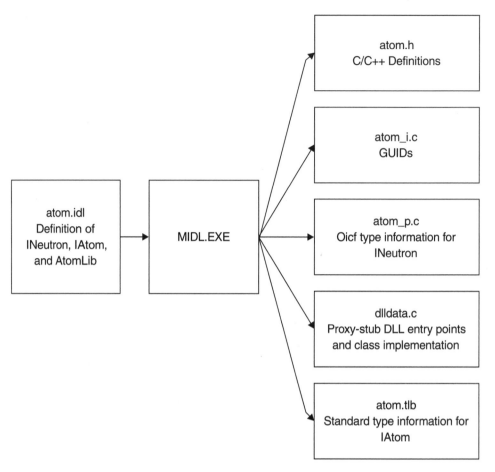

Figure 2.1   MIDL compiler output

needed by COM to locate the DLL at runtime. The entries for INeutron are shown below.

```
[HKCR\Interface\
{380E3D07-A4D0-412A-9582-BE10547612BF}]
@="INeutron"
[HKCR\Interface\
{380E3D07-A4D0-412A-9582-BE10547612BF}\ProxyStubClsid]
@="{380E3D07-A4D0-412A-9582-BE10547612BF}"
[HKCR\Interface\
{380E3D07-A4D0-412A-9582-BE10547612BF}\
ProxyStubClsid32]
@="{380E3D07-A4D0-412A-9582-BE10547612BF}"
```

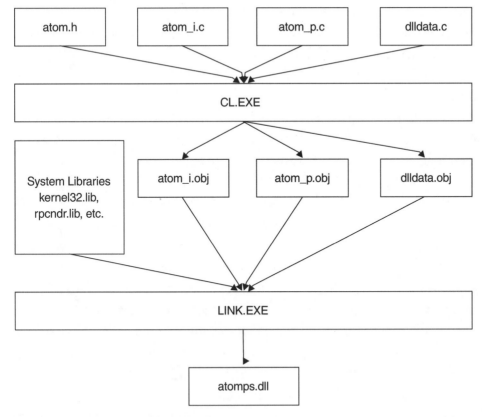

Figure 2.2   Building a proxy-stub DLL

The entries for INeutron differ from those for IAtom in three places. First, they use the IID for INeutron as the top-level key under HKEY_CLASSES _ROOT\Interface. Second, there is no Typelib key, because it is not needed owing to the fact that the Oicf type information is contained within the proxy-stub DLL. Third, the ProxyStubClsid32 does not refer to the universal marshaler but rather to the class provided by the proxy-stub DLL that implements IPSFactoryBuffer. The class is registered under HKEY _CLASSES_ROOT\CLSID.

```
[HKCR\CLSID\{380E3D07-A4D0-412A-9582-BE10547612BF}]
@="PSFactoryBuffer"
[HKCR\CLSID\{380E3D07-A4D0-412A-9582-BE10547612BF}\InProcServer32]
@="atomps.dll"
"ThreadingModel"="Both"
```

Note that the CLSID of the proxy-stub is identical to the IID of `INeutron`. The MIDL compiler uses the IID of the first interface defined outside the library block as the CLSID for the proxy-stub.

Recall that whenever COM needs an interceptor for an interface it searches `HKEY_CLASSES_ROOT\Interface` using the IID of the interface as the key and extracts the CLSID stored in the `ProxyStubClsid32` key. COM then creates an instance of the class and calls `CreateProxy` or `CreateStub` as appropriate. In the case of `INeutron` or any other interface whose interceptor is built from Oicf type information, the implementation of `IPSFactoryBuffer` passes the Oicf string to a piece of system code, hereafter the generic marshaler, that is able to generate an interceptor dynamically. The implementation of `IPSFactoryBuffer` provided by the MIDL compiler is merely a thin veneer on top of the generic marshaler and the universal marshaler is just a slightly thicker veneer. Having loaded the type library, the universal marshaler converts standard type information into Oicf type information and passes the resulting Oicf string to the generic marshaler, which creates the required interceptor. Owing to this conversion step, creating an interceptor from standard type information takes slightly longer than creating one from Oicf type information.

Compiling multiple IDL files will result in multiple proxy, interface identifier, and header files, all of which can be compiled together to produce a single proxy-stub DLL. However, only one dlldata file will be generated. The MIDL compiler will modify any existing dlldata file rather than overwriting it. Thus, this single file will contain references to each of the generated proxy files. Note that this applies only to IDL files that are compiled in the same directory or that explicitly target the same dlldata file. For example, compiling the files `i1.idl` and `i2.idl` in a directory `c:\myfiles` will result in a dlldata file that references each of the generated proxy files `i1_p.c` and `i2_p.c`. If a third IDL file, `i3.idl`, is compiled in a separate directory, `c:\otherfiles`, then a second dlldata file will be generated that references only `i3_p.c`, as illustrated in Figure 2.3.

To force the reference to `i3_p.c` into `c:\myfiles\dlldata.c`, use the `/dlldata` command line switch when compiling `i3.idl`.

```
midl /dlldata c:\myfiles\dlldata.c i3.idl
```

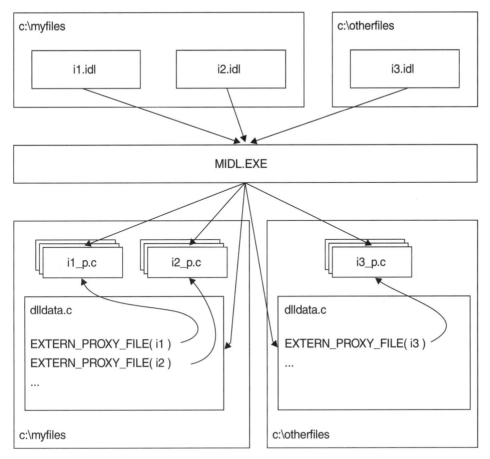

Figure 2.3   Compiling multiple IDL files

Note that if an IDL file is deleted or moved from a given directory, any dlldata.c file in that directory will still contain a reference to the generated proxy file. To work around this issue, the dlldata.c file must be deleted and any remaining IDL files recompiled.

Interface Definitions, Type Libraries, and the oleautomation Attribute

With the IDL file shown in Listing 2.4, the definition of INeutron appears in the Oicf type information and the header file. The IID also appears in the interface identifier file. No information about INeutron is present in the type library, and so the interface is unavailable to development environments such as Visual Basic. To force the definition of INeutron to appear in the generated type library in addition to appearing in the Oicf type information, header file, and interface identifier file, a reference to INeutron should be placed inside the library block, as shown in Listing 2.5.

Listing 2.5 Reference to INeutron in library block

```
// atom.idl
import "unknwn.idl";
[
  uuid(380E3D07-A4D0-412A-9582-BE10547612BF),
  object
]
interface INeutron : IUnknown {
  HRESULT Split ( [out] long* pnParticles );
}
[
  uuid(48705370-DE6A-4347-9C51-A8F2D1947C0B),
  version(1.0)
]
library AtomLib {
  interface INeutron; // Reference to INeutron
  [
    uuid(FAC852FF-35FE-48D3-B3FC-89D1364839AB),
    object,
    oleautomation
  ]
  interface IAtom : IUnknown {
    HRESULT Collide ( [in] IAtom* pAtom );
  }
}
```

INeutron is not annotated with the [oleautomation] attribute, and with good reason. It is the presence of this attribute that determines whether the universal marshaler is used to produce interception code. In fact, this is the sole purpose of the [oleautomation] attribute. If INeutron were annotated with the [oleautomation] attribute and referenced in the library block, as in Listing 2.5, the universal marshaler would be used when building interception code. For this reason, care should be taken when applying the [oleautomation] attribute to interfaces defined outside a library block. If such an interface is ever referenced in a library block, even in a completely separate IDL file, then, when the resulting type library is registered, it will overwrite the registry entries for the proxy-stub DLL and replace them with the entries for the universal marshaler. If the interface uses IDL constructs that cannot be described in standard type information, this will have disastrous consequences for the resulting interception code. Unfortunately, the MIDL compiler does not generate any warnings or errors when such IDL constructs are used in an interface marked with the `[oleautomation]` keyword.

The Local Attribute

Some interfaces may never need interception code or may contain method signatures for which interception code cannot be generated. Such interfaces should be annotated with the `[local]` attribute to signify that no interception code is required. Interfaces marked as `[local]` may be referenced inside a library block, in which case the interface definition will appear in the type library. This will enable development tools such as Visual Basic to call and implement the interface. The `[oleautomation]` attribute specifies that interception code should be used and hence overrides the `[local]` attribute. Consequently, interface definitions that contain the `[local]` attribute should not contain the `[oleautomation]` attribute.

The `[local]` attribute is often applied to interfaces that are used for private communication between two objects. Provided the two objects are always in the same context, this is a reasonable approach. If the objects are ever separated by a context boundary, then all `QueryInterface` requests for local interfaces will fail, because the COM runtime will be unable to build an interceptor.

Method signatures in interfaces marked as `[local]` need not return an HRESULT. Any primitive data type, including pointers and `void`, may be used as a return type. Listing 2.6 shows an interface annotated with the `[local]` attribute.

Listing 2.6 Interface annotated with the [local] attribute

```
[
  object,
  uuid(39C22A0B-D80A-4138-836E-C14E994A5901),
  local
]
interface IAtomStuff : IUnknown {
```

Table 2.1   Interception code choices for an interface definition

Relation to Library Block	IDL Interface Attributes	Appears in C Header?	Appears in Type Library?	Interception Code
Inside	None	If generated	Yes	None
Inside	local	If generated	Yes	None
Inside	oleautomation	If generated	Yes	Universal marshaler
Outside	None	Yes	Only if referenced	Proxy-stub DLL
Outside	local	Yes	Only if referenced	None
Outside	oleautomation	Yes	Only if referenced	Last one registered

```
    short Protons();
    short Neutrons();
    short Electrons();
    void AddParticle ( [in] IParticle* p );
}
```

For style reasons, it may be preferable to have the methods return HRESULTs and continue to use [out,retval] for logical return values. Table 2.1 shows the various combinations of [local] and [oleautomation] along with the position of the interface definition in the IDL file and the effect they have on the resulting interface interception code or lack thereof.

Note that interface definitions inside the library block will appear in the C header file if one is generated. Header file generation will occur if at least one type definition occurs outside the library block or if the /header command line switch is used.

Importing Other Files

A given interface definition will typically contain method signatures taking a variety of parameter types. Those parameter types must be available to the MIDL compiler to enable it to parse the interface definition. For example, consider the IDL shown in Listing 2.7.

Listing 2.7   Initial atomcracker.idl
```
// atomcracker.idl
[
  uuid(D71F215A-391D-4ddb-832D-495892EE2A85),
  object
]
```

```
interface IAtomCracker : IUnknown {
  HRESULT CrackAtom ( [in] IAtom*pAtom,
                      [out] long* pnEnergy );
}
```

The `IAtomCracker` interface needs the definition of `IAtom`, which is used as a parameter type. The IDL file above will not compile because the definition of `IAtom` is not available. Having to define all required types within every IDL file that needed them would be very tedious and error-prone. Fortunately, IDL provides facilities for referencing an external file. The types defined in the external file may then be used. One approach is to use the `#include` directive to bring the content of `atom.idl` into `atomcracker.idl`. The definitions in `atom.idl` are then available for use in `atomcracker.idl`. The modified `atomcracker.idl` is shown in Listing 2.8.

Listing 2.8 Use of #include in atomcracker.idl

```
// atomcracker.idl
#include "atom.idl"
[
  uuid(D71F215A-391D-4ddb-832D-495892EE2A85),
  object
]
interface IAtomCracker : IUnknown {
  HRESULT CrackAtom ( [in] IAtom*pAtom,
                      [out] long* pnEnergy );
}
```

Using the `#include` directive is identical to pasting the entire content of the external file into the IDL file. As far as the MIDL compiler is concerned, the file above looks exactly as it would if the content of `atom.idl` were pasted at the top of `atomcracker.idl`. This has the unfortunate side effect of placing the Oicf type information for `INeutron` in the proxy file, `atomcracker_p.c`, in addition to the Oicf type information for `IAtomCracker`. All the associated definitions for `INeutron` will also be present in the header and interface identifier files. Typically this is not what is required, as the type information and definitions for `INeutron` are already present in the output from `atom.idl`.[17]

---

[17] The type information and associated definitions for `IAtom` will not be present because it is defined in a library block.

Because of this side effect, `#include` is rarely used to bring in IDL files. It is occasionally used to bring in a C header file, a common example being `mtx-attr.h`, which defines several custom type library attributes that the MTS and COM+ catalog manager understands.

If the filename is enclosed in quotation marks, the `#include` directive searches the current directory, followed by the directories listed in the INCLUDE environment variable. If the filename is in angle brackets, the current directory is not searched. The `/I` command line switch allows extra directories to be specified. If the `/I` switch is used, the directories specified are searched before the INCLUDE environment variable.

Because of the behavior of `#include`, the `import` keyword is typically used to bring in external IDL files. The `import` keyword is followed by a comma-separated list of filenames, with each filename enclosed in quotation marks. The statement must be terminated with a semicolon. The `import` statement may appear anywhere within an IDL file, including inside the library block, although this usage should be avoided as explained later in this chapter. Amending `atomcracker.idl` to use `import` instead of `#include` produces the IDL shown in Listing 2.9.

Listing 2.9 Use of import in atomcracker.idl

```
// atomcracker.idl
import "unknwn.idl";
import "atom.idl";
[
  uuid(D71F215A-391D-4ddb-832D-495892EE2A85),
  object
]
interface IAtomCracker : IUnknown {
  HRESULT CrackAtom ( [in] IAtom*pAtom,
                      [out] long* pnEnergy );
}
```

Note that the system IDL file, `unknwn.idl`, has also been imported. This file contains the definition of `IUnknown` and is required because `IUnknown` is the base interface for `IAtomCracker`.[18]

---

[18] This is also the reason that the `atom.idl` examples shown in Listings 2.4 and 2.5 needed to import `unknwn.idl`.

The `import` keyword should be used whenever the contents of an external IDL file are required. For any types used as method parameters or fields of user-defined types, the `import` statement must appear before the reference to the type. However, for types used as base interfaces, the `import` statement may appear after the reference to the type. Because the `import` keyword is idempotent, it is also perfectly legal to import a particular IDL file more than once.

These facts lead to the following usage pattern. Place `import` statements immediately inside interface definitions that use the imported types. Then, if the interface definition is moved to another file, the required imports automatically move with it. For example, the IDL shown in Listing 2.10 shows two interfaces, both of which derive from `IUnknown` and use `IAtom` as a method parameter type. Both interfaces import `unknwn.idl` and `atom.idl`. The import for `unknwn.idl` in the first interface, `IMolecule`, occurs after `IUnknown` is referenced as the base interface.

Listing 2.10 Usage pattern for import statements

```
// atomstuff.h
 [
  uuid(1A83223B-9C70-4E80-867B-58D302B91894),
  object
]
interface IMolecule : IUnknown {
  import "unknwn.idl"
  import "atom.idl";
  HRESULT AddAtom ( [in] IAtom* pAtom );
}
[
  uuid(506EE69B-ECDB-449D-929B-73DEEF4C5996),
  object
]
interface IAtomSmasher : IUnknown {
  import "unknwn.idl"
  import "atom.idl";
  HRESULT SmashAtom ( [in] IAtom* pAtom,
                      [out] long* pParticles );
}
```

Now assume that at some later date the file containing `IMolecule` and `IAtomSmasher` is split into two separate IDL files, perhaps `molecule.idl` and `atomsmasher.idl`. Because the required `import` statements are contained within the interface definition, both files will compile correctly. This avoids having to keep track of which imports are needed for which interface definitions; each interface contains within it all the required `import` statements for all referenced types.[19]

The resulting header file for any IDL file that uses the `import` keyword will have a corresponding `#include` statement to bring in the appropriate header file when building the proxy-stub DLL or C++ components or clients. The `#include` statements appear in the same order as the import statements and appear only once regardless of the number of times the corresponding IDL file is imported. The header file for `atomstuff.idl` above would contain the following lines.

```
/* header files for imported files */
#include "unknwn.h"
#include "atom.h"
```

The only exception to this behavior is when the `import` statement appears inside a library block; in this case, no corresponding `#include` statement appears in the generated header file. For this reason, avoid placing `import` statements inside the library block of an IDL file.

When compiling C or C++ code that includes MIDL-generated header files, it is important that the directories containing any imported IDL files be added to the INCLUDE list so that the corresponding header files can be found. The MIDL-generated header files for the system IDL files are in the same directory as the IDL files, and this is usually the case for other IDL files as well.

When trying to locate IDL files, the `import` keyword searches the current directory, followed by the directories listed in the INCLUDE environment variable. The `/I` MIDL command line switch can also be used with the import keyword, in which case the directories specified are searched before the INCLUDE environment variable.

---

[19] Versions of the MIDL compiler prior to 5.01.0164 could not import an external IDL file that contained a library block into an IDL file that itself contained a library block, generating the error 'MIDL2016 : two library blocks'. If you are using a version of MIDL prior to 5.01.0164, consider defining interfaces in IDL files that do not contain a library block to avoid the problem.

Importing Files in the Library Block

Interface and other definitions that are brought in via the `import` keyword may be referenced both inside and outside the library block. However, types referenced inside the library block will appear in the resulting type library. This includes system types such as `IUnknown`. Consider the IDL file shown in Listing 2.11.

Listing 2.11   quark.idl without importlib
```
// quark.idl
[
  uuid(60DF5144-700B-44BB-A032-D58CEA735D70)
]
library QuarkLib {
  [
    uuid(C601105D-845C-4253-812B-4F9B164D7BD0),
    object,
    oleautomation
  ]
  interface IQuark : IUnknown {
    HRESULT Spin ( [in] short s );
  }
}
```

The resulting type library will contain the definition of `IUnknown` in addition to the definition of `IQuark`. To avoid this unnecessary duplication of information, IDL provides the `importlib` keyword. This keyword is used to bring in an external type library. This is very similar to the use of `import` to bring in an external IDL file. The types defined in the imported type library may be referenced in the library block. Rather than duplicating the information, references to the types defined in the external type library are placed in the new type library. These references include the LIBID of the external type library and the index number of the referenced type. `IUnknown` is defined in `stdole2.tlb`, and the first statement in all library blocks should import this type library, as shown in Listing 2.12.

Listing 2.12   Use of importlib in quark.idl
```
// quark.idl
[
  uuid(60DF5144-700B-44BB-A032-D58CEA735D70)
]
```

```
library QuarkLib {
  // Import standard system types; Iunknown, etc.
  importlib ( "stdole2.tlb" );
  [
    uuid(C601105D-845C-4253-812B-4F9B164D7BD0),
    object,
    oleautomation
  ]
  interface IQuark : IUnknown {
    HRESULT Spin ( [in] short s );
  }
}
```

Various other system types are also defined in stdole2.tlb, such as IDispatch and the GUID structure. There is another version of stdole2.tlb, which is named stdole32.tlb. Both type libraries have the same GUID: stdole2.tlb is version 2.0, while stdole32.tlb is version 1.0. Only the more recent type library is needed, and if both type libraries are imported, only the later version will be referenced.[20]

The importlib statement must come before any reference to types defined in the imported type library. The only exception to this is when the IDL file that corresponds to the type library is also imported. For example, the IDL file shown in Listing 2.13 will not compile, because the MIDL compiler will be unable to find the definition of IAtom at the point at which it is referenced.

Listing 2.13 Erroneous use of importlib
```
// quark.idl
import "unknwn.idl";
[
  uuid(60DF5144-700B-44BB-A032-D58CEA735D70)
]
library QuarkLib {
  importlib ( "stdole2.tlb" );
  [
    uuid(C601105D-845C-4253-812B-4F9B164D7BD0),
    object,
    oleautomation
  ]
```

---

[20] Why some development tools specifically use importlib to bring in both versions is a mystery.

```
interface IQuark : IUnknown {
  HRESULT Spin ( [in] short s );
}
[
  uuid(BA5F54C2-0CCF-4de2-B2CD-C023ABF0FD0A),
  object
]
interface ICreateAtoms : IUnknown {
  HRESULT AddQuark ( [in] IQuark* pQuark );
  HRESULT CreateAtom ( [out,retval] IAtom**ppAtom );
}
importlib ( "atom.tlb" );
}
```

Moving the importlib statement for atom.tlb to the top of the library block would solve the problem, as would adding an import statement for atom.idl at the top of the file.[21]

When looking for type libraries, the importlib statement searches the current directory, any directories specified by the /I switch, directories in the INCLUDE environment variable, and then directories in the PATH environment variable.

Coclasses

In addition to interface and other data type definitions, IDL allows classes to be described. Classes are defined using the coclass keyword. For example:

```
[
  uuid(D0DB3F0A-E956-476C-B6D6-CAA99242792D)
]
coclass Neutron {
  [default] interface INeutron;
  interface ISubatomicParticle;
}
```

The [uuid] attribute is mandatory for coclasses. Various other attributes may be applied to a coclass statement, as detailed in Chapter 8. A coclass statement can occur inside or outside the library block. If it appears inside the library

---

[21] Perversely, the importlib ("stdole2.tlb") statement can appear at the end of the library block because the MIDL compiler automatically adds an implicit import statement for oaidl.idl whenever it encounters a library block. The oaidl.idl file causes objidl.idl, unknwn.idl, and wtypes.idl to be imported also.

block or if the coclass is referenced inside the library block, the type information for the coclass will appear in the generated type library.

Inside the `coclass` statement, interfaces are listed. Ideally, all the domain-specific interfaces that a given coclass implements would be listed in its `coclass` definition. Unfortunately, there is no enforcement of this in the COM runtime. It is perfectly possible to list a subset of interfaces or even to list interfaces that the coclass does not implement.

Providing a `coclass` statement makes the UUID for the class available to Visual Basic. This allows the use of the `New` keyword.

```
Dim obj As Neutron
Set obj = New Neutron
```

The `coclass` statement is also used by the MTS and COM+ catalogs. When a new class is imported into MTS or COM+, the catalog manager uses information in the `coclass` statement to determine which interfaces to list in the catalog under the component. This is important if any interface- or method-level attributes are going to be applied, such as role-based security. If the interfaces are not listed in the `coclass` statement, they will not appear in the MTS or COM+ catalog. Such interfaces will still get interception code; it is only the interface and method level declarative attributes that will be unavailable. As MTS and COM+ become more prevalent, it is even more important to ensure that the `coclass` statement accurately represents the class it is describing.

The `[default]` attribute on the interface `INeutron` causes Visual Basic to hide the interface in the object browser and make the methods of that interface accessible through the class name. If the class supports `IDispatch`, then the default interface is, by convention, also accessible through `IDispatch`. If the `[default]` attribute is not specified for any interface in the coclass, the MIDL compiler will choose the first interface in the list that does not have the `[restricted]` attribute in the interface definition.

So, in the example above, the methods of `INeutron` would be accessible through any reference of type `Neutron`. The `INeutron` interface can also be used, but it will not appear in the Visual Basic statement completion field. To circumvent this behavior, list `IUnknown` as the `[default]` interface of the coclass.[22]

The `coclass` statement also causes the MIDL compiler to emit the UUID, `CLSID_Neutron`, into the interface identifier file. A class declaration with the UUID attached will be placed in the header file.

```
class
DECLSPEC_UUID("D0DB3F0A-E956-476C-B6D6-CAA99242792D")
Neutron;
```

Again, `__uuidof` can be used to retrieve the CLSID inside C++ applications.

```
IUnknown* punk = 0;
HR(CoCreateInstance ( __uuidof ( Neutron ), 0,
  CLSCTX_ALL, __uuidof ( pUnk ), (void**)&pUnk ));
```

Conclusions

Correct placement of type definitions in IDL files is critical to ensure that the required kinds of type information are emitted. Managing IDL files and the resultant output can be problematic, especially in large projects where there may be a correspondingly large number of interfaces and components. Listed below are some guidelines to make IDL file management easier.

1. If the universal marshaler is to be used, use the `[oleautomation]` attribute and place the interface definitions inside the library block. Corollary: Do not use the `[oleautomation]` attribute on interfaces that are to use Oicf type information. Getting this right will ensure that the registry entries for the proxy-stub DLL are never overwritten by those of the universal marshaler.
2. Put related interface definitions into a single IDL file. For example, if `IAtom2` derives from `IAtom`, place both interface definitions in a single IDL file.
3. For interface definitions outside the library block, place `import` statements inside the interface definition.
4. Do not use `import` inside a library block; rather, use `importlib` to bring in external definitions. This will avoid type library bloat.

---

[22] The only time this approach should not be used is if the class is to be deployed in MTS, because the presence of IUnknown in the coclass confuses the MTS runtime. COM+ suffers from no such confusion.

5. Consider writing 'wrapper' IDL files that contain no definitions of their own—just import multiple IDL files. Then use the `/header` command line switch at compile time to force MIDL to generate a header file. This will allow other developers to import a single IDL file rather than having to import each IDL file separately.

6. Write `coclass` statements that accurately reflect the domain-specific interfaces implemented by the class. This will enable the Visual Basic developers and the MTS and COM+ runtimes to discover the capabilities of a class without instantiating it.

7. Keep coclass definitions and interface definitions in separate files. This will provide a clean separation of class and interface and will make file management easier.

Chapter 3

Data Types and Interface Issues

Primitive Data Types

IDL supports several primitive data types, including integer types, floating point types, and string types. These types may be used as method parameters directly or as fields in structures and other user-defined types. The IDL primitive types and the appropriate language mappings are shown in Table 3.1.

Because not all IDL types have mappings into all implementation languages, care should be taken in making type choices at interface design time. Interfaces that are to be used from or implemented by C/C++ may use any of the IDL primitives. However, interfaces that are to be used or implemented by Visual Basic should restrict themselves to types that Visual Basic can deal with—for example, they should avoid use of the hyper data type. Interfaces designed for use from scripting languages such as VBScript and JavaScript must restrict even further the set of types to be used.

With regard to type information, each primitive type has two mappings, one of which is used in standard type information and the other in Oicf type information. The mapping values are shown in Table 3.2. In the case of type library mappings, corresponding constants are defined in the system IDL file `wtypes.idl`. Note that standard type information sees `boolean` and `char` as the same type, whereas Oicf type information distinguishes between them.

Signed and Unsigned Data Types

The primitive types can have various type modifiers applied to them. The integer data types—`small`, `short`, `int`, `long`, and `hyper`/`__int64`—and the `char` data type may be qualified with the `signed` or `unsigned` modifier. The `signed` and `unsigned` modifiers further illustrate the original purpose of

Table 3.1 Mapping of IDL types to language types

IDL Type	C/C++ Type	Visual Basic Type	Supported in Script?
boolean	unsigned char	No mapping	No
byte	unsigned char	Byte	Yes
char	unsigned char	No mapping	No
double	double	Double	Yes
float	float	Single	Yes
hyper	__int64	No mapping	No
int	int	Long	Yes
__int64	__int64	No mapping	No
long	long	Long	Yes
short	short	Integer	Yes
small	char	No mapping	No
wchar_t	unsigned short	No mapping	No

Table 3.2 Mapping of IDL types to type information

IDL Type	TLB Mapping	TLB Constant	Oicf String
boolean	0x10	VT_I1	0x03
byte	0x11	VT_UI1	0x01
char	0x10	VT_I1	0x02
double	0x05	VT_R8	0x0c
float	0x04	VT_R4	0x0a
hyper	0x14	VT_I8	0x0b
int	0x16	VT_INT	0x08
__int64	0x14	VT_I8	0x0b
long	0x03	VT_I4	0x08
short	0x02	VT_I2	0x06
small	0x10	VT_I1	0x03
wchar_t	0x12	VT_UI2	0x05

the two forms of type information. Whether a data type is signed or unsigned is irrelevant during marshaling, hence Oicf type information does not store the modifier. When IDL types are mapped to language-level types, the presence of such modifiers is important. Consequently, standard type information reflects the signed or unsigned nature of a data type, as shown in Table 3.3.

The int data type should be avoided completely. While Oicf type information treats int as long, there is no guarantee that the C++ compiler will do the same. Always explicitly use the long data type in IDL instead of int.

The char data type should be used with care, because the MIDL compiler treats an unmodified char as unsigned when generating C/C++ language mappings. Unfortunately, when generating the type library it treats an unmodified char as signed. This can cause confusion during building and use of components that use char types as method parameters. There are two solutions to this problem, the simpler of which is to qualify explicitly all occurrences of the char type as either signed or unsigned. The second solution is to compile the IDL with the /char unsigned command line switch, which causes MIDL to

Table 3.3 Type library and Oicf mapping for signed/unsigned types

IDL Type	TLB Mapping	TLB Constant	Oicf String
signed char	0x10	VT_I1	0x02
unsigned char	0x11	VT_UI1	0x02
signed hyper	0x14	VT_I8	0x0b
unsigned hyper	0x15	VT_UI8	0x0b
signed int	0x16	VT_INT	0x08
unsigned int	0x17	VT_UINT	0x08
signed __int64	0x14	VT_I8	0x0b
unsigned __int64	0x15	VT_UI8	0x0b
signed long	0x03	VT_I4	0x08
unsigned long	0x13	VT_UI4	0x08
signed short	0x01	VT_I2	0x06
unsigned short	0x12	VT_UI2	0x06
signed small	0x10	VT_I1	0x03
unsigned small	0x11	VT_UI1	0x03

generate type libraries that contain `unsigned char` and C/C++ source files that contain an unmodified `char`. The C/C++ source files can then be compiled with the `/J` switch, which for Visual C++ specifies that unmodified `char` types should be treated as unsigned. This second solution involves changing the compile options for all source files that use interface definitions that contain `char` data types, and consequently the first solution should be preferred.

Although the signed and unsigned parts of a data type are present in the type library, Visual Basic is unable to use unsigned 16- and 32-bit integers. It is also unable to use signed 8-bit integers. Interfaces that contain these types may not be used or implemented by Visual Basic, so the interface shown in Listing 3.1 would be useless to a Visual Basic programmer.

Listing 3.1   An interface that Visual Basic cannot use

```
[
  uuid(3955E6C8-FB8D-4a0f-BA4A-3B0849C687DD)
  object
]
interface ICannotBeUsedFromVB : IUnknown {
  HRESULT M1 ( [in] char c );
  HRESULT M2 ( [in] small s );
  HRESULT M3 ( [in] unsigned short n );
  HRESULT M4 ( [in] unsigned long l );
  HRESULT M5 ( [in] unsigned int i );
}
```

Because of the issues with unsigned numbers, interfaces designed for use or implementation by Visual Basic should refrain from using unsigned 16- and 32-bit integers and signed 8-bit integers as method parameters or structure members.

Char versus Byte

The `unsigned char` and `byte` data types may at first glance appear to be more or less synonymous. However, as far as IDL is concerned, they are two completely different types. Although the underlying language mapping for `unsigned char` and `byte` may be identical, the two types are treated very differently by the MIDL compiler; the `char` data type is subject to format conversion on the wire, whereas the `byte` type is not. If the client is running on an ASCII system and the object is running on an EBCDIC system, any `char` types in method calls, be they signed or unsigned, will be converted at unmarshal time owing to the reader-makes-right protocol. This conversion does not occur for parameters of `byte` type, so when binary data needs to be transmitted, use the `byte` type rather than the `char` type.

Char versus Wchar_t

All 32-bit implementations of COM use Unicode to represent text strings. All COM APIs and system interface methods that deal with strings use Unicode rather than 8-bit characters. The primitive IDL type `wchar_t` is used to specify a Unicode character. When coupled with the `[string]` attribute, the `wchar_t` type represents a null-terminated Unicode string. COM prefers the `wchar_t` type over the `char` type for passing strings, because of the greater flexibility with respect to character sets that Unicode characters provide. So while the interface shown in Listing 3.2 is legal IDL, a wide character version, as shown in Listing 3.3, is preferred because it is usable in a greater number of international locations.

Listing 3.2   An interface that uses 8-bit characters and strings

```
[
  uuid(1EC21232-ABEB-4973-BA1F-7EDBDD10A54D),
  object
]
interface I8BitCharacterStrings : IUnknown {
  HRESULT TakeAChar ( [in] char c );
  HRESULT TakeAString ( [in,string] char*psz );
}
```

Listing 3.3 An interface that uses wide characters and strings

```
[
  uuid(F2489026-C572-4cf4-87AA-B7108C8F4816),
  object
]
interface IWideCharacterStrings : IUnknown {
  HRESULT TakeAWideChar ( [in] wchar_t wc );
  HRESULT TakeAWideString ( [in,
                            string] wchar_t* pwsz );
}
```

The system IDL file, `wtypes.idl`, has a type definition or alias, `LPOLESTR`, that includes the `[string]` attribute:

```
typedef [string] OLECHAR* LPOLESTR;
```

where OLECHAR is a type definition for wchar_t. The [string] attribute specifies that the length of the string will be determined at runtime by looking for the termination character, typically NULL. So the definition of TakeAWideString could have been written as

```
HRESULT TakeAWideString ( [in] LPOLESTR pwsz );
```

Given that the wchar_t type is preferred for single characters and strings and that the byte type should be used for transmitting binary data, the char data type is of limited use in COM interface definitions.

LPOLESTR versus BSTR

Visual Basic stores strings as Unicode and has its own internal string type, String, which maps directly to the IDL type BSTR. The BSTR data type is a wide character string that is NULL terminated. However, it may contain embedded NULL characters and is preceded in memory by a 4-byte count of the length of the string in bytes, not characters. The in-memory representation of the string 'BSTR' as a BSTR is shown in Figure 3.1.

When interfaces are designed for use or implementation by Visual Basic, the BSTR data type should be used, rather than the LPOLESTR type, where string parameters are needed. In C++, the BSTR data type is a pointer to the first character in the string; however, the 4-byte count still exists in C++ environments, and consequently BSTRs should always be managed using the system APIs designed for that purpose. These APIs are shown in Listing 3.4.

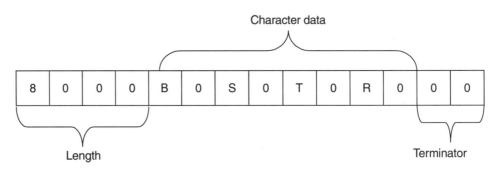

Figure 3.1 In-memory representation of a BSTR

Listing 3.4 System APIs for managing BSTRs

```
// Create a BSTR based on wide character string
BSTR SysAllocString(const OLECHAR *);
// Reallocate a BSTR based on a wide character string
INT SysReAllocString(BSTR *, const OLECHAR *);
// Create a BSTR based on a wide character string
// and a length
BSTR SysAllocStringLen(const OLECHAR *, UINT);
// Reallocate a BSTR based on a wide character string
// and a length
INT SysReAllocStringLen(BSTR *, const OLECHAR *, UINT);
// Destroy a BSTR
void SysFreeString(BSTR);
// Length of BSTR in characters
UINT SysStringLen(BSTR);
// Length of BSTR in bytes
UINT SysStringByteLen(BSTR bstr);
// Create a BSTR based on a character string
// and a length
BSTR SysAllocStringByteLen(LPCSTR psz, UINT len);
```

Note that the method SysAllocStringByteLen takes an 8-bit character string as input; however, it does not convert the input string into a wide character string. The function is supposedly for passing binary data inside a BSTR. This should be avoided, because the reader-makes-right protocol may perform unwanted conversion. If binary data is to be transmitted, use an array of bytes as described in Chapter 4.

It should be clear from Figure 3.1 that the BSTR data type is very different from the LPOLESTR data type. Unfortunately for C/C++ developers, there is a type definition in the system header file, wtypes.h:

```
typedef OLECHAR* BSTR;
```

which allows C/C++ programs to treat BSTR and OLECHAR* as synonymous. This allows the following usage.

```
// Function prototype
void TakeAnLPOLESTR ( LPOLESTR pwsz );
void TakeABSTR ( BSTR bstr ) {
  // Pass BSTR to LPOLESTR function
  TakeAnLPOLESTR ( bstr );
}
```

In the majority of cases, this will work as expected, the only caveat being that if the BSTR contains embedded NULL characters, the function TakeAnLPOLESTR will not see all the data passed in the BSTR, but only the data preceding the first NULL character.

A much more serious problem arises with the following incorrect usage.

```
// Function prototype
void TakeABSTR ( BSTR bstr );
void TakeAnLPOLESTR ( LPOLESTR pwsz ) {
  // Pass LPOLESTR to BSTR function
  TakeABSTR ( pwsz );
}
```

The compiler is powerless to catch this error owing to the aliasing of BSTR and OLECHAR*. Unfortunately, the chances of the four bytes preceding the LPOLESTR in memory containing the correct value are 1 in 2^{32}. Care should be taken to ensure that when calling methods that take BSTRs as parameters from C++, an LPOLESTR is not passed by mistake.

Enumerated Types

Often in interface design, a particular parameter will have a limited number of possible values. It is useful in these situations to be able to define enumerations for those values. Consider the following interface definition.

```
[
  uuid(E20F508A-7AFE-4565-A384-3E1C77FD825A),
  object
]
interface ISubAtomicParticle : IUnknown {
  HRESULT Spin ( [in] long nSpin );
}
```

If the only possible values of the parameter nSpin are −1, 0, and +1, IDL allows an enumerated type to be defined as

```
enum SPIN {
  ANTICLOCKWISE = -1,
  NEUTRAL,
  CLOCKWISE
};
```

which would assign the values −1, 0, and 1 to the enumeration constants `ANTICLOCKWISE`, `NEUTRAL`, and `CLOCKWISE`, respectively. The definition of `Spin` can then be amended to read

```
HRESULT Spin ( [in] enum SPIN nSpin );
```

The C++ compiler will ensure that when the `Spin` method is called, a member of the `SPIN` enumeration is passed as a parameter. Unfortunately, a determined C++ developer could still pass an incorrect value by using a cast:

```
pObj->Spin ( reinterpret_cast<enum SPIN>(10));
```

Similarly, there is nothing to stop a Visual Basic developer from passing any 32-bit value. This type of error can be caught at runtime inside the implementation of `Spin`, or if interception code exists between the client and the object, the `[range]` attribute can be used.

```
HRESULT Spin( [in, range(ANTICLOCKWISE,CLOCKWISE)]
              enum SPIN nSpin )
```

The interception code will generate the error 0x800706f7, "The stub received bad data" if a value outside the allowed range is supplied at call time. Range checking can be used only where the required values are contiguous and the parameter type is either an enumeration or a 32-, 16-, or 8-bit integer type. It is also applicable only to `[in]` parameters.

It should be noted that the `[range]` attribute is supported only on Windows 2000 and that to take advantage of it IDL files must be compiled with the `/robust` command line switch. The resulting source files should be compiled with the `/D_WIN32_WINNT=0x0500` command line parameter or appropriate entry in the make file when building the proxy-stub DLL. The `[range]` attribute does not appear in any resulting type library, and consequently if the universal marshaler is used, range checking does not occur.

Constants defined in an enumerated type may be qualified with an explicit value, as in the case of `ANTICLOCKWISE` above. If no explicit value is supplied, the number 1 higher than the previous constant is used, as shown in the `Spin` example. If no starting value is supplied, then zero is assumed. It is legal for several constants to have the same numerical value, as shown in Listing 3.5, and for there to be gaps or out-of-order values in the numerical sequence, as shown in Listing 3.6.

Listing 3.5 Enumeration with two constants that have the same value

```
enum SPIN {
  ANTICLOCKWISE = -1,
  NEUTRAL,
  NONE = 0,
  CLOCKWISE
};
```

Listing 3.6 Enumeration with noncontiguous values

```
enum SOMEVALUES {
  POS_X = 100,
  POS_Y = 200,
  POS_Z = -1000
};
```

Note that range checking using the [range] attribute would be much less useful in the case of the enumeration defined in Listing 3.6 because the enumeration values are not contiguous.

Enumerated types can appear inside a library block either as a reference or as a definition. Either way, the resulting type library will contain the definition of the enumeration. The type library generated from the IDL file shown in Listing 3.7 would contain the SPIN enumeration.

Listing 3.7 Putting an enumeration into a type library

```
enum SPIN {
  ANTICLOCKWISE = -1,
  NEUTRAL,
  NONE = 0,
  CLOCKWISE
};

[
  uuid(F5186FD3-1677-44dd-8303-B194654E6447),
  version(1.0)
]
library EnumLib {
  enum SPIN;
}
```

Enumerated types are always stored in 32 bits in memory, but by default they are represented in 16 bits when marshaled. This can result in loss of information at marshaling time. An enumeration can be annotated with the `[v1_enum]` attribute, which causes the attributed type to be transmitted as a 32-bit value, ensuring that no information is lost.

```
[v1_enum] enum SPIN {
   ANTICLOCKWISE = -1,
   NEUTRAL,
   NONE = 0,
   CLOCKWISE
};
```

The `[v1_enum]` attribute should always be used, and an examination of the system IDL files finds that all system-defined enumerations use the `[v1_enum]` attribute. Various other IDL attributes may be applied to enumerations; these attributes are detailed in Chapters 9 and 10.

Enumerated types are available directly in C/C++, along with the constants they define. The C/C++ mapping of the SPIN enumeration defined in Listing 3.5 would be

```
enum SPIN {
   ANTICLOCKWISE = -1,
   NEUTRAL = ANTICLOCKWISE + 1,
   NONE = 0,
   CLOCKWISE = NONE + 1
};
```

thus making all the constants available for use as well as the data type itself. If the enumeration appears in a referenced type library, the Visual Basic IDE will make the relevant constants available through a drop-down list when passing method parameters. The underlying enumerated type will also be available as a declarable data type, allowing the following two usage patterns.

```
' First pattern
obj.Spin ANTICLOCKWISE
' Second pattern
Dim sp as SPIN;
sp = CLOCKWISE;
obj.Spin sp
```

As mentioned earlier, neither the Visual Basic runtime nor the Visual Basic compiler performs any range checking, so invalid parameter values could be passed. Because of this and the lack of range checking support either when using the universal marshaler or when running on platforms predating Windows 2000, the safest approach is to perform range checks inside the method implementation. This is reasonably straightforward in the case of the SPIN enumeration defined in Listing 3.5, because the values form a discrete range. The method implementation in C++ would look something like this:

```
HRESULT Spin ( enum Spin nSpin ) {
  // Check range
  if ( ANTICLOCKWISE > nSpin || CLOCKWISE < nSpin )
    return E_INVALIDARG;
  // Method implementation goes here
}
```

For more complex enumerations whose values do not form a discrete range, the checking code becomes more complex. For the SOMEVALUES enumeration shown in Listing 3.6, the code would look like this:

```
HRESULT TakeSomeValue ( enum SOMEVALUES val ) {
  // Check value
  if ( POS_X != val && POS_Y != val && POS_Z != val )
    return E_INVALIDARG;
  // Method implementation goes here
}
```

While the code is fairly concise for this enumeration, imagine how verbose the code would be for an enumeration containing a significant number of constants, say 20 or more.

Object References

In addition to dealing with primitive data types, COM developers often need to pass references to COM objects into and out of methods. Describing such methods in IDL is straightforward.

```
HRESULT TakeAnObjRef ( [in] IAtom* pAtom );
HRESULT ReturnAnObjRef (
  [out,retval] IAtom** ppAtom );
```

Method definitions such as these, with strongly typed object references, are very common in COM interfaces. The object reference is strongly typed because it is known at design time and at compile time what the interface type will be. Calling the former method from C++ would look like this:

```
IAtom* pAtom;
// Initialize pAtom
HR(pObj->TakeAnObjRef ( pAtom ));
```

while a call to the latter would look something like this:

```
IAtom* pAtom = 0;
HR(pObj->ReturnAnObjRef ( &pAtom));
// Do something with returned object
pAtom->Release();
```

The Visual Basic call sequence for input would be

```
Dim pAtom As IAtom
' Initialize pAtom
pObj.TakeAnObjRef pAtom
```

and the output example would be

```
Dim pAtom as IAtom
Set pAtom = pObj.ReturnAnObjRef
' Do something with returned object
Set pAtom = Nothing
```

Sometimes it may not be possible to specify a strongly typed parameter, perhaps because a method is capable of working with a variety of interfaces. For example, consider a method that persisted an object and was able to do so using IPersistStream, IPersistStorage, or IPersistXML. While defining a method that takes one of these interfaces as input would be typesafe, it would restrict the number of objects that the method could work with to those that implemented that particular interface. For greater flexibility, what is needed is a method that can take an untyped object reference. Such a method would look like this in IDL:

```
HRESULT PersistObject ( [in] IUnknown*pUnk );
```

This would allow the following call sequence.

```
IPersistStream*p1;
IPersistXML*p2;
IPersistStorage*p3;
// p1, p2 and p3 initialized here
HR(pObj->PersistObject ( p1 ));
HR(pObj->PersistObject ( p2 ));
HR(pObj->PersistObject ( p3 ));
```

Because all interfaces are type-compatible with IUnknown, each of the object references is a valid parameter to the PersistObject method. The implementation of the PersistObject method is shown in Listing 3.8.

Listing 3.8 Brute force implementation of PersistObject

```
STDMETHODIMP PersistObject ( IUnknown*pUnk ){
  IPersistStream*pps = 0;
  HRESULT hr = pUnk->QueryInterface ( __uuidof ( pps ),
                                      (void**)&pps );
  if ( SUCCEEDED (hr)) {
    // Persist object into a stream
  }
  else {
    IPersistStorage*ppst = 0;
    hr = pUnk->QueryInterface ( __uuidof ( ppst ),
                                (void**)&ppst );
    if ( SUCCEEDED ( hr )) {
      // Persist object to storage
    }
    else {
      // Deal with IPersistXML case...
    }
  }

  return S_OK;
}
```

The problem with this approach is that the method parameter is not type-safe. Multiple calls to QueryInterface and therefore multiple round trips to the input object passed in by the client may be required before a usable interface is found. Effectively, the object is providing type safety at runtime. It is likely that the input object implements only one of the persistence interfaces, so all but one call to QueryInterface are doomed to failure. Furthermore, the object reference passed into the method call by the client is actually strongly typed to a specific persistence interface. In all likelihood, it will be this interface that the method implementation ends up using to persist the object. If the implementation of `PersistObject` knew which persistence interface the client had passed into the method, no calls to `QueryInterface` would be required. Unfortunately, the client was unable to communicate anything about the actual interface type to the object.

The [iid_is] Attribute

The IDL attribute `[iid_is]` exists to help with this problem, allowing the caller of a method to type strongly an object reference at runtime, rather than at compile time. The strongly typed object reference is then available to the method implementation without further calls to `QueryInterface`. To use `[iid_is]`, the method signature would be amended thus:

```
HRESULT PersistObject ( [in] REFIID riid,
            [in,iid_is(riid)] IUnknown*pUnk );
```

Note the additional parameter, `riid`, and the `[iid_is]` attribute attached to the second parameter. The interception code uses the relationship between the two parameters to marshal a typed object reference into the method implementation rather than merely marshaling `IUnknown`. The client-side call sequence would be amended to pass the IID with the call.

```
IPersistStream*p1;
IPersistXML*p2;
IPersistStorage*p3;
// p1, p2 and p3 initialized here
HR(pObj->PersistObject ( IID_IPersistStream, p1 ));
HR(pObj->PersistObject ( IID_IPersistXML, p2 ));
HR(pObj->PersistObject ( IID_IPersistStorage, p3 ));
```

The interception code will always call `QueryInterface` through the object reference passed in `pUnk` for the IID provided in the `riid` parameter. If the object referred to by `pUnk` does not support the IID passed in `riid`, then the interceptor will fail the call to `PersistObject`, returning `E_NOINTERFACE`. Thus, the interceptor ensures that the implementation of `PersistObject` never receives mismatched parameters. However, it is still important for the client to ensure that the IID and the type of the object reference actually match, because, in the absence of interception code, an incorrectly typed object reference could still be passed. For example, it would be very easy to make the mistake

```
IPersistStream*p;
// p initialized here
HR(pObj->PersistObject ( IID_IPersistStorage, p ));
```

and have the implementation of `PersistObject` receive an `IPersistStream` that it thinks is an `IPersistStorage`. The `__uuidof` operator is very useful in this case and ensures that the correct IID is extracted from the object reference and passed into the method.

```
IPersistStream*p1;
IPersistXML*p2;
IPersistStorage*p3;
// p1, p2 and p3 initialized here
HR(pObj->PersistObject ( __uuidof ( p1 ), p1 ));
HR(pObj->PersistObject ( __uuidof ( p2 ), p2 ));
HR(pObj->PersistObject ( __uuidof ( p3 ), p3 ));
```

Use of the `[iid_is]` attribute makes the method implementation much simpler, as shown in Listing 3.9.

Listing 3.9 [iid_is] implementation of PersistObject
```
STDMETHODIMP PersistObject ( REFIID riid,
                             IUnknown* pUnk ) {
  if ( IID_IPersistStream == riid ) {
    IPersistStream*pps = (IPersistStream*)pUnk;
    // Persist object into a stream
  }
  else if ( IID_IPersistStorage == riid ) {
    IPersistStorage* ppst = (IPersistStorage*)pUnk;
    // Persist object to storage
  }
  else {
    // Deal with other cases…
  }
  return S_OK;
}
```

Note that the method never calls `QueryInterface` and thus incurs no round trips to the input object. Casting `pUnk` to the appropriate interface is safe in this case, because the object reference passed in is not merely an `IUnknown` but is more strongly typed. Sometimes the following signature will be used.

```
HRESULT PersistObject ( [in] REFIID riid,
              [in,iid_is(riid)] void*pUnk );
```

This signature forces the client to perform a cast in order to make the call and is of little real benefit.

```
IPersistStream*p1;
IPersistXML*p2;
IPersistStorage*p3;
// p1, p2 and p3 initialized here
HR(pObj->PersistObject ( __uuidof ( p1 ), (void*)p1 ));
HR(pObj->PersistObject ( __uuidof ( p2 ), (void*)p2 ));
HR(pObj->PersistObject ( __uuidof ( p3 ), (void*)p3 ));
```

The method implementation has to perform a cast with both parameter types, and so there is little difference from its perspective.

The [iid_is] attribute can also be used when returning object references from methods. `QueryInterface` is an example of this technique.

```
HRESULT QueryInterface ( [in] REFIID riid,
               [out,iid_is(riid)] void**ppv );
```

Note that with `QueryInterface` the client is specifying the required type through the input parameter `riid` and the interception layer returns a typed object reference. This makes it critical that `QueryInterface` actually return a pointer to the correct interface. The use of `void**` rather than `IUnknown**` for the type of the second parameter is largely stylistic, because the caller would have to cast the second parameter in order to make the call even if `IUnknown**` were used. Making the parameter type `void**` highlights the fact that type safety may be in jeopardy and the client must ensure that the IID matches the type of the object reference passed in the second parameter.[1]

In some cases, the method implementation will determine the type of the returned interface. For example, imagine a version of `PersistObject` that returned a dynamically typed object reference to the storage medium to which

---

[1] For a detailed discussion of this and other aspects of `QueryInterface`, see *Essential COM* (Box, Addison-Wesley, 1998), Chapter 2.

the input object was persisted. For example, if the input object supported `IPersistStream`, the method would return the `IStream` into which the object was written, whereas if the input object supported `IPersistStorage`, an `IStorage` would be returned. The IDL for such a method would look like this:

```
HRESULT
PersistObjectAndReturnMedium ( [in] REFIID riidobj,
                    [in,iid_is(riidobj)] IUnknown*pObj,
                                [out] REFIID riidmed,
                    [out,iid_is(riidmed)] void**ppMed );
```

The implementation is shown in Listing 3.10. Note that the `riidmed` parameter is set to the type of the object reference returned in `ppMed`.

Listing 3.10 Implementation of PersistObjectAndReturnMedium

```
STDMETHODIMP
PersistObjectAndReturnMedium ( REFIID riidobj,
                                IUnknown*pObj,
                                REFIID riidmed,
                                void**ppMed ) {
  if ( IID_IPersistStream == riidobj ) {
    IPersistStream*pps = (IPersistStream*)pObj;
    IStream* pStream = 0;
    // Create a stream object and persist object
    // Set type of returned object reference
    riidmed = IID_IStream;
    // About to make a copy of pStream
    pStream->AddRef();
    // Copy pStream into output parameter
    *ppMed = pStream;
    // Release pStream reference acquired when
    // stream object was created
    pStream->Release();
  }
  else {
    // Deal with other cases…
  }
  return S_OK;
}
```

The client-side call sequence is shown in Listing 3.11. Note that the object reference returned in `pMedium` can be safely cast to a strongly typed object reference just as the implementation of `PersistObjectAndReturnMedium` shown in Listing 3.10 can safely cast the input parameter, `pObj`.

Listing 3.11 Client-side call sequence for PersistObjectAndReturnMedium

```
IPersistStream*p1;
// p1 initialized here
IID iidMedium;
IUnknown* pMedium = 0;
HR(pObj->PersistObjectAndReturnMedium( __uuidof ( p1 ),
                                       p1,
                                       &iidMedium,
                                       &pMedium ));
// Check for IStream
if ( IID_IStream == iidMedium ) {
  IStream* pStream = reinterpret_cast<IStream*>(pMedium);
  // Do something with stream
}
else {
// Check for other mediums
}
```

Information about the `[iid_is]` attribute is not present in type libraries and so should be avoided for interfaces marked `[oleautomation]` or `[dual]`—that is, for those that use the universal marshaler. Unfortunately, the MIDL compiler will not generate an error when compiling the interface shown in Listing 3.12.

Listing 3.12 Erroneous use of [iid_is] and [oleautomation]

```
[
  uuid(03676C26-38AC-4E0E-ABA8-CE44C98DBC1D),
  object,
  oleautomation
]
interface IBadIIDIs : IUnknown {
  HRESULT TakeAnObjRef ( [in] REFIID riid,
          [in, iid_is(riid)] IUnknown* pUnk );
  HRESULT TakeAnObjRef2 ( [in] REFIID riid,
            [in, iid_is(riid)] void*p );
}
```

Any `QueryInterface` request for `IBadIIDIs` will fail, with the HRESULT 0x80020008, 'Bad variable type'. This refers to the `void*` in the method `TakeAnObjRef2`. In the absence of `[iid_is]`, `void*` is invalid as a parameter type in a remoted interface because the interception code has no way of knowing what the pointer refers to and so is unable to marshal it. Because the [iid_is] attribute is not present in standard type information, it is effectively missing from both the methods in Listing 3.12. Removing the second method will allow QueryInterface to succeed. In this case, the interception code will at least marshal an object reference to the caller, albeit of type IUnknown rather than anything more specific. Unfortunately, any attempt to cast the IUnknown to a stronger type will not work as expected. Therefore, interfaces that use the universal marshaler must either use strongly typed object references or force the method implementation to use QueryInterface, as shown in the implementation of PersistObject in Listing 3.8.

Type Information and Object References

As noted in the previous chapter, despite there being two forms of type information there is only one marshaling architecture. Interfaces whose interceptors are built from Oicf type information can handle references to interfaces whose interceptors are built from standard type information, and vice versa. For example, the IDL shown in Listing 3.13 is perfectly legal.

Listing 3.13 Examples of the use of interfaces marshaled using standard and Oicf type information as method parameters

```
import "objidl.idl";
[
  object,
  uuid(350C3E56-2625-40D8-8EA2-207BFE570396)
]
interface IOicf : IUnknown {
  HRESULT DoSomething ( [in] BSTR bstr );
}
// Forward reference to ITlb which is defined in
// the library block but used in ITakeObjRefsOicf
interface ITlb;
[
  object,
  uuid(5C5426E2-F679-457D-B9B5-5B33B35ABCA4)
]
interface ITakeObjRefsOicf : IUnknown {
  HRESULT TakeAnOicfObjRef ( [in] IOicf * p );
  HRESULT TakeATlbObjRef ( [in] ITlb * p );
}
```

```
[
  uuid(C640F6F4-8F61-4E4B-9859-160CBF3F7EED),
  version(1.0)
]
library OBJREFLib {
  importlib("stdole2.tlb");
  [
    object,
    uuid(11FC2290-89AA-4EB7-B85C-8AEC7953ECA9),
    oleautomation
  ]
  interface ITlb : IUnknown {
    HRESULT DoSomething ( [in] BSTR bstr );
  }

  [
    object,
    uuid(655136D7-91F2-405E-B934-181DBFF9E93F),
    oleautomation
  ]
  interface ITakeObjRefsTlb : IUnknown {
    HRESULT TakeAnOicfObjRef ( [in] IOicf * p );
    HRESULT TakeATlbObjRef ( [in] ITlb * p );
  };
}
```

Note that interceptors for `ITakeObjRefsOicf` and `IOicf` are built from Oicf type information whereas interceptors for `ITakeObjRefsTlb` and `ITlb` are built from standard type information. Both `ITakeObjRefsOicf` and `ITakeObjrefsTlb` have methods with parameters of types `IOicf` and `ITlb`.

Structures

Although primitive types are very useful, and form the basis for all other types in IDL, few developers can manage with primitive types alone. Similarly, while passing object references is a straightforward way of making complex and encapsulated data available to a method implementation or returning such data to a client, it is not always the most efficient mechanism. Certainly, when standard marshaling is used, object references, as their name implies, marshal by reference, and a round trip to the object is required to retrieve any data, which is inefficient.

IDL also supports the creation of user-defined types or structures, which are a more efficient way of passing data. Because structures are marshaled by value, rather than by reference, the data is directly accessible and requires no extra round trips to retrieve. As with any efficiency gain, there are tradeoffs. First, the amount of space taken up on the wire by the structure may well exceed that of an object reference, and second, the size of the structure in memory may exceed the size of a proxy required in the case of an object reference. A third tradeoff is that the recipient has direct access to the data; it is no longer encapsulated behind a programmatic interface.

When a structure is being defined, the `struct` keyword is used. It is always followed by a name and opening and closing curly braces and is terminated by a semicolon. This syntax, like many other type definitions in IDL, is identical to the C programming language syntax. Field definitions appear between the curly braces, and after definition the new type may be used as a method parameter or as a field in another structure. Listing 3.14 shows a structure definition `MyPoint`, which contains simple field types, and a second structure definition `MyRect`, which contains fields of type `MyPoint` along with an associated interface.[2]

Listing 3.14 Structure definitions in IDL

```
struct MyPoint {
  long x,y;
};
struct MyRect {
  struct MyPoint topleft;
  struct MyPoint bottomright;
};
[
  uuid(E652F456-ADF4-4503-A2BB-847EB1DB5174),
  object
]
interface IStruct : IUnknown {
  HRESULT TakeAPoint ( [in] struct MyPoint pt );
  HRESULT TakeARect ( [in] struct MyRect rect );
}
```

---

[2] `Point` and `Rect` types are defined in `wtypes.idl`; hence the use of the names `MyPoint` and `MyRect`.

A given structure definition maps directly in C++, so the `MyPoint` and `MyRect` structures would appear verbatim in the MIDL-generated header file. The C++ implementation of `IStruct` is shown below.

```
STDMETHODIMP TakeAPoint ( struct MyPoint pt ) {
   // Method implementation goes here
}
STDMETHODIMP TakeARect ( struct MyRect rect ) {
   // Method implementation goes here
}
```

The C++ client-side call sequence is shown in Listing 3.15.

Listing 3.15 Passing user-defined types in C++
```
IStruct* pObj;
// Initialize pObj here
MyPoint pt;
pt.x = 50;
pt.y = 50;
HR(pObj->TakeAPoint ( pt ));
MyRect square;
square.topleft = pt;
square.bottomright.x = 100;
square.bottomright.y = 100;
HR( pObj->TakeARect ( rect ));
```

In Visual Basic, the `MyPoint` and `MyRect` types may be used as data types provided they appear in a referenced type library. An example usage is shown in Listing 3.16.

Listing 3.16 Using user-defined types in Visual Basic
```
Dim pt As MyPoint
Dim square As MyRect
pt1.x = 0
pt1.y = 0
square.topleft = pt1
square.bottomright.x = 10
square.bottomright.y = 10
```

Structures may also be used as method parameters, but only when passed by reference, because Visual Basic does not support passing of user-defined types by value. This restriction applies both to the calling of methods that take user-defined types by value and to the implementation of those methods.

Consequently, a different interface is needed to allow Visual Basic to handle the MyPoint and MyRect datatypes as method parameters.

```
[
  uuid(3b1f6b5b-6101-4338-8409-bcc585390f89),
  object
]
interface IStructVB : IUnknown {
  HRESULT TakeAPointByRef ( [in] struct MyPoint* pPt );
  HRESULT TakeARectByRef ( [in] struct MyRect* pRect );
}
```

This translates to the following Visual Basic implementation code.

```
Implements IStructVB
Private Sub _
IStructVB_TakeAPointByRef( ByRef pPt As MyPoint)
' Method implementation goes here
End Sub
Private Sub _
IStructVB_TakeARectByRef( ByRef pRect As MyRect)
' Method implementation goes here
End Sub
```

The Visual Basic client-side call sequence is shown in Listing 3.17.

Listing 3.17 Passing user-defined types in Visual Basic
```
Sub CallIStructVB ( pObj As IStructVB )
  Dim pt As MyPoint
  pt1.x = 50
  pt1.y = 50
  pObj.TakeAPointByRef pt
  Dim square As MyRect
  square.topleft = pt1
  square.bottomright.x = 100
  square.bottomright.y = 100
  pObj.TakeARectByRef rect
End Sub
```

Visual Basic is unable to implement or call the methods of IStruct, because the environment generates the 'User-defined type may not be passed ByVal' error at compile time. So, when designing interfaces for use or implementation by Visual Basic always use pointers to user-defined types—that is, pass by reference rather than by value. Reference types as method parameters and use of reference types within structures are covered in detail in Chapter 4.

It is sometimes necessary to attach a UUID to a structure, typically in order to pass the structure in a VARIANT or SAFEARRAY (the former is detailed later in this chapter, and the latter is covered in Chapter 4). The IDL in Listing 3.18 shows a structure with an attached `[uuid]` and a corresponding interface.

Listing 3.18   Structure with [uuid] attribute

```
[
  uuid(7BC4679E-236F-41eb-A4D8-030DBB195322)
]
struct MyPoint {
  long x;
  long y;
};


[
  uuid(DB2E7543-9F68-451b-BB02-6B23CE6DD2BC),
  object
]
interface ITakePoints : IUnknown {
  HRESULT TakeAPoint ( [in] struct MyPoint pt );
}
```

Unfortunately, owing to a bug in the MIDL compiler, if the IDL above is contained within a library block, the following appears in the C++ header file.

```
MIDL_INTERFACE("7BC4679E-236F-41eb-A4D8-030DBB195322")
ITakePoints : public IUnknown {
public:
  HRESULT TakeAPoint ( /* [in] */ struct MyPoint pt ) = 0;
};
```

The UUID attached to the `ITakePoints` interface is the UUID of the `MyPoint` structure rather than the UUID of `ITakePoints`. Note that this error occurs whenever a structure definition with a `[uuid]` attribute immediately precedes an interface definition within a library block. There are three workarounds for this bug. The first is to describe all structures with attached UUIDs in separate IDL files. This completely removes the problem. The second approach is to ensure that all structure definitions with attached UUIDs appear outside a library block. This approach works well with one caveat: if a reference to a structure immediately precedes the interface definition inside the library block, the error will still occur. So the IDL shown in Listing 3.19 would still exhibit the problem.

Listing 3.19 Structure reference inside library block

```
[
  uuid(7BC4679E-236F-41eb-A4D8-030DBB195322)
]
struct MyPoint {
  long x;
  long y;
};

[
  uuid(D9610FBC-A5CF-4d51-AC46-5AC2D48C021C),
  version(1.0)
]
library BugLib {
  importlib("stdole2.tlb");
  struct MyPoint; // This line causes the problem
  [
    uuid(DB2E7543-9F68-451b-BB02-6B23CE6DD2BC),
    object
  ]
  interface ITakePoints : IUnknown {
    HRESULT TakeAPoint ( [in] struct MyPoint pt );
  }
}
```

The problem recurs because of the reference to `struct MyPoint` inside the library block. The third solution is to place all structure definitions at the end of the library block, as shown in Listing 3.20. Even though `struct MyPoint` is referenced inside the interface `ITakePoints`, ostensibly before it is defined, the IDL compiles correctly without error. Of the three approaches, the first is perhaps the cleanest, while the third is the simplest to implement.

Listing 3.20 Structure definition at the end of the library block

```
[
  uuid(53a52db0-3fa2-4588-900d-dfc83fd523a7),
  version(1.0)
]
```

```
library GoodLib {
  importlib("stdole2.tlb");
  [
    uuid(DB2E7543-9F68-451b-BB02-6B23CE6DD2BC),
    object
  ]
  interface ITakePoints : IUnknown {
    HRESULT TakeAPoint ( [in] struct MyPoint foo );
  }

  [
    uuid(7BC4679E-236F-41eb-A4D8-030DBB195322)
  ]
  struct MyPoint {
    long x;
    long y;
  };
}
```

Unions

In addition to structures, many developers also make use of union data types. A union is similar to a structure in that it has multiple fields; however, the fields all overlap in memory, and consequently only one field has meaning at any given moment. Unions are useful for reducing storage requirements and, more importantly, can be used where the type of a method parameter is not known until runtime. Unions are supported only in C/C++, and inside a given application a programmer typically knows which field in the union is valid at any given point in the program based on some information that is external to the union itself—the value of a structure field or method parameter, for example. Such information discriminates between the fields in the union and is known as the discriminant.

Consider the pseudo-IDL fragment shown in Listing 3.21 and the corresponding client-side call sequence shown in Listing 3.22. The union models a person's salary, which may need to be represented as a 16- or 32-bit unsigned integer or a double-precision floating point number. People paid in Sterling will use the 16- or 32-bit integer as appropriate based on the amount they get paid. Those paid in Troy ounces of gold will use the floating point number, because precision to one 100th of an ounce is important. The method parameter `nField` is the discriminant, informing the method implementation which field in the union is valid during any given call, where the values 1, 2, and 3 correspond to the fields `s`, `l`, and `lf`, respectively. A sample method implementation is shown in Listing 3.23.

Listing 3.21 Pseudo-IDL definition of Salary union

```
union Salary {
  short s;
  long l;
  double lf;
};


[
  uuid(5F4B4A9E-165B-45e0-9DEB-31B7FD47AE3D),
  object
]
interface IDoUnions : IUnknown {
  HRESULT ProcessSalary ( [in] short nField,
                          [in] union Salary sal );
}
```

Listing 3.22 Client-side call sequence for pseudo-IDL Salary union

```
union Salary somesal;
u.s = 45000;
HR(p->ProcessSalary ( 1, somesal ));
u.l = 0xFEFIF000;
HR(p->ProcessSalary ( 2, somesal ));
u.lf = 54.654;
HR(p->ProcessSalary ( 3, somesal ));
```

Listing 3.23 Implementation of IDoUnions::ProcessSalary

```
STDMETHODIMP ProcessSalary ( short nField,
                             union Salary sal ) {
  if ( SMALLSALARY == nField ) {
    // Do something with sal.s
  }
  else if ( LARGESALARY == nField ) {
    // Do something with sal.l
  }
  else if ( GOLDSALARY == nField ) {
    // Do something with sal.lf
  }
```

```
    else
      return E_INVALIDARG;

    return S_OK;
  }
```

Although this call sequence is fine in straight C/C++ in the absence of
COM, with this invalid IDL definition of a union, an interceptor has no way of
knowing which field to marshal on any given cross-context call. Although
the client and the method implementation are aware of the relationship
between the value of the discriminant and the fields in the union, the interception code has no knowledge of that relationship. It is important for the
interception code to know which field to marshal on any given call for data-
conversion reasons. The stub may have to perform byte ordering and floating
point conversions at unmarshal time, and if the proxy does not know which
field is valid at call time, the stub cannot know how to unmarshal it correctly.
This means that the discriminant, the nField parameter in this case, must be
linked in some way to the union in order to tell the interception layer which
field to marshal.

IDL provides two ways of specifying the discriminant for a union type.
The first approach uses the union keyword along with the [switch_type],
[switch_is], and [case] attributes. The union keyword is followed by
the name of the union and a pair of curly braces. Inside the curly braces,
the union fields are listed. Each field is annotated with the [case] attribute,
which takes a value as an argument. The argument denotes which discriminant value refers to that field in the union. The attribute is applied to the
union definition and specifies the IDL type of the discriminant, which must be
one of boolean, byte, small, short, int, long, char, or an enumerated
type.

Whenever the union type is used as a method parameter or structure field,
the [switch_is] attribute is used. This attribute takes as an argument the
name of the method parameter or structure field that is to be used as the discriminant. This provides the link between the discriminant and the union itself.
The type of the method parameter or structure field specified by the
[switch_is] attribute must match the type specified by the [switch_type]

attribute. Recoding Listing 3.21 to use these constructs gives the IDL shown in Listing 3.24.

Listing 3.24 Salary union using [switch_type] and [switch_is]

```
[switch_type ( short )] union Salary {
  [case(1)] short ;
  [case(2)] long l;
  [case(3)] double lf;
};

[
  uuid(ac93fa4f-938f-48b8-9859-f21052d89bf1),
  object
]
interface IReallyDoUnions : IUnknown {
  HRESULT ProcessSalary ( [in] short nField,
       [in,switch_is(nField)] union Salary sal );
}
```

Note that the `union` keyword is followed by the tag name for the union, `Salary` in this case. The client-side calling code for calls to `ProcessSalary` would be exactly the same as that shown in Listing 3.22, and the method implementation would be as shown in Listing 3.23. Because of the relationship between the `nField` parameter and the union parameter `sal`, any interception code is able to marshal the data correctly.

A second approach to unions is to use what IDL calls an encapsulated union. An encapsulated union is one for which, after processing by the MIDL compiler, the union and the discriminant are wrapped or encapsulated by a structure. Such unions are defined using the `union`, `switch`, and `case` keywords. The `union` keyword is followed by the name to be assigned to the encapsulating structure. The `switch` keyword follows the structure name and takes the type and name of the discriminant as an argument. An optional name for the union follows the `switch` keyword and is itself followed by curly braces. The `case` keyword appears inside the curly braces along with the field definitions and is used to denote which discriminant values refer to which field in the union. Recoding the union from Listing 3.21 as an encapsulated union gives the IDL shown in Listing 3.25.

Listing 3.25 Salary union as an encapsulated union

```
union Salary switch ( short nField ) _Salary {
  case 1: short s;
  case 2: long l;
  case 3: double lf;
};
```

The resulting C/C++ header file would contain a wrapper structure and a union with a strange tag name, as shown in Listing 3.26.

Listing 3.26 Wrapper structure generated for encapsulated union

```
struct Salary {
  short nField;
  union __MIDL___MIDL_itf_salary_0000_0002 {
    float f;
    double lf;
    short s;
    long l;
  } _Salary;
};
```

Note that the wrapper structure takes the first name in the union definition, `Salary`, and that the embedded union takes the second name, `_Salary`, as its field name within the wrapper structure. If the second name is omitted, the embedded union field is given the name `tagged_union`. The union is given the type name `__MIDL___MIDL_itf_salary_0000_0001`, where the salary part is based on the filename in which the union was defined, `salary.idl` in this case. The number at the end of the name specifies that the union was the first construct in this file to be assigned a name by the MIDL compiler, further data types would be assigned incrementing numbers resulting in `__MIDL___MIDL_itf_salary_0000_0002`, and so on. When methods that take a `Salary` union as a parameter are defined in IDL, the `union` keyword is used.

```
HRESULT ProcessSalary ( [in] union Salary sal );
```

However, the resulting method signature in the header file takes the structure as its parameter.

```
HRESULT SetSalary ( struct Salary sal );
```

So the client-side call sequence is as shown in Listing 3.27.

Listing 3.27 Client-side call sequence for encapsulated union
```
struct Salary somesal;
u.nField = 1;
u.s = 45000;
HR(p->ProcessSalary ( somesal ));
u.nField = 2;
u.l = 0xFEFIF000;
HR(p->ProcessSalary (somesal ));
u.nField = 3;
u.lf = 54.654;
HR(p->ProcessSalary (somesal ));
```

It may be useful to use an enumeration when defining a union, so `Salary` could be redefined as shown in Listing 3.28.

Listing 3.28 Union definition using an enumeration
```
[v1_enum] enum SALARYSIZE {
  SMALLSALARY,
  LARGESALARY,
  GOLDSALARY
};
union Salary
switch ( enum SALARYSIZE nField ) _Salary {
  case SMALLSALARY: short s;
  case LARGESALARY: long l;
  case GOLDSALARY:  double lf;
};
```

The client-side call sequence would be modified to use the enumerated constants as shown in Listing 3.29.

Listing 3.29 Client-side call sequence using enumerated constants
```
struct Salary somesal;
u.nField = SMALLSALARY;
u.s = 45000;
HR(p->ProcessSalary ( somesal ));
u.nField = LARGESALARY;
u.l = 0xFEFIF000;
HR(p->ProcessSalary (somesal ));
u.nField = GOLDSALARY;
u.lf = 54.654;
HR(p->ProcessSalary (somesal ));
```

Using enumerations with unions makes the union definition and the calling code easier to read. Enumeration constants could also be used in the method implementation, aiding readability there also. Listing 3.30 shows an example method implementation.

Listing 3.30   Implementation of ProcessSalary using encapsulated union

```
STDMETHODIMP ProcessSalary ( struct Salary sal ) {
  if ( SMALLSALARY == sal.nField ) {
    // Process small salary
  }
  else if ( LARGESALARY == sal.nField ) {
    // Process large salary
  }
  else if ( GOLDSALARY == sal.nField ) {
    // Process gold salary
  }
  else
    return E_INVALIDARG;

  return S_OK;
}
```

The choice between encapsulated and nonencapsulated unions is mainly one of style. The author prefers encapsulated unions, but the system IDL files are almost evenly split between the two forms. It should be noted that marshaling of union types is not supported by standard type information, so the `[oleautomation]` and `[dual]` keywords should not be used for any interface that takes a union, or a structure that contains a union, as a parameter.

The VARIANT

User-defined unions can be used only from C/C++, but Visual Basic developers still have a requirement to pass parameters whose types are not known until runtime. Fortunately, IDL has a particular discriminated union data type, called VARIANT, that can be used from both C/C++ and Visual Basic. The VARIANT is a fixed union in that it contains a predefined set of types, but the type list is very comprehensive. In IDL, the VARIANT is actually a structure containing a union, rather than a typical IDL encapsulated union. The definition of the VARIANT can be found in the system IDL file `oaidl.idl`. The structure has a discriminant field, `vt`, that is used to determine which field in the union is currently valid, just like the discriminant in an encapsulated union.

The `vt` field can contain a variety of constants, each specifying a different data type and corresponding union field. Each supported data type has a specific constant, and there are modifiers to allow values to be passed by reference and to allow arrays of values to be passed. The supported primitive types and the associated constants and field names are listed in Table 3.4.

Note that the `VT_` values used for the `VARIANT` discriminator are the same as those used in the type library representation of the various IDL types shown earlier in Table 3.2. Note also that the list of types is comprehensive, covering all IDL character, integer, and floating point types. In fact, a VARIANT can contain more that just primitive IDL types: it can also contain more complex types such as strings, dates, currency values, and object references. These types are listed in Table 3.5.

Table 3.4   Primitive VARIANT types

IDL Type	Typedef	vt Value	Variant Field Name
signed char	CHAR	VT_I1	cVal
unsigned char	BYTE	VT_UI1	bVal
signed hyper	LONGLONG	VT_I8	llVal
unsigned hyper	ULONGLONG	VT_UI8	ullVal
signed int	INT	VT_INT	intVal
unsigned int	UINT	VT_UINT	uintVal
signed __int64	LONGLONG	VT_I8	llVal
unsigned __int64	ULONGLONG	VT_UI8	ullVal
signed long	LONG	VT_I4	lVal
unsigned long	ULONG	VT_UI4	ulVal
signed short	SHORT	VT_I2	iVal
unsigned short	USHORT	VT_UI2	uiVal
signed small	CHAR	VT_I1	cVal
unsigned small	BYTE	VT_UI1	bVal
double	DOUBLE	VT_R8	dblVal
float	FLOAT	VT_R4	fltVal

Table 3.5 Complex VARIANT types

IDL Type	Typedef	vt Value	Variant Field Name
VARIANT_BOOL	VARIANT_BOOL	VT_BOOL	boolVal
CY	CY	VT_CY	cyVal
DATE	DATE	VT_DATE	date
BSTR	BSTR	VT_BSTR	bstrVal
IUnknown*	IUnknown*	VT_UNKNOWN	punkVal
IDispatch*	IDispatch*	VT_DISPATCH	pdispVal
User-defined type	Not applicable	VT_RECORD	pvRecord
SAFEARRAY*	SAFEARRAY*	VT_ARRAY	parray

Using VARIANTs in Visual Basic is very natural; any declared variable whose type is not specified is implicitly a VARIANT.

```
Dim x As Long
Dim y
```

While `x` is explicitly typed as `Long`, `y` is a VARIANT. Note that `y` would be a VARIANT in the following fragment also.

```
Dim y, x As Long
```

This is because the `As Long` clause refers only to the variable to its immediate left—that is, x—so `y` does not have a specific type and hence is of type VARIANT. Variables can also be declared explicitly as being of type VARIANT.

```
Dim x As Variant, y As Variant
```

Variables in scripting languages, such as Visual Basic Script and JavaScript, are of type VARIANT because these languages do not support typed variables.

Assigning numeric or string values to a VARIANT is straightforward.

```
Dim x
x = 10
x = 2.456
x = "Hello World"
```

VARIANTs can be passed into various methods, and the Visual Basic runtime will coerce the type as necessary; consider the following IDL.

```
HRESULT TakeALong ( [in] long l );
```

In the call sequence shown in Listing 3.31, the Visual Basic runtime will convert the 16-bit integer to a 32-bit integer in the first call and will convert the string to a 32-bit integer in the second call.

Listing 3.31 Using VARIANTs from Visual Basic
```
Dim x
x = 1000
pObj.TakeALong x
x = "2345"
pObj.TakeALong x
```

Dealing with VARIANTs from C/C++ requires more work than in Visual Basic. The VARIANT is a structure containing a nested union and has some associated APIs for construction, copy construction, destruction, and type coercion. These APIs are shown in Listing 3.32.[3]

Listing 3.32 System APIs for managing VARIANTs
```
// Constructor: Initialize a VARIANT ( zero memory )
void VariantInit ( VARIANTARG * pvarg);
// Destructor: Clear a VARIANT ( release embedded
// resources )
 HRESULT VariantClear ( VARIANTARG * pvarg);
// Copy constructor: Copy a VARIANT ( copy embedded
// resources )
HRESULT VariantCopy ( VARIANTARG * pvargDest,
                      VARIANTARG * pvargSrc);
// Copy constructor: Copy a VARIANT with BYREF and
// make it BYVAL
HRESULT VariantCopyInd ( VARIANT * pvarDest,
                         VARIANTARG * pvargSrc);
// Type coercion: Coerce a VARIANT from one type to
// another
HRESULT VariantChangeType ( VARIANTARG * pvargDest,
                            VARIANTARG * pvarSrc,
                            USHORT wFlags, VARTYPE vt);
```

---

[3] Most C++ developers use a wrapper class when dealing with VARIANTs and hence do not call these APIs directly. The author prefers the ATL `CComVariant` wrapper.

```
// Type coercion: Coerce a VARIANT from one type to
// another for a specific locale
HRESULT VariantChangeTypeEx ( VARIANTARG * pvargDest,
                              VARIANTARG * pvarSrc,
                              LCID lcid, USHORT wFlags,
                              VARTYPE vt);
```

Note that, strictly speaking, VARIANTARG should be used for method parameters and VARIANT should be used for method return values. However, the two types are syntactically synonymous and are typically used interchangeably. Unlike in Visual Basic, where the runtime performs coercion automatically when calling methods from C++, the program must perform coercion explicitly. Converting the Visual Basic call sequence shown in Listing 3.31 to C++ gives the source code shown in Listing 3.33.

Listing 3.33 Using VARIANTs from C++
```
VARIANT x;
VariantInit ( &x );
x.vt = VT_I2;
x.iVal = 1000;
VariantChangeType ( &x, &x, 0, VT_I4 );
pObj->TakeALong ( x.lVal );
x.vt = VT_BSTR;
x.bstrVal = SysAllocString ( L"2345" );
VariantChangeType ( &x, &x, 0, VT_I4 );
pObj->TakeALong ( x.lVal );
VariantClear ( &x );
```

Note that, in addition to setting the correct field of the VARIANT, the vt field must also be set to the correct value just like the discriminated union shown earlier.

Structures can also be assigned to VARIANTs provided they are described in a type library. Consider the IDL definition of an interface ITransform shown in Listing 3.34.

Listing 3.34 IDL for ITransform interface
```
import "oaidl.idl";
[
  uuid(7DB2944C-918B-4323-8F71-B58BD6427824),
  version(1.0)
]
```

```
library VTStructLib {
  [
    object,
    uuid(2561E7B5-B752-468c-A15B-29925066FD5E),
    oleautomation
  ]
  interface ITransform : IUnknown {
    HRESULT Transform( [in] VARIANT vtFirst,
                       [in] VARIANT vtSecond,
                 [out,retval] VARIANT* vtOutput  );
  }
  [
    uuid(934526BA-2310-4989-B18C-69E7C77C0F43)
  ]
  struct MyPoint {
    long x;
    long y;
  };
  [
    uuid(D2A67F09-7D6F-43b6-8F6B-13744C9E5172)
  ]
  struct MyRect {
    struct MyPoint topleft;
    struct MyPoint bottomright;
  };
}
```

The Transform method can take any combination of Point or Rect structures and returns either a MyPoint or a MyRect structure. The client must specify at runtime which combination of parameter types is being provided, and the object must specify which type is being returned.

In order to pass a structure in a VARIANT from C++, an IRecordInfo describing the structure must be used. Application developers never implement and seldom call IRecordInfo; rather, interception code uses it to determine the layout of a structure in memory and thus transmit it correctly. The system provides an implementation of IRecordInfo that can be retrieved using either GetRecordInfoFromTypeInfo or GetRecordInfoFromGuids, the latter being a wrapper around the former. Both APIs return an IRecordInfo for a particular structure based on type information for that structure. Listing 3.35 shows a C++ call sequence that uses both APIs.

Listing 3.35 Passing structures in VARIANTs in C++

```cpp
// Get the IRecordInfo for Point using the
// GetRecordInfoFromTypeInfo API
CComPtr<ITypeLib> sptl = 0;
HR(LoadRegTypeLib ( LIBID_VTStructLib,
                       1, 0, 0, &sptl ));
CComPtr<ITypeInfo> sptipt = 0;
HR(ptl->GetTypeInfoOfGuid ( __uuidof ( struct MyPoint ),
                               &sptipt ));
IRecordInfo* pript = 0;
HR(GetRecordInfoFromTypeInfo ( ptipt, &pript ));
// Initialize a Point structure
struct MyPoint pt;
pt.x = 10; pt.y = 20;

// Get the IRecordInfo for Rect using the
// GetRecordInfoFromGuids API
IRecordInfo* prirect = 0;
HR(GetRecordInfoFromGuids ( LIBID_VTStructLib, 1, 0,
                              0, __uuidof ( struct MyRect ),
                              &prirect ));
// Initialize a Rect structure
struct MyRect rect;
rect.topleft.x = 45; rect.topleft.y = 90;
rect.bottomright.x = 55; rect.bottomright.y = 100;

// Set up VARIANTs
VARIANT vtFirst, vtSecond, vtOutput;
vtFirst.vt = VT_RECORD;
vtFirst.pvRecord = &pt;      // Address of MyPoint
pript->AddRef();             // About to make a copy
vtFirst.pRecInfo = pript;    // IRecordInfo for MyPoint
vtSecond.vt = VT_RECORD;
vtSecond.pvRecord = &rect;   // Address of MyRect
prirect->AddRef();           // About to make a copy
vtSecond.pRecInfo = prirect; // IRecordInfo for MyRect

HR(pObj->Transform ( vtFirst, vtSecond, &vtOutput ));

// Process output
if ( VT_RECORD == vtOutput.vt ){
  GUID guid;
  HR(vtOutput.pRecInfo->GetGuid ( &guid ));
```

```
    if ( __uuidof ( struct MyPoint ) == guid ) {
      struct MyPoint output =
        *(struct MyPoint*)vtOutput.pvRecord;
      // Do something with MyPoint
    }
    else if ( __uuidof ( struct MyRect ) == guid ) {
      struct MyRect output =
        *(struct MyRect*)vtOutput.pvRecord;
      // Do something with MyRect
    }
  }
  pript->Release();
  prirect->Release();
  VariantClear ( &vtFirst );
  VariantClear ( &vtSecond );
  VariantClear ( &vtOutput );
```

Note the initialization of the input VARIANTs; the address of the structure to be transmitted is passed, along with the appropriate IRecordInfo. Also note the use of IRecordInfo::GetGuid to retrieve the type of the returned VARIANT and process it accordingly.

The Visual Basic call sequence is more straightforward and is shown in Listing 3.36.

Listing 3.36 Passing structures in VARIANTs in Visual Basic
```
Dim pt As MyPoint
Dim rect As MyRect
pt.x = 10
pt.y = 20

rect.topleft.x = 45
rect.topleft.y = 90
rect.bottomright.x = 55
rect.bottomright.y = 100

Dim answer As Variant

answer = obj.Transform(p1, r2)
If TypeName ( answer ) = "MyPoint" Then
  ' Do something with MyPoint
ElseIf TypeName ( answer ) = "MyRect" Then
  ' Do something with MyRect
End If
```

The Visual Basic runtime packs the parameters into VARIANTs before making the method call and also deals with unpacking the fields of the resulting structure. Note the use of the `TypeName` function to determine whether a `MyPoint` or a `MyRect` was returned by the method.

The method implementation needs to determine the types of the parameters and process them accordingly. The C++ implementation of the `Transform` method is shown in Listing 3.37.

Listing 3.37 C++ implementation of Transform method

```
STDMETHODIMP Transform ( VARIANT vtFirst,
                         VARIANT vtSecond,
                         VARIANT *pvtOutput ) {
  ::VariantInit( pvtOutput );
  if ( VT_RECORD != vtFirst.vt ||
       VT_RECORD != vtSecond.vt )
    return E_INVALIDARG;

  GUID guid1, guid2;
  HR(vtFirst.pRecInfo->GetGuid(&guid1));
  HR(vtSecond.pRecInfo->GetGuid(&guid2));
  if ( __uuidof ( struct MyPoint ) == guid1 &&
       __uuidof ( struct MyPoint ) == guid2 ) {
    // Two points
    // Extract input structures
    struct MyPoint pt1 =
      *(struct MyPoint*)vtFirst.pvRecord;
    struct MyPoint pt2 =
      *(struct MyPoint*)vtSecond.pvRecord;
    // Calculate result
    struct MyPoint ptRes;
    ptRes.x = pt1.x * pt2.x;
    ptRes.y = pt1.y * pt2.y;

    IRecordInfo* pri = 0;
    HR(GetRecordInfoFromGuids (
      LIBID_VTStructLib, 1, 0, 0,
      __uuidof ( struct MyPoint ), &pri ));

    // Set up output parameter
    pvtOutput->vt = VT_RECORD;
    pvtOutput->pvRecord =
      CoTaskMemAlloc ( sizeof ( struct MyPoint ));
    pvtOutput->pRecInfo = pri;
```

```
        *(struct MyPoint*)pvtOutput->pvRecord = ptRes;
    }
    else { // Deal with other cases
    }
    return S_OK;
}
```

Note that the method uses `IRecordInfo::GetGuid` to determine which structure type was passed in each of the input parameters, just as the client-side code used `IRecordInfo::GetGuid` to determine the type of the output parameter.

The Visual Basic implementation of the method is shown in Listing 3.38.

Listing 3.38 Visual Basic implementation of Transform method
```
Private Function ITransform_Transform ( _
ByVal vtFirst As Variant, _
ByVal vtSecond As Variant) As Variant

If TypeName(vtFirst) = "MyPoint" And _
TypeName(vtSecond) = "MyPoint" Then
  Dim outpt As MyPoint
  outpt.x = vtFirst.x * vtSecond.x
  outpt.y = vtFirst.y * vtSecond.y
  ITransform_Transform = outpt
Else ' Deal with other cases
End If
End Function
```

Again, note the use of the `TypeName` function to determine the type of the input parameters.

Typedefs

It is often useful to define an alias for a particular type, often with the purpose of making source code more readable. Such aliases, also known as type definitions, or typedefs, are defined using the IDL keyword `typedef`. The syntax for a `typedef` is

```
typedef <typename> <alias>;
```

For example, here are some simple type definitions that appear in the system IDL file, `wtypes.idl`.

```
typedef byte BYTE;
typedef unsigned int UINT;
typedef int  INT;
typedef long BOOL;
typedef unsigned long DWORD;
```

Type definitions for reference types are also supported; again, here are some examples from `wtypes.idl`.

```
typedef WORD *LPWORD;
typedef DWORD *LPDWORD;
typedef IID *REFIID;
```

Once defined, a type definition can be used in place of the original type name. For example, the method

```
HRESULT TakeUnsignedInt ( [in] unsigned int n );
```

could be rewritten as

```
HRESULT TakeUnsignedInt ( [in] UINT n );
```

Type definitions can be defined for more complex data types. An example `typedef` for an enumeration is shown in Listing 3.39, although it is more common to see the `typedef` and the declaration appear in a single statement, as shown in Listing 3.40.

Listing 3.39 Typedef for an enumeration
```
enum SPIN {
  ANTICLOCKWISE = -1,
  NEUTRAL,
  CLOCKWISE
};
typedef enum SPIN SPINENUM;
typedef enum SPIN* PSPINENUM;
```

Listing 3.40 Typedef and declaration in a single statement
```
typedef enum Spin {
  ANTICLOCKWISE = -1,
  NEUTRAL,
  CLOCKWISE
} SPIN;
typedef SPIN* PSPIN;
```

Note that a `typedef` can be used as the basis for other type definitions, as in the definition of PSPIN in Listing 3.40. It is also possible to define both a value and a reference type definition in a single statement. Listing 3.41 provides an example.

Listing 3.41 Value and reference typedef in a single statement

```
typedef enum Spin {
  ANTICLOCKWISE = -1,
  NEUTRAL,
  CLOCKWISE
} SPIN, *PSPIN;
```

IDL attributes can also be included in type definitions—in which case, whenever the `typedef` is used, the IDL attributes apply. So, for the example shown in Listing 3.42, the `[v1_enum]` attribute would apply to any use of the SPIN or PSPIN type definition.

Listing 3.42 Typedef with IDL attributes

```
typedef [v1_enum] enum Spin {
  ANTICLOCKWISE = -1,
  NEUTRAL,
  CLOCKWISE
} SPIN, *PSPIN;
```

In addition to being able to alias primitive and enumerated types, type definitions can be defined for structures, unions, and object references. With structures and unions, as with enumerated types, it is typical to define the structure and the alias in a single statement.

```
typedef struct MyPoint {
  long x;
  long y;
} MYPOINT, *PMYPOINT;
```

Type definitions appear more or less verbatim in the C++ header file. The `typedef` above appears as:

```
typedef struct MyPoint {
  long x;
  long y;
} MYPOINT;
typedef struct MyPoint *PMYPOINT;
```

The only difference between the IDL and the C++ is the separation of the two aliases into two separate `typedef` statements in C++.

Aliases may also appear in type libraries, either because they are defined inside a library block or because they are referenced by something that is defined inside a library block, such as in a method parameter. In the IDL shown in Listing 3.43, the `MyPoint` type definition will appear in the generated type library because it is referenced inside the `ITrigonometry` interface definition.

Listing 3.43   Type definitions and type libraries
```
import "wtypes.idl";
typedef struct MyPoint {
    long x;
    long y;
} MYPOINT;

[
  uuid(F3AA6C8B-5976-477A-8C1B-130C4D51712F),
  version(1.0)
]
library TypedefLib {
  importlib ( "stdole2.tlb" );

  [
    object,
    uuid(5CDC7620-6710-4BFC-93E4-4EF890B7958D),
    oleautomation
  ]
  interface ITrigonometry : IUnknown {
    HRESULT AddPoint ( [in] MYPOINT* pPoint );
  }
}
```

Care should be taken when using type definitions in type libraries; the `typedef` that appears in the type library is based on the type name of the structure rather than the type name of the alias. Listing 3.44 shows the resulting `typedef` and method signature that appear in the type library generated from Listing 3.43.

Listing 3.44   Typedefs that appear in type library generated from Listing 3.43
```
// typedef
typedef struct tagMyPoint {
```

```
    long x;
    long y;
    } MyPoint;
    // method signature
    HRESULT AddPoint ( [in] MyPoint* pPoint );
```

Note that the `typedef` is called `MyPoint` in mixed case rather than `MYPOINT` in uppercase and that the tag name for the structure is `tagMyPoint` rather than `MyPoint`. The method signature uses `MyPoint` rather than `MYPOINT` as the parameter type. Because of this behavior, the common C++ practice of defining type definitions for structures using tag<name> should be avoided. For example:

```
    typedef struct tagMyPoint {
      long x;
      long y;
    } MyPoint;
```

would result in a `typedef` for `tagMyPoint` and in a tag name of `tagtagMyPoint` being placed in the type library.

```
    typedef struct tagtagMyPoint {
      long x;
      long y;
    } tagMyPoint;
```

If it is important that the C++ name and the name used in the type library, and hence in Visual Basic, be the same, then consider using identical tokens in both places:

```
    typedef struct MYPOINT {
      long x;
      long y;
    } MYPOINT;
```

Note that both tokens use exactly the same character sequence, including case. This will allow the following call sequence from C/C++:

```
    MYPOINT pt = { 5, 10 };
    HR(pObj->AddPoint ( &pt ));
```

and a similar sequence in Visual Basic:

```
Dim pt As MYPOINT
pt.x = 5
pt.y = 10
pObj.AddPoint pt
```

Alternatively, the `[public]` attribute can be used on the `typedef`. This will cause the MIDL compiler to enter two aliases into the type library; the first aliasing the structure definition to the structure tag name and the second aliasing the structure tag name to the name of the type definition. Listing 3.45 shows such a `typedef`, while Listing 3.46 shows the type definitions that appear in the type library.

Listing 3.45   Structure type definition with [public] attribute
```
[public]
typedef struct tagMyPoint {
   long x;
   long y;
} MYPOINT;
```

Listing 3.46   Typedefs appearing in type library for typedef in Listing 3.45
```
typedef struct tagtagMyPoint {
   long x;
   long y;
} tagMyPoint;
typedef [public] tagMyPoint MYPOINT;
```

Note that the first `typedef` aliases the structure definition to the token `tagMyPoint` and that the second aliases `tagMyPoint` to the token `MYPOINT`.

Type definitions can be annotated with the `[uuid]` attribute, as shown in Listing 3.47.

Listing 3.47   Typedef annotated with [uuid] attribute
```
[
   uuid(85F6ADA3-2A04-4D75-8ADC-F3945B050A1C),
   public
]
typedef struct tagMyPoint {
   long x;
   long y;
} MYPOINT;
```

If the alias above is defined or referenced inside a library block, the MIDL compiler will generate a warning, saying that it cannot attach a UUID to `tagMyPoint`. This warning is benign; the UUID is correctly attached to the `MYPOINT` typedef instead. Note that attaching the `[uuid]` attribute to a `typedef` implies the `[public]` attribute; even if the `[public]` attribute is not specified, the resulting type library is the same.

The generated C++ header file apparently has the UUID attached to the typedef.

```
typedef /* [public][uuid] */
DECLSPEC_UUID("85F6ADA3-2A04-4D75-8ADC-F3945B050A1C")
struct tagMyPoint MYPOINT;
```

Unfortunately, the `DECLSPEC_UUID` is in the wrong place; it should appear between the `struct` keyword and the tag name, `tagMyPoint`. This bug means that `__uuidof` will not work with either `struct tagMyPoint` or `MYPOINT`. The workaround for this bug is complicated and nonintuitive, the problem being ensuring that the UUID is present in both the type library and the C++ header file. The workaround consists of four steps.

1. In order to persuade the MIDL compiler to generate the `DECLSPEC_UUID` in the correct place, the `[uuid]` attribute must annotate the structure directly rather than annotating a `typedef`. This will allow `__uuidof` to be used with a combination of the `struct` keyword and the structure name.
2. A `typedef` allowing the use of the structure name without the `struct` keyword must not appear in the IDL. If such a `typedef` is required in the C/C++ header file, it must appear in a `cpp_quote`[4] statement. This will allow `__uuidof` to be used with the structure name alone, without the `struct` keyword.
3. A reference to the structure must appear inside the library block.
4. A `typedef` for the structure annotated with the `[public]` attribute must appear inside the library block. The alias must have a different name from that of the structure. Changing the case of a name does not make it a different name for this purpose.

The reference defined in step 3 and the typedef can appear in the same statement. These last two steps ensure that the UUID ends up in the type library

---

[4] See Chapter 9, "IDL Keywords", for a description of `cpp_quote`.

and enables APIs such as `GetRecordInfoFromGuids`. Combining Listing 3.43 and Listing 3.47 in light of the information above produces the IDL shown in Listing 3.48.

Listing 3.48 Getting the UUID into the type library and the header file

```
import "wtypes.idl";
// Step 1: Structure definition
[
  uuid(85F6ADA3-2A04-4D75-8ADC-F3945B050A1C),
]
struct MyPoint {
  long x;
  long y;
};
// Step 2: Emit C++ typedef into header file
cpp_quote ( "typedef struct MyPoint MyPoint;" )
[
  uuid(F3AA6C8B-5976-477A-8C1B-130C4D51712F),
  version(1.0)
]
library TypedefLib {
  importlib ( "stdole2.tlb" );
  // Steps 3 and 4: reference and typedef
  [public]
  typedef struct MyPoint* PMYPOINT;

  [
    object,
    uuid(5CDC7620-6710-4BFC-93E4-4EF890B7958D),
    oleautomation  ]
  interface ITrigonometry : IUnknown {
    HRESULT AddPoint ( [in] PMYPOINT pPoint );
  }
}
```

The structure definition in step 1 will allow the use of __uuidof (struct MyPoint) in C++ code, while step 2 allows the use of __uuidof (MyPoint). Steps 3 and 4 put the UUID for struct MyPoint into the type library. Note the use of the PMYPOINT type definition, rather than MyPoint* as used in Listing 3.43, in the method of ITrigonometry. It is critical that the name of the alias be different from the name of the structure. If the names are the same, the MIDL compiler will be unable to generate the type library.

Properties

It is common in object-based systems to expose certain aspects of an object as properties rather than as methods. COM interfaces can contain only methods, but IDL supplies several attributes that allow runtime environments such as Visual Basic and scripting languages to treat certain method calls as if they were properties, giving the illusion of direct access to the exposed data of the object. Note, however, that this is merely syntactic trickery; all access to an object occurs through the methods of its interfaces.

To describe a property in IDL, a method is annotated with one of three possible attributes: [propget], [propput], or [propputref]. Typically, properties are read/write, but it is possible to define read-only and write-only properties by omitting the [propput] and [propget] versions of a property declaration, respectively. The IDL in Listing 3.49 shows a read/write property and a read-only property.

Listing 3.49   IMolecule interface with properties

```
[
  object,
  uuid(C19F26D5-E148-4cea-8CF7-8B69C5A9F12F)
]
interface IMolecule : IUnknown {
  // Normal method
  HRESULT AddAtom ( [in] short nPosition,
                    [in] IAtom* pAtom );
  // Read/write property
  [propget] HRESULT Name (
    [out,retval] BSTR* pbstrName );
  [propput] HRESULT Name ( [in] BSTR bstrName );
  // Read only property
  [propget] HRESULT Weight (
    [out,retval] float* pfWeight );
}
```

Having two methods with the same name in a single interface definition is illegal in IDL, and at first glance it appears that this is the case in the interface above. However, IDL is able to differentiate between the two Name methods because, as far as IDL is concerned, they do not have the same name. Methods annotated with [propput] and [propget] are prefixed with put_ and get_, respectively. The C++ mapping for IMolecule is shown in Listing 3.50.

Listing 3.50 C++ mapping of IMolecule

```
MIDL_INTERFACE("C19F26D5-E148-4cea-8CF7-8B69C5A9F12F")
IMolecule : public IUnknown {
public:
  HRESULT AddAtom( /* [in] */ short nPosition,
                   /* [in] */ IAtom* pAtom ) = 0;
  /*[propget]*/ HRESULT get_Name(BSTR* pbstrName) = 0;
  /*[propput]*/ HRESULT put_Name(BSTR bstrName) = 0;
  /*[propget]*/ HRESULT get_Weight(float*pfWeight) = 0;
};
```

Note that for C++ clients, apart from the prefixes on the method names, the method calls look just as they would if the property attributes had been omitted from the IDL, as shown in Listing 3.51. In Visual Basic, however, the property name is used without the `put_` or `get_` prefix, and the position of the property with respect to the assignment operator determines whether a `[propput]` or a `[propget]` will be used. If the property appears on the left-hand side of the assignment operator, a `[propput]` will occur. Conversely, a `[propget]` is used whenever a property appears on the right-hand side of the assignment operator. Listing 3.52 shows an example Visual Basic call sequence.

Listing 3.51 Using properties from C++

```
HRESULT DoThingsWithAMolecule ( IMolecule* pMol ) {
  BSTR bstrName;
  HR(pMol->get_Name ( &bstrName ));
  if ( lstrcmpW ( L"methane", bstrName ) == 0 ) {
    BSTR bstrNewName = SysAllocString ( L"CH4" );
    HR(pMol->put_Name ( bstrNewName ));
    SysFreeString ( bstrNewName );
  }
  SysFreeString ( bstrName );
  float fWeight;
  HR(pMol->get_Weight ( &fWeight ));
  return S_OK;
}
```

Listing 3.52 Using properties from Visual Basic

```
Private Sub DoThingsWithAMolecule( mol As IMolecule )
If "methane" = mol.Name Then
  mol.Name = "CH4"
End If
```

```
Dim fWeight As Single
fWeight = mol.Weight
End Sub
```

When implementing methods annotated with property attributes in Visual Basic, [propget] translates to a Property Get and [propput] translates to a Property Let, as shown in Listing 3.53.

Listing 3.53 Implementing properties in Visual Basic
```
Private Sub _
IMolecule_AddAtom(ByVal nPosition As Integer, _
                  ByVal pAtom As IAtom)
End Sub
Private Property _
Let IMolecule_Name(ByVal RHS As String)
End Property
Private Property Get IMolecule_Name() As String
End Property
Private Property Get IMolecule_Weight() As Float
End Property
```

Properties annotated with [propput] may have more than one method parameter—for example, the Name property could be rewritten as:

```
propput] HRESULT Name ( [in] BSTR bstrCommonName,
                        [in] BSTR bstrChemicalName,
                        [in] BSTR bstrFormula );
```

In theory, the corresponding [propget] would look like this:

```
[propget] HRESULT Name ( [out] BSTR* pbstrCommonName,
                         [out] BSTR* pbstrChemicalName,
                  [out,retval] BSTR* pbstrFormula );
```

Although get_Name is correctly defined in the C/C++ header file, the MIDL compiler is unable to produce a type library mapping for the property. In order for a [propget] property to appear in a type library, the last parameter must be marked [out,retval] and all preceding parameters, if any, must be marked [in], which is not terribly useful in the case above. When the Visual Basic usage of properties is considered, this makes sense, because it is impossible to have two items on the left-hand side of an assignment operator. No such restrictions apply to [propput] properties. Note, however, that the number and type of the parameters of the [propget] must match those of the [propput] in all aspects save the level of indirection of the last parameter. For example,

```
[propput] HRESULT Item( [in] short nIndex,
                        [in] long lItem );
[propget] HRESULT Item ( [in] short nIndex,
                    [out,retval] long* plItem );
```

is legal, whereas

```
[propput] HRESULT Item( [in] short nIndex,
                        [in] long lItem );
[propget] HRESULT Item ( [in] long nIndex,
                    [out,retval] long* plItem );
```

is not, because the type of the nIndex parameter for the [propget] method does not match the type of the nIndex parameter for the [propput] method.

The [propputref] attribute is applicable only for object references and makes a real difference only for Visual Basic. A property annotated with [propputref] requires the use of the Set keyword, whereas a property annotated with [propput] does not. An example interface containing such a property is shown in Listing 3.54.

Listing 3.54 Interface containing a [propputref] property

```
[
  uuid(a400f1e5-847d-4221-a38e-184b96933b6c),
  object
]
interface IAtomsOfMolecule : IUnknown {
  [propget] HRESULT Atom( [in] short nPosition,
                    [out,retval] IAtom** ppAtom );
  [propput] HRESULT Atom( [in] short nPosition,
                          [in] IAtom* pAtom );
  [propputref] HRESULT Atom( [in] short nPosition,
                        [in] IAtom* pAtom );
}
```

The Visual Basic client-side usage of the interface shown in Listing 3.54 would be

```
Dim atom1 As IAtomsOfMolecule
Set atom1 = pObj.Atom ( 1 ) ' [propget]
```

```
Dim atom2 As IAtomsOfMolecule
Set atom2 = New Atom
pObj.Atom ( 2 ) = atom2        ' [propput]
Set pObj.Atom ( 2 ) = atom2 ' [propputref]
```

Note the presence of the `Set` keyword when the `[propputref]` version of the property is used and its absence when the `[propput]` version is used. Because the `Set` keyword is required when one object reference is assigned to another in Visual Basic, it makes sense to use the same syntax when dealing with properties that are object references. Therefore, use `[propputref]` rather than `[propput]` for such properties.

The method implementation for the `Atom` property is shown in Listing 3.55. The `[propputref]` translates to a `Property Set` in the method implementation. In C++, the property has `putref_` prepended to the name instead of `put_`. Note that while the MIDL compiler will accept a `[propputref]` on methods that take types other than object references as parameters, Visual Basic will not accept such properties and will be unable to implement any interface containing them.

Listing 3.55 Implementing [propputref] in Visual Basic

```
Implements IAtomsOfMolecule
Dim m_atoms(10) As IAtom
' [propputref]
Private Property Set IAtomsOfMolecule_Atom ( _
  ByVal nPosition As Integer, _
  ByVal RHS As PropLIB.IDriver)
Set m_atoms(nPosition) = RHS
End Property

' [propput]
Private Property Let IAtomsOfMolecule_Atom ( _
  ByVal nPosition As Integer, _
  ByVal RHS As PropLIB.IDriver)
Set m_atoms(nPosition) = RHS
End Property

' [propget]
Private Property Get IAtomsOfMolecule_Atom ( _
  ByVal nPosition As Integer) As PropLIB.IDriver
Set IAtomsOfMolecule_Atom = m_atoms(nPosition)
End Property
```

Interface Inheritance

Inheritance is a technique used in object-oriented languages to achieve code reuse and polymorphism. The polymorphism comes from the fact that a derived type is type-compatible with any base types that it inherits from and can be used anywhere a base type is expected.

IDL supports interface inheritance. One interface can derive from another base interface, inheriting all the methods of the base interface. The most common example of a base interface is Iunknown.

```
[
  uuid(FC498275-C259-4AB0-98AB-218E563730F4),
  object
]
interface IAnimal : IUnknown {
  [propget] HRESULT Age ( [out,retval] long* pnSeconds );
}
```

All COM interfaces must have IUnknown as their ultimate base interface, but it is not necessary to derive directly from IUnknown. For example, Listing 3.56 describes two interfaces that derive from IAnimal.

Listing 3.56 Two interfaces that derive from IAnimal

```
[
   uuid(AA423CAD-8C8A-4876-AFDD-22D21BE2AC17),
   object
]
interface IDog : IAnimal {
  HRESULT Bark();
  HRESULT Fetch ();
}
[
  uuid(FE5465A7-4ED9-4765-8A6D-4459E37AF580),
  object
]
interface ICat : IAnimal {
  HRESULT Sleep();
}
```

The v-tables for both ICat and IDog include the methods of IAnimal. From an object-oriented-language perspective, ICat and IDog are considered type-compatible with IAnimal. In IDL, this allows the interface designer to express type relationships and also forces implementers of derived interfaces to implement all the methods of the base interface. For example, implementers of ICat and IDog must also provide code for the methods of IAnimal. COM is trying to provide an object-oriented framework that will work with languages that are not inherently object-oriented. Because of this, interface inheritance cannot provide the runtime type relationships that are present in languages that are inherently object-oriented, such as C++. Consider the following interface.

```
[
  uuid(65515A6D-64B5-40DA-9A49-61D407B2433B),
  object
]
interface IPetShop : IUnknown {
  HRESULT AddAnimal ( [in] IAnimal* pAnimal );
}
```

A C++ client could pass an IAnimal*, an IDog*, or an ICat* to the AddAnimal method, and the C++ compiler would allow the call because of the type relationship between the interfaces. For example:

```
HRESULT Menagerie ( IPetShop*pPetShop, IDog *pDog,
                    ICat*pCat, IAnimal* pSomething ) {
  HR(pPetShop->AddAnimal ( pDog ));
  HR(pPetShop->AddAnimal ( pCat ));
  HR(pPetShop->AddAnimal ( pSomething ));
}
```

However, the type relationship above may be meaningful only at compile time. For instance, the underlying interception code is unaware of this compile time type relationship and will call QueryInterface through the provided object reference, asking explicitly for IAnimal in each case. Note also that other environments—Visual Basic, for example—will always call QueryInterface for the type that the method call actually expects. Here is the method above implemented in Visual Basic.

```
Public Sub Menagerie ( pPetShop As IPetShop, pDog As IDog,
                       pCat As ICat, pSomething As IAnimal )
  pPetShop.AddAnimal pDog
  pPetShop.AddAnimal pCat
  pPetShop.AddAnimal pSomething
End Sub
```

In each case, the Visual Basic runtime will call `QueryInterface`, asking for `IAnimal` before making the call to `AddAnimal`, regardless of whether any interception code is involved.

Now, `QueryInterface` is implemented at the class level, and so in COM it is the class that determines the runtime type relationship between interfaces rather than the IDL definition. If the `QueryInterface` implementation of the class responds to requests for `IDog` but does not respond to requests for `IAnimal`, then, as far as the interception code or the Visual Basic runtime is concerned, the type relationship between `IDog` and `IAnimal` does not exist.

IDL allows interface designers to express type relationships and build hierarchies of related types. It is the responsibility of the implementer of a given class to ensure that those type relationships are maintained. This means implementing `QueryInterface` such that it responds positively to requests for the derived interfaces and any base interfaces.

Note that when classes are implemented in Visual Basic, interface inheritance should be avoided, because Visual Basic cannot implement any interface that does not derive directly from either `IUnknown` or `IDispatch`. This is a limitation of the Visual Basic runtime.

Dispatch Interfaces

Scripting clients call into COM objects through the `IDispatch` interface rather than through any problem domain interface provided by the object. Thus, any object that wishes to be callable from script must provide an implementation of `IDispatch`.[5] The methods and properties of an object that are available through `IDispatch` can be described in IDL by defining a dispatch interface or dispinterface. Listing 3.57 shows an example dispatch interface with both properties and methods.

Listing 3.57   An example dispinterface

```
[
   uuid(62BE173B-1A46-42B5-9A98-C5F835E1380D)
]
dispinterface _Timer {
```

---

[5] For further information about `IDispatch`, see *Essential COM* (Box, Addison-Wesley, 1998), Chapter 7, *ATL Internals* (Rector and Sells, Addison-Wesley, 1999), Chapter 3, or *Effective COM* (Box, et al., Addison-Wesley, 1999), Item 11.

```
properties:
  [id(1)] long Time;
  [id(2)] short Interval;
methods:
  [id(100)] void Start();
  [id(101)] void Stop();
}
```

Both the properties section and the methods section must be present even if they are empty; the MIDL compiler generates an error if either of them is missing. The [id] attributes define the dispatch id's for the methods and properties. Any non-negative integer is a valid dispatch id. The [id] attribute is mandatory for methods and properties in a dispatch interface, and each dispatch id must be a distinct value.

The interface above is callable only through IDispatch; there are no v-table entries corresponding to the properties and methods listed in the dispinterface. The definition of _Timer in the generated C++ header file contains only the v-table for IDispatch. A second syntax is supported, allowing a dispatch interface to be defined in terms of a v-table interface. Listing 3.58 contains such a definition for the _Timer interface.

Listing 3.58   dispinterface based on a v-table interface

```
[
  uuid(57e745fd-6f91-4b63-b1de-d5178f24457d),
  object
]
interface ITimer : IUnknown {
  [propput, id(1)]
  HRESULT Time ( [in] long lTime );
  [propget, id(1)]
  HRESULT Time ( [out,retval] long* plTime );
  [propput, id(2)]
  HRESULT Interval ( [in] short nInterval );
  [propget, id(2)]
  HRESULT Interval ( [out,retval] short* pnInterval );
  [id(100)] HRESULT Start();
  [id(101)] HRESULT Stop();
}

[
  uuid(62BE173B-1A46-42B5-9A98-C5F835E1380D)
]
```

```
dispinterface _Timer {
  interface ITimer;
}
```

Note that the declaration of the dispatch interface contains just a single inter-face statement. The properties and methods provided by the dispatch interface are the same as those in Listing 3.57.

It is also possible to combine the dispatch interface and the v-table inter-face into a single interface definition. Such interfaces are known as dual inter-faces and are v-table interfaces that derive from either IDispatch or another dual interface. Rewriting the _Timer example so as to use a dual interface gives the IDL shown in Listing 3.59.

Listing 3.59 A dual interface

```
[
  uuid(59120BBE-2240-445A-8C86-FDB3423C2D05),
  object,
  dual
]
interface ITimer : IDispatch {
  [propput, id(1)]
  HRESULT Time ( [in] long lTime );
  [propget, id(1)]
  HRESULT Time ( [out,retval] long* plTime );
  [propput, id(2)]
  HRESULT Interval ( [in] short nInterval );
  [propget, id(2)]
  HRESULT Interval ( [out,retval] short* pnInterval );
  [id(100)] HRESULT Start();
  [id(101)] HRESULT Stop();
}
```

Note that the ITimer interface is annotated with the [dual] attribute. This attribute indicates that the interface is callable through a v-table and through IDispatch. Because of this, IDispatch must appear in the interface hier-archy of all dual interfaces. Dispatch id's are optional for dual interfaces; if they are not specified in the IDL, the MIDL compiler will generate default values. The [dual] attribute also implies the [oleautomation] attribute, hence dual interfaces typically use the universal marshaler.

Of the three approaches—pure dispinterface, dispinterface based on v-table interface, and dual interface—one of the latter two is generally preferred, because a v-table interface is typically already available for use as the basis for the dispatch interface. Moreover, most modern implementations of IDispatch delegate to the system-provided implementation of ITypeInfo, which implements IDispatch functionality based on a v-table interface.

The advantage of using a dual interface over using a standard v-table interface is that only one v-table entry is required. The nondual approach requires two entries: one for the problem domain v-table interface and one for IDispatch. Thus, using a dual interface saves 4 bytes per object instance.

Both v-table approaches are perfectly reasonable for an object that has a single interface. However, problems occur when an object has more than one v-table interface. Which one should be used as the basis for IDispatch? Choosing any one v-table interface would limit the functionality available to scripting clients. It is far better to define an extra v-table interface that provides the union of all the v-table interfaces on the object. For example, Listing 3.60 shows two problem domain v-table interfaces, IClock and ILEDClock; a corresponding union v-table interface _HiddenUnion; and a dispinterface _Clock based on _HiddenUnion.

Listing 3.60 A dispatch interface based on a union interface

```
[
  object,
  uuid(D2D2DAE9-63F4-466c-921D-4BD67DBF0159)
]
interface IClock : IUnknown {
  [propget] HRESULT Hours ( [out,retval] byte* pnHours );
  [propput] HRESULT Hours ( [in] byte nHours );
  [propget] HRESULT Minutes ( [out,retval] byte* pnMinutes );
  [propput] HRESULT Minutes ( [in] byte nMinutes );
}
[
  object,
  uuid(B9696E9D-833F-41aa-AF23-3055021B623A)
]
interface ILEDClock : IUnknown {
  [propput] HRESULT Luminosity ( [in] short nLum );
}

[
  object,
```

```
  uuid(258A7B47-B211-470f-B095-7F2ADC75902C),
  hidden
]
interface _IHiddenUnion : IUnknown {
  // Methods of IClock
  [propget] HRESULT Hours ( [out,retval] byte* pnHours );
  [propput] HRESULT Hours ( [in] byte nHours );
  [propget] HRESULT Minutes ( [out,retval] byte* pnMinutes );
  [propput] HRESULT Minutes ( [in] byte nMinutes );
  // Methods of ILEDClock
  [propput] HRESULT Luminosity ( [in] short nLum );
}
[
  uuid(15EE2623-8D17-460b-8312-65B5DD586619)
]
dispinterface _IClock {
  interface _IHiddenUnion;
}
```

The `_IHiddenUnion` interface can then be used as the basis for the
`IDispatch` implementation. Because the methods of `_IHiddenUnion` are
identical to those found in `IClock` and `ILEDClock`, only one implementation
needs to be provided; the C++ compiler will fill in the v-table entries appropriately. Note that `_HiddenUnion` need not appear in any `coclass` statement
in IDL or in the `QueryInterface` implementation for the class. A `coclass`
statement for an implementation class `CoClock` is shown in Listing 3.61.

Listing 3.61 coclass statement for CoClock
```
[
  uuid(f38bc3f9-e0c1-46ea-be87-28849349a15e)
]
coclass CoClock {
  interface _Clock;
  interface IClock;
  interface ILCDClock;
}
```

A dual interface could also be used for the hidden union interface; this
would again result in a 4-byte-per-instance saving.[6] It is also appropriate to

---

[6] For more information on techniques for exposing multiple interfaces to scripting clients, see
http://www.sellsbrothers.com/tools/multidisp/index.htm.

annotate the union interface with the [hidden] attribute, hiding the interface definition from development environments such as Visual Basic. Clients do not need the v-table definition of the interface, because it cannot be called directly, but only through IDispatch.

Conclusions

IDL supports a broad set of base types and gives interface designers great flexibility in creating and using user-defined types. Various IDL constructs can be used to provide more natural support for certain development environments—for example, property support for Visual Basic and interface inheritance for C++. Listed below are some guidelines for using the IDL constructs presented in this chapter.

1. Restrict data type usage to those with which the calling environment can deal.
2. Do not use the char data type; use wchar_t instead.
3. Do not use unsigned 16- or 32-bit integers or signed 8-bit integers in interfaces intended for use by Visual Basic.
4. Whenever possible, use enumerations coupled with the [range] attribute if /Oicf type information is being used.
5. Use properties where appropriate; it makes life easier for Visual Basic developers.
6. Be aware of the limitations of interface inheritance, and do not use it if implementing interfaces in Visual Basic.

Chapter 4

Pointers and Arrays

Pointer Basics

Reference types are part of most modern programming languages. A reference type is one that refers or points to a concrete instance of a type, rather than being the concrete instance itself. Reference types are also known as pointer types, or more commonly, simply as pointers. Passing pointers as method parameters is an important programmatic technique and is supported by C++ and Visual Basic and in fact in Visual Basic is the default. At the programming language level, pointers provide three things:

1. Efficient passing of data, because copying of data is avoided
2. The ability for the called method to modify data passed in by the caller
3. Construction of complex data types such as lists and queues

In COM, efficient passing of data is dealt with partly by using IDL directionality attributes and partly by designing efficient data structures in the first place. Clients and objects are often separated by a context boundary, and in such situations copying the data typically cannot be avoided. The latter two issues are applicable to COM, and in addition pointers are the only way for data to be returned from an object to a client.

Pointers are declared in IDL using C pointer syntax—namely, the * operator. For example:

```
// Pass by value
HRESULT TakeALong ( [in] long x );
// Pass by reference
HRESULT TakeALongByRef ( [in] long* px );
```

This is a very simple example, but notice that for `TakeALongByRef` the parameter is a pointer type rather than a value type; a level of indirection has been added. This is called "pass by reference," because a reference to an instance is being passed rather than the instance itself. Parameters that pass an instance directly are called "pass by value" parameters, because the value of the instance is passed into the method call. For `[in]` parameters, pass by value or pass by reference may be used. Pass by value is the most common choice for simple scalar values. Pass by reference is often used for complex `[in]` parameters such as structures, because, in the absence of interception code, passing a pointer rather than a copy of the structure is more efficient. This is because only the pointer value, typically 4 bytes, needs to be passed into the method call rather than the entire structure. Where interception code exists between the caller and the callee, there is not much difference in execution speed, because in either case the entire structure must be copied by the proxy and re-created by the stub.

Whereas `[in]` parameters can be value or reference types, `[out]` or `[in,out]` parameters must be reference types. For example:

```
HRESULT ReturnALong ( [out] long* px );
HRESULT TakeAndReturnALong ( [in,out] long* px );
```

Reference types are needed because parameters marked `[out]` or `[in,out]` will be modified by the call. For parameters passed by value, only a copy is given to the proxy, so modifying that value will not suffice. Consider the following call sequence and the associated stack frame shown in Figure 4.1.

```
long x = 10;
// Copy of x placed on stack
HR(pObj->TakeALong ( x ));
```

A copy of the value stored in the local variable x is placed on the stack. If the method call, and hence any interception code that may be present, were to modify the value, the change would not be reflected in the local variable, because the modification has been performed on the copy.

Pointers are necessary for all parameters marked with the `[out]` attribute, because the proxy needs somewhere to place the returned value when the method call completes. When a pointer is passed as a method parameter, the pointer value, which is the address of the variable, is placed on the stack. This gives the following call sequence and the associated stack frame shown in Figure 4.2.

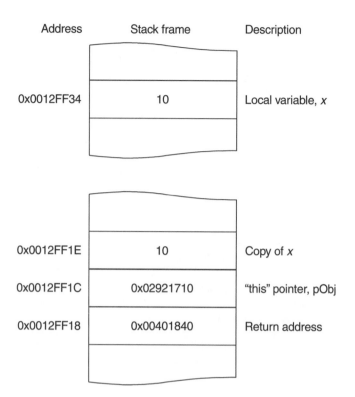

Address	Stack frame	Description
0x0012FF34	10	Local variable, *x*

Address	Stack frame	Description
0x0012FF1E	10	Copy of *x*
0x0012FF1C	0x02921710	"this" pointer, pObj
0x0012FF18	0x00401840	Return address

Figure 4.1   Stack frame for TakeALong

```
long x;
// Address of x placed on stack
HR(pObj->ReturnALong ( &x ));
```

In this case, the address of the local variable x, rather than the value of the variable, is placed on the stack. The proxy dereferences this address to store the returned value when the method call returns. When the proxy returns control to the client, the value stored in the local variable will have been modified.

The MIDL compiler will enforce the requirement that all parameters annotated with the [out] attribute be pointers. Any attempt to compile a method signature similar to

```
HRESULT Foo ( [out] long l );
```

will result in the error MIDL2042: "[out] parameter is not a pointer".

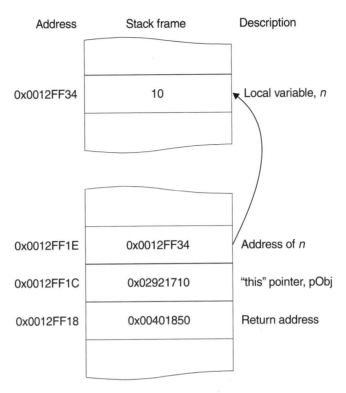

Address	Stack frame	Description

0x0012FF34   10   Local variable, *n*

0x0012FF1E   0x0012FF34   Address of *n*

0x0012FF1C   0x02921710   "this" pointer, pObj

0x0012FF18   0x00401850   Return address

Figure 4.2   Stack frame for ReturnALong

Pointers may also be used inside user-defined types, either structures or unions. The syntax is straightforward, using the * operator once again.

```
struct Person {
   short nAge;
   // Pointer to tax information
   struct TaxInfo* pTaxInfo;
};
```

The type pointed to, `struct TaxInfo` in this case, may also contain pointer types, possibly referring back to the `Person` structure.

```
struct TaxInfo {
   BSTR bstrTaxCode;
   long lSalary;
   struct Person* pOwner;
};
```

   ESSENTIAL IDL

Hence, arbitrarily complex trees of data may be described. A structure may also contain a pointer to its own type, enabling linked lists to be described. The IDL shown in Listing 4.1 contains structures describing a linked list of `PointNode` structures. Each `PointNode` has a pointer to a `MyPoint`, the actual data, and a pointer to another `PointNode`, the next node in the list.[1]

Listing 4.1 Linked-list structure

```
struct MyPoint {
  long x,y;
};
struct PointNode {
  struct MyPoint* pPoint;
  struct PointNode* pNext;
};
```

The MIDL compiler will happily compile the structure definition in Listing 4.1 and the following associated method signature:

```
HRESULT TakeAList ( [in] struct PointNode* pList );
```

and, provided Oicf type information is used, everything will work correctly. Unfortunately, the universal marshaler is unable to deal with self-referential structures and causes an access violation at `QueryInterface` time. When dealing with self-referential data structures, Oicf type information should always be used. It should also be noted that Visual Basic is unable to deal with user-defined types that contain pointer types, so the `PointNode` structure above could not be used from Visual Basic.

Pointers and const

The `const` modifier is often used in C++ to ensure that a given parameter value or pointer cannot be modified by the called function. For pointer parameters annotated with the `[in]` attribute in IDL, the `const` modifier makes sense, because it correctly describes the semantics of the call—namely, that the pointer value may not be modified. Even if the method implementation did modify the pointer or the value it points to, the changes would not propagate back to the client, because the parameter is passed only from client to object.

---

[1] As in Chapter 3, the MyPoint structure is used to avoid conflict with the Point structure defined in wtypes.idl.

The following method signature specifies that neither the pointer, `pvt`, nor its content, `*pvt`, may be modified by the method.

```
HRESULT TakeAVariant ( [in] const VARIANT * const pvt );
```

For `[out]` parameters, the value itself needs to be modifiable, but the pointer that holds the value should remain constant. The method signature below specifies that the parameter `px` cannot be modified, but `*pl` can be changed.

```
HRESULT ReturnALong ( [out] long * const px );
```

While this method signature describes the correct semantics, the MIDL compiler will generate the warning MIDL2279: "[out] parameters may not have 'const'", although the correct signature will appear in the C++ header file. The warning can be suppressed by using a typedef:

```
typedef long * const CPLONG;
HRESULT ReturnALong ( [out] CPLONG px );
```

Note that having the `const` after the * operator specifies that the `constness` applies to the pointer rather than the thing to which the pointer points. The following method signature is incorrect because it specifies that the long value itself, `*px`, is `const`, rather than the pointer, `px`.

```
HRESULT ReturnALong ( [out] const long *px );
```

`Constness` is of syntactic use only to C++ developers, because Visual Basic has no notion of `const` and the constness of a given element is not preserved in the type library. However, the presence of `const` in the IDL conveys some semantic meaning over and above the standard method declaration and is therefore useful.

Pointer Semantics

In C++, a pointer is a pointer is a pointer. In IDL, however, not all pointers are created equal. IDL defines three basic pointer types, each having different semantics. Consider the following structure and the associated diagram shown in Figure 4.3.

```
struct Node {
  BSTR bstrName;
  struct Node* pParent;
```

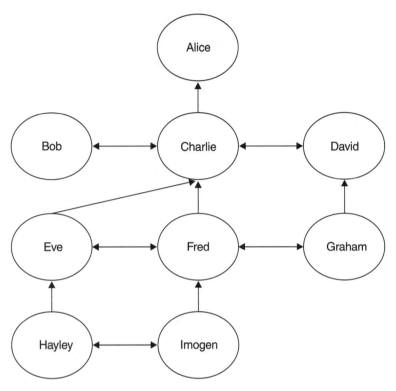

Figure 4.3 Tree of Node structures

```
    struct Node* pPrevious;
    struct Node* pNext;
}
```

Passing the node Hayley to the following C++ function, which counts the number of nodes, is perfectly reasonable and works as expected, returning a value of 10.

```
int CountNodes ( struct Node* pNode );
```

Because everything exists in the same address space, the method implementation is able to follow all the various pointers and count the number of nodes passed into the function. How could this treelike structure be passed into a COM method? The method signature is going to look very similar:

```
HRESULT CountNodes ( [in] struct Node* pNode,
                [out,retval] long* pCount );
```

The interception code is going to have to copy the entire tree structure and re-create it on the object side, including all the pointers and back-pointers. During the marshaling process, the proxy must detect pointer cycles, such as the one that exists between Hayley and Imogen, who have a pointer to each other. The proxy is also going to have to deal with duplicate pointers in the data structure. For example, both Eve and Fred have pointers to Charlie.

To support such structures, IDL provides a pointer semantic that is identical to the standard C++ semantic. Such pointers are known as full pointers, because they provide full C++ semantics. Full pointers are specified using the [ptr] attribute. They provide cycle and duplicate detection, ensuring that a given pointer value is marshaled only once. When a particular pointer value is encountered a second time, it is not dereferenced a second time, but instead the interception code writes a record into the marshal packet referring back to the previously marshaled data. For all this to work for the example above, the structure needs to be modified to use full pointers, as shown in Listing 4.2.

Listing 4.2 Node structure using full pointers

```
struct Node {
  BSTR bstrName;
  [ptr] struct Node* pParent;
  [ptr] struct Node* pPrevious;
  [ptr] struct Node* pNext;
}
```

The method signature also needs to be modified as follows.

```
HRESULT CountNodes ( [in,ptr] struct Node* pNode,
                 [out,retval] long* pCount );
```

It may be preferable to use a typedef instead of decorating each member or parameter separately, as shown in Listing 4.3.

Listing 4.3 Using [ptr] in a typedef

```
typedef [ptr] struct Node*PNODE;
struct Node {
  BSTR bstrName;
  PNODE pParent;
  PNODE pPrevious;
  PNODE pNext;
}
HRESULT CountNodes ( [in] PNODE pNode,
             [out,retval] long* pCount );
```

All the work that the interception code has to do to deal with cycles and duplicates takes time and space, CPU cycles, and memory locations. When it is known in advance that no duplicates or cycles exist, full pointers are in effect overkill. IDL provides a second pointer type, unique, for exactly this situation. Amending the previous data structure to be a linked list instead of a treelike structure provides an example. A diagram of the list is shown in Figure 4.4.

```
struct ListNode {
  BSTR bstrName;
  struct ListNode*pNext;
};
HRESULT TakeAList ( [in] struct ListNode* pList );
```

Each node has a pointer to the next node in the list with the exception of Imogen, who is at the end of the list and hence has a null pointer in her pNext member. All the pointer values in the list are unique: each value occurs exactly once. To make the MIDL compiler aware of this fact, the pointers are annotated with the [unique] attribute.

```
struct ListNode {
  BSTR bstrName;
  [unique] struct ListNode* pNext;
};
```

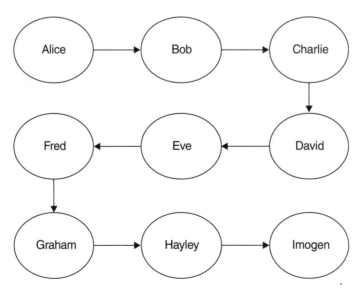

Figure 4.4   Linked list of ListNodes

```
HRESULT
TakeAList ( [in,unique] struct ListNode* pList );
```

As in the full pointer example, a typedef may be used if desired. When marshaling this data structure, the proxy will first check that a pointer is non-null. Provided a pointer satisfies this restraint, the proxy will dereference the pointer, marshaling the data to which the pointer refers. In the example above, passing the Alice node as the parameter to `TakeAList` would result in the proxy following each pointer in turn, through Bob and each following node until reaching Imogen. The marshaling would stop at Imogen, because `pNext` is null.

Note that the assumption made by the interception code in the case of unique pointers is that they are just that—unique. If a given pointer value appears in the data structure more than once, unique pointers will not marshal the data correctly. Exactly what happens will depend on the data structure. At best, the interception code will get into an infinite loop and eventually run out of storage space. This would occur with a circular list, for example. At worst, data will be marshaled more than once, and the resulting structure created at unmarshal time will be incorrect. Consider the following structure and the associated diagram shown in Figure 4.5. Each node has pointers to the next two nodes in the list.

```
struct BadNode {
  BSTR bstrName;
  [unique] struct BadNode*p1;
  [unique] struct BadNode*p2;
};
```

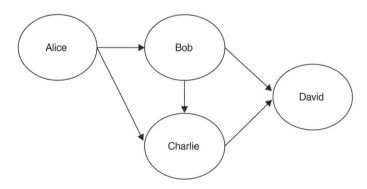

Figure 4.5   List of BadNode structures

```
HRESULT CountNodes ( [in,unique] struct BadNode* pNode,
                     [out,retval] long* pCount );
```

When marshaled, the structure will be re-created on the object side, as shown in Figure 4.6. This is obviously not what was intended, because node Charlie appears twice and node David three times. This kind of error is more difficult to detect than an infinite loop. Care should be taken when choosing pointer semantics for data structures; unique pointers should be used only when the pointers in the structure really are unique.

When marshaling unique pointers, the interception code checks for null as each pointer is encountered. If it is known that a given pointer will never be null, then the third IDL pointer type, reference, may be used. Such a pointer is annotated with the `[ref]` attribute. Consider the following IDL.

```
struct Point {
   long x, y;
};
struct Line {
   [ref] struct Point* pstart;
   [ref] struct Point* pend;
};
```

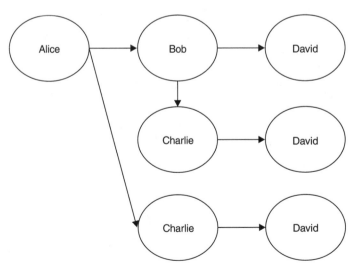

Figure 4.6   List of BadNode structures after unmarshaling

Table 4.1   Pointer semantics

Pointer Type	Attribute	Can Be Null?	Duplicates Allowed?
Reference	ref	No	No
Unique	unique	Yes	No
Full	ptr	Yes	Yes

A line, by definition, always has a starting point and an endpoint, and thus the two pointers in the structure can never be null. For reference pointers, an exception will be generated by the interception code if a null value is encountered. Reference pointers carry the least overhead of all three pointer types. The three pointer types are summarized in Table 4.1.

Top-Level vs. Embedded Pointers

In addition to providing three separate pointer types—full, unique, and reference—IDL also categorizes pointers according to level of indirection. Pointers with a single level of indirection are known as top-level pointers. Top-level pointers are always method parameters, typically local variables. Pointers with two or more levels of indirection are called embedded pointers. Consider the double indirection in the following IDL.

```
HRESULT DoubleIndirectionIn ( [in] long** ppx );
```

The method parameter ppx, the long**, is the top-level pointer, whereas *ppx, the long*, is the embedded pointer. This is illustrated in the following call sequence.

```
long x;
long *px = &x;
*px = 45;
HR(pObj->DoubleIndirectionIn ( &px ));
```

Note that the address of px, itself a pointer to a long, is passed as the method parameter. It is this address that is the top-level pointer, while px is the embedded pointer. The stack frame for the call is shown in Figure 4.7.

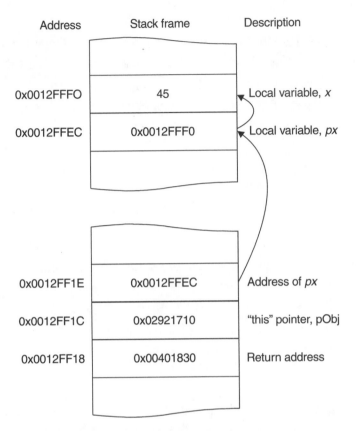

Address	Stack frame	Description

0x0012FFF0   45   Local variable, *x*

0x0012FFEC   0x0012FFF0   Local variable, *px*

0x0012FF1E   0x0012FFEC   Address of *px*

0x0012FF1C   0x02921710   "this" pointer, pObj

0x0012FF18   0x00401830   Return address

Figure 4.7   Stack frame for call to DoubleIndirectionIn

The reason that IDL differentiates between top-level and embedded pointers is not immediately obvious from the example above. However, consider the following, slightly different method signature:

```
HRESULT DoubleIndirectionOut ( [out] long** ppx );
```

and the appropriately modified call sequence:

```
long*px = 0;
HR(pObj->DoubleIndirectionOut ( &px ));
printf ( "The value is %d\n", *px );
```

The variable `px` points to address zero before the call to `Double IndirectionOut` but can be safely dereferenced after the call, as shown in the `printf` statement. If the pointer can be safely dereferenced, it must point to a valid memory location—but who is responsible for that memory, who allocated it, and who is responsible for freeing it when it is no longer needed?

In COM, the client and the object share responsibility for the memory. The object is responsible for allocating the memory inside the method call. This must be done using the COM memory allocator IMalloc, typically through the wrapper API, CoTaskMemAlloc, for example:

```
STDMETHODIMP DoubleIndirectionOut ( long** ppx ) {
    *ppx = (long*)CoTaskMemAlloc ( sizeof ( long ));
    **ppx = 45; // return the value 45 to the caller
    return S_OK;
}
```

When the method call returns, ownership of the memory passes to the client, who is responsible for freeing the memory once it is no longer needed, again using the system IMalloc or the wrapper CoTaskMemFree. This gives the following call sequence.

```
long*px = 0;
HR(pObj->DoubleIndirectionOut ( &px );
printf ( "The value is %d\n", *px );
CoTaskMemFree ( px );
```

To help visualize what is actually happening, the stack frames before and after the call to DoubleIndirectionOut are shown in Figures 4.8 and 4.9, respectively.

Before the call the local variable px contains a null pointer and points at no concrete instance. Inside the method, memory is allocated from the COM heap. The address of this memory block is stored in px, through the address of px, passed as the method parameter. After the call, the local variable px points at the memory block in the COM heap, which was initialized inside the method to contain the value 45. Ownership of the memory block at address 0x00FC0010 has been transferred from the object to the client. The client is responsible for freeing the memory block once it no longer needs the contents.

This is a very common usage pattern for embedded [out] parameters in COM; the object allocates a particular resource, in this case the memory block, and the client frees the resource once it is no longer needed. The same pattern is used for object references, strings including BSTRs, and arrays, as shown later in this chapter.

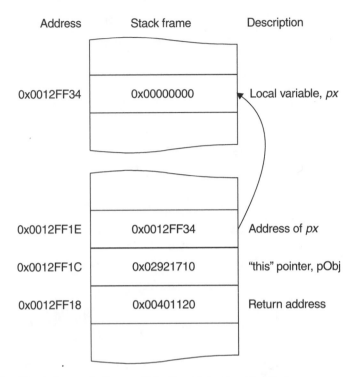

Address	Stack frame	Description

0x0012FF34   0x00000000   Local variable, *px*

0x0012FF1E   0x0012FF34   Address of *px*

0x0012FF1C   0x02921710   "this" pointer, pObj

0x0012FF18   0x00401120   Return address

Figure 4.8 Stack frame before call to DoubleIndirectionOut

Memory for `[in]` parameters, whether top-level or embedded, is always managed by the client and may be allocated using any memory management API the client chooses. However, it is very important that the memory for embedded `[out]` parameters be allocated using the COM memory allocator. The reason for this is not immediately obvious; indeed, the RPC layer on which COM is built takes a completely different approach, requiring each executable to provide two entry points. The first entry point, `midl_user_alloc`, is used to allocate memory, while the second, `midl_user_free`, is used to free memory once it is no longer needed. The typical implementation of these methods is shown in Listing 4.4.

Listing 4.4 Implementation of midl_user_alloc and midl_user_free

```
void* midl_user_alloc ( size_t size ) {
  return malloc ( size );
}
void midl_user_free ( void* p ) {
  free ( p );
}
```

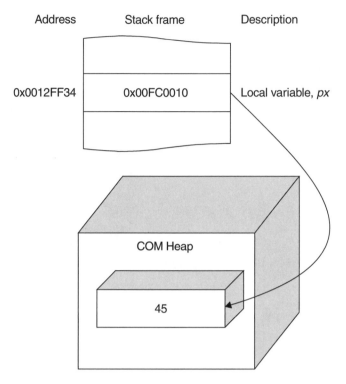

Figure 4.9   Stack frame after call to DoubleIndirectionOut

The RPC proxies and stubs call these methods at the appropriate point during marshaling of method parameters. Consider an RPC implementation of the `DoubleIndirectionOut` method call:

```
void DoubleIndirectionOut ( long** ppx ) {
   *ppx = midl_user_alloc ( sizeof ( long ));
   **ppx = 45;
}
```

The client-side calling code looks like this:

```
long* px = 0;
p->DoubleIndirectionOut ( &px );
printf ( "The value is %d\n", *px );
midl_user_free ( px );
```

Figure 4.10 shows the sequence of calls to both client- and server-side memory allocation functions.

ESSENTIAL IDL

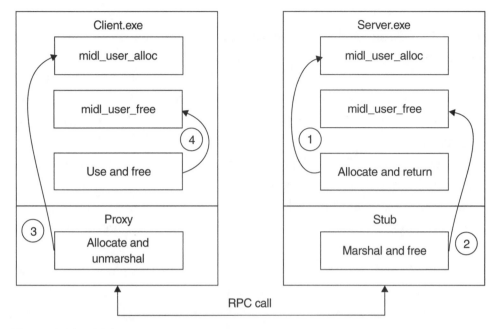

Figure 4.10 RPC memory management sequence

For the purpose of this discussion it is assumed that the client and the server are using different memory management APIs in the implementations of `midl_user_alloc` and `midl_user_free`; the server is using the Win32 APIs `HeapAlloc` and `HeapFree` while the client is using the more traditional C runtime functions `malloc` and `free`.

In step 1, the method implementation in the server allocates memory using the server-side implementation of `midl_user_alloc`, hence using `HeapAlloc`. The method returns to the stub, which marshals the data into the marshal packet and frees the memory block using the server implementation of `midl_user_free` in step 2. This will result in a call to `HeapFree`, which matches the call to `HeapAlloc` in step 1. The data is transferred from the server back to the client where the proxy, in step 3, allocates memory for the data using the client-side implementation of `midl_user_alloc`, resulting in a call to `malloc`. The data is copied out of the marshal packet into the newly allocated memory block, and the proxy returns to the client. The client uses the data as it sees fit, in a call to `printf` in this case, and then frees the memory by making a call to the client-side implementation of `midl_user_free` in step 4. This results in a call to `free`, which matches the `malloc` call made in step 3. Because the memory allocation and deallocation calls match on both sides, everything works as expected. The advantage of this approach is that the participants are able to choose their own memory management strategies. High-performance servers may wish to use a highly optimized third-party heap manager rather than the standard C runtime heap in order to get a performance increase.

So why did the COM designers not take the same approach as RPC? One reason is that the proxy-stub model in RPC is very different from that found in COM. RPC proxies are statically linked into the client code, and the corresponding stubs are statically linked into the server executable. Because of the monolithic nature of RPC clients and servers, the proxies and stubs are able to bind easily to the `midl_user_alloc` and `midl_user_free` implementations at link time. Conversely, COM proxies and stubs are loaded dynamically at `QueryInterface` time. In order for a COM proxy or stub to bind to `midl_user_allocate` and `midl_user_free`, it would have to find the addresses of both methods in the EXE into which it was loaded. Although this is no easy task, it is probably achievable with some effort. So there must be another, more compelling reason for the COM approach.

Although Figure 4.10 is an illustration of an RPC call, it looks very similar to the way a remote COM call would look. The word "remote" is the key to the solution. Not all COM calls go through a proxy; some are made directly on the object. The case where no proxy is used is illustrated in Figure 4.11.

For step 1, inside the method implementation, the server allocates memory using its own implementation of `midl_user_alloc`. The method returns to the client, who uses the returned data. In step 2, the client frees the data using its own implementation of `midl_user_free`. Unfortunately, if the server and client are still using different memory management APIs, there is now a mismatch between the API used to allocate memory and the API used to deallocate memory. Typically, this results in some form of heap corruption.

COM could mandate that any DLL, be it proxy-stub DLL or server DLL, must bind at load time to the `midl_user_alloc` and `midl_user_free` implementations provided by the host executable. However, this puts extra burden on both client and server implementers. The client implementer must provide

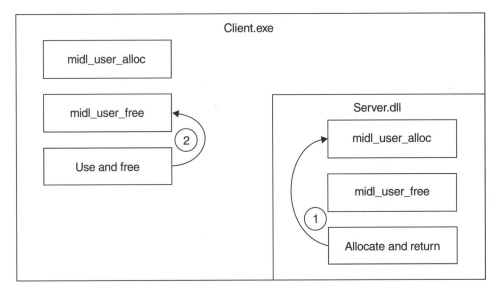

Figure 4.11 Hybrid COM/RPC memory management

implementation of `midl_user_alloc` and `midl_user_free`. The functions must also be exported from the executable so that any dynamically loaded COM DLL can locate them. The server implementer must add code to locate the memory management APIs and bind to them at DLL load time.

In order to keep things simple and relieve some of the burden on the application developer, COM takes the approach of mandating an API that must be used for embedded `[out]` pointers. Figure 4.12 shows the sequence of events for a cross-context COM call.

Because both the server method code and the stub use the COM memory management APIs, memory management is handled correctly on the server side. Similarly, on the client side both the proxy and the client code use the same API. For a direct call, the situation is as shown in Figure 4.13.

The server method code allocates the memory using `CoTaskMemAlloc`, and the client code frees the memory using `CoTaskMemFree`.

Note that the rules applying to embedded `[out]` parameters also apply to `[in,out]` parameters. For `[in,out]` parameters, the memory on the client side must be allocated from the COM heap. The server is then free to reallocate the memory block if required. The client then frees the memory when the method call returns using the `CoTaskMemFree` API.

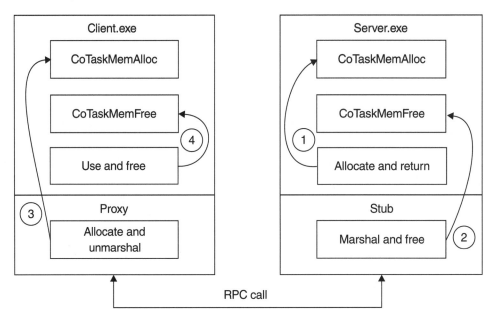

Figure 4.12   Intercontext memory management in COM

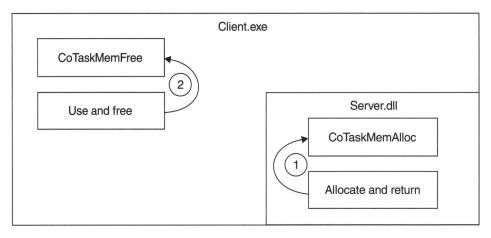

Figure 4.13   Intracontext memory management in COM

So IDL differentiates between top-level and embedded pointers for memory management reasons. IDL also specifies different restrictions on pointer semantics for top-level and embedded pointers based on directionality. Top-level [in] parameters may be of any pointer semantic. By default, they are reference pointers, but this may be modified on a per-parameter basis. Top-level [out] parameters must be reference pointers, and no other semantic is supported. This is perfectly reasonable because only reference pointers cannot be null. Both other pointer types can be null, which does not make sense for a top-level [out] parameter because the proxy would have no place to put the data returned from the method. Hence, the following method signature will not compile, giving the error MIDL2121: "[out] only parameter must not derive from a top-level [unique] or [ptr] pointer/array".[2]

```
HRESULT BadReturnALong ( [out, unique] long * px );
```

Curiously, IDL does not require [in,out] pointers to be reference pointers. The MIDL compiler will happily compile the following method signature.

```
HRESULT TakeAndReturnALong ( [in,out,unique] long*pl );
```

Because a null value is transmitted from client to server by the interception layer the stub passes a null pointer into the method call. Contrast this with an [out] only parameter where the stub always passes a non-null pointer value to the method. The only reason for using a method signature such as that shown above would be if for certain calls no input was to be supplied and the results were not required. If this were never the case, a reference pointer would suffice.

Embedded pointers are treated slightly differently by IDL. Regardless of directionality, embedded pointers may use any of the three pointer semantics. The default semantic for embedded pointers is defined by an interface level attribute, [pointer_default], which takes one of ref, unique, or full as an argument. Listing 4.5 contains an interface annotated with the [pointer_default] attribute.

Listing 4.5 Interface annotated with [pointer_default]
```
[
    uuid(3D71832A-77C0-46fc-BEE3-6BEC17DAD165),
    object,
    pointer_default(unique)
]
```

---

[2] Sadly, the error is generated only if the method definition appears outside a library block. If the method were defined inside a library block, no error would be generated. This is clearly a bug in the current MIDL compiler.

```
interface IReturnData : IUnknown {
  HRESULT DoubleIndirectionOut ( [out] long** ppx );
}
```

The top-level pointer, `ppx`, is assumed to be and must be a reference pointer. The embedded pointer, `*ppx`, is assumed to be a unique pointer because of the `[pointer_default]` attribute on the interface.

Strictly speaking, there is no default for the `[pointer_default]` attribute, and the MIDL compiler should generate an error for any interface definition that contains embedded pointers but has no `[pointer_default]` attribute. However, the interface definition shown in Listing 4.6 compiles with versions of MIDL up to 5.03.0280 despite the presence of an embedded pointer and the absence of a `[pointer_default]` attribute. The same C++ header file and Oicf type information are generated as for the interface definition in Listing 4.5. This aberrant behavior is not guaranteed, and it is good practice always to specify a pointer default for a given interface just in case a future version of the MIDL compiler should start enforcing the law.

Listing 4.6 Interface with embedded pointer and no [pointer_default]
```
[
  uuid(D1188347-AA22-4736-A1F6-A94E966E2401),
  object
]
interface IReturnDataToo : IUnknown {
  HRESULT DoubleIndirectionOut ( [out] long** ppx );
}
```

The `[pointer_default]` attribute is very subtle when used with structures. Consider the `Node` structure defined in Listing 4.7.

Listing 4.7 Node structure with unqualified pointers
```
struct Node {
  BSTR bstrName;
  struct Node* pParent;
  struct Node* pPrevious;
  struct Node* pNext;
}
```

This is a slightly modified version of the example shown in Listing 4.2 in that it does not qualify the semantics of the embedded pointers, and consequently the `[pointer_default]` will be used. However, consider the two interfaces shown in Listing 4.8. The `Node` structure will behave differently depending on which interface method is called. This is probably not what is required, and the only way around the problem is to qualify the embedded pointers in the `Node` structure. So while the `[pointer_default]` attribute is very useful for standard IDL types, care should be taken whenever structures are used.

Listing 4.8 Interaction between [pointer_default] and structures

```
[
  uuid(A80A0FCE-ABCD-43a1-8284-DEBF2D8A13E5),
  object,
  pointer_default(unique)
]
interface ITakeNodes : IUnknown {
  HRESULT TakeANode ( [in] Node* pHead );
}
[
  uuid(9B98A810-083F-4dff-9484-9EB8E0D5A013),
  object,
  pointer_default(ptr)
]
interface IAlsoTakeNodes : IUnknown {
  HRESULT TakeANode ( [in] Node* pHead );
}
```

The semantic and memory management rules for the various directions and levels of pointers are summarized in Table 4.2.

Table 4.2   Pointer attributes and memory management rules

Pointer Type	Allocated By	Allocation API	Default Semantic	Notes
Top-level				
[in]	Caller	Any	[ref]	
[out]	Caller	Any	[ref]	Must be [ref]
[in,out]	Caller	Any	[ref]	Should be [ref]
Embedded				
[in]	Caller	Any	[pointer_default]	
[out]	Callee	CoTaskMemXXX	[pointer_default]	
[in,out]	Caller/Callee	CoTaskMemXXX	[pointer_default]	

It is worth noting that pointer semantics are honored only when Oicf type information is being used to build interception code. The universal marshaler treats all top-level pointers as reference pointers, regardless of attributes. Likewise, all embedded pointers are treated as unique pointers. The MIDL compiler will not generate any errors or warnings when it encounters conflicting attributes in interfaces marked [oleautomation] or [dual].

Pointers and Language Mappings

It is important to understand how IDL pointer types map to a given development language. For C++, the mapping is totally straightforward: the IDL maps directly to the generated constructs in the C++ header file. For example, the interface definition shown in Listing 4.9 maps directly to the C++ header file fragment shown in Listing 4.10; the only real difference is that the structure definition appears at global scope, rather than inside the interface declaration. Because of this direct mapping, C++ clients and objects can use any pointer type with any number of levels of indirection for both method parameters and pointers in user-defined types.

Listing 4.9 IDL definition of IDoStuff

```
import "unknwn.idl";

[
  object,
  uuid(FE03C7BF-72BE-4CF9-8F09-8B1579D6EEFF),
  pointer_default(unique)
]
interface IDoStuff : IUnknown {
  struct Stuff {
    BSTR bstrName;
    struct Stuff* pNext;
  };
  HRESULT TakeStuff([in] struct Stuff* pStuff );
  HRESULT ReturnStuff([out] struct Stuff** ppStuff );
}
```

Listing 4.10 C++ definition of IDoStuff

```
struct Stuff {
  BSTR bstrName;
  struct Stuff __RPC_FAR *pNext;
};
MIDL_INTERFACE("FE03C7BF-72BE-4CF9-8F09-8B1579D6EEFF")
```

```
IDoStuff : public IUnknown {
public:
  virtual HRESULT STDMETHODCALLTYPE
  TakeStuff( struct Stuff *pStuff) = 0;
  virtual HRESULT STDMETHODCALLTYPE
  ReturnStuff( struct Stuff **ppStuff) = 0;
};
```

Visual Basic is a little more restricted in the pointers that it supports; specifically, it cannot deal with more than one level of indirection for method parameters nor can it handle user-defined types with embedded pointers. The interface defined in Listing 4.9 would be unusable from Visual Basic, but the interface definition in Listing 4.11 would work perfectly well.

Listing 4.11   IDL definition of VB-friendly interface
```
[
  object,
  oleautomation,
  uuid(D8313038-7178-4424-BA11-887C2B2B75D2)
]
interface IMakeVBHappy : IUnknown {
  typedef struct VBStuff {
    BSTR bstrName;
    byte nAge;
    long lSalary;
  } VBStuff;
  HRESULT TakeAVBStuff([in] VBStuff* pStuff );
  HRESULT ReturnAVBStuff([out,retval] VBStuff* pStuff );
}
```

A Visual Basic implementation of the interface is shown in Listing 4.12.

Listing 4.12   Visual Basic implementation of IMakeVBHappy
```
' List interfaces this class implements
Implements IMakeVBHappy
Dim data as VBStuff
Private Function _
IMakeVBHappy _ReturnAVBStuff() As VBStuff
  IMakeVBHappy _ReturnAVBStuff = data
End Function
Private Sub _
IMakeVBHappy _TakeAVBStuff ( ByRef pStuff As VBStuff )
  data = pStuff
End Sub
```

Note the `ByRef` keyword on the parameter to the `TakeAVBStuff` method; this indicates that a single level of indirection is being used. `ByRef` is the default in Visual Basic, the other possibility being `ByVal`, which means that no indirection is being used. For example, the method

```
HRESULT TakeALongByValAndOneByRef ( [in] long x,
                                    [in] long*px );
```

would translate to the implementation

```
Private Sub _
ISomeInterface_ TakeALongByValAndOneByRef ( _
  ByVal l as Long, ByRef pl as Long )
End Sub
```

It is also worth noting that Visual Basic is unable to implement interfaces that have method parameters marked as `[out]` only. Parameters marked as `[out,retval]` or `[in,out]` cause no such problems. Also, calling a method with `[out]` only parameters works fine; it is only the implementation of such a method that is not supported. So Visual Basic can call but not implement the following method.

```
HRESULT ReturnAStringAndALong ( [out] BSTR bstr,
                      [out,retval] long l );
```

This leads to the following conclusion: when designing interfaces for implementation by Visual Basic, avoid `[out]` only parameters.

Examining the mapping from IDL parameter attributes to language level types proves to be an interesting exercise, especially when the output generated by the MIDL compiler is considered. Table 4.3 shows the mapping between IDL attributes and C++ types, while Table 4.4 shows the mapping between IDL attributes and Visual Basic types. In both tables, the left-hand column contains the IDL parameter declaration. The middle column of Table 4.3 shows the mapping MIDL provides in the C++ header file, while the same column in Table 4.4 shows the mapping Visual Basic uses based on the content of the type library. In both tables, the third column shows the most accurate language level mapping for the IDL semantics.[3]

---

[3] `[out,unique]` and `[out,ptr]` are not legal in IDL, as explained earlier.

Table 4.3   IDL attribute to C++ type mapping

IDL Parameter Declaration	IDL Mapping in Header File	Natural Mapping
[in] short s	short s	short s
[in,ref] short* ps	short* ps	const short& s
[in,unique] short* ps	short* ps	None
[in,ptr] short* ps	short* ps	const short * const ps
[out,ref] short* ps	short* ps	None
[in,out,ref] short* ps	short* ps	short * const ps

Table 4.4   IDL attribute to Visual Basic type mapping

IDL Parameter Declaration	Mapping from Type Library	Natural Mapping
[in] short s	ByVal s As Integer	ByVal s As Integer
[in,ref] short* ps	ByRef s As Integer	None
[in,unique] short* ps	ByRef s As Integer	None
[in,ptr] short* ps	ByRef s As Integer	None
[out,ref] short* ps	None	None
[in,out,ref] short* ps	ByRef s As Integer	ByRef s As Integer

Where no natural mapping exists, calls that do not go through the interception layer may violate the specified IDL semantics. It is interesting to note that for both languages the IDL mapping of all pointer types elicits `[in,out]` behavior. It is also interesting that neither language has a natural mapping for `[out]` only parameters.

Object References and Pointers

With regard to pointer attributes, object references are treated as special cases by the IDL compiler, always being treated as `[unique]`. Any attempt to change the pointer semantics of object reference parameters will meet with failure; specifically, the warning MIDL2314 : "explicit pointer attribute [ptr] [ref] ignored for interface pointers" will be generated. Specifying full pointer semantics is unnecessary for object references, because the standard marshaling architecture already provides such semantics. Because reference pointers are not supported, there is no way to specify that a valid object reference must be passed into a method. A caller could always pass a null reference and the proxy would not complain, although the method implementation might do so. When object references are used as `[out]` parameters, then, like all other `[out]` parameters, the top-level pointer must be marked as `[ref]` either implicitly or explicitly.

Note that an object reference is an embedded resource in the output case, and hence ownership is transferred from object to client when the method completes, just as it is for embedded memory. It is therefore the responsibility of the client to free up the resource when it is no longer needed by calling `IUnknown::Release`. Object references used as structure members are inherently embedded and must be released by the client whenever such a structure is returned from a method.

Arrays

Developers often need to pass multiple values of the same type into or out of a method. Many constructs exist to support this, such as linked lists as described previously. However, not all applications store data in linked lists—in fact, arrays are a much more common data representation. Moreover, linked lists are not particularly efficient when transmitted across a context boundary, because the interception code has to follow all the pointers and copy each list element into the network buffer. A reference to the next element also needs to be written into the network buffer, making the transmission size larger than necessary. A more efficient transmission format is an array. IDL supports many types of arrays, including fixed-size arrays and arrays whose size is determined at runtime.

Fixed-Size Arrays

Fixed-size arrays are declared using the `[]` syntax, specifying the size between the square brackets. Because the array size is fixed, the interception code will always copy the same amount of data, regardless of how many elements in the array are actually valid at call time. Listing 4.13 shows an interface in which each of the methods takes some form of array as an input parameter, with each array being of a fixed size. The C++ client-side call sequence for the interface is shown in Listing 4.14. In the case of the call to `TakeMyStrings`, the array allocated by the client is larger than the size specified in the IDL. The interception code will transmit only the number of elements specified in the IDL; any extra elements will not be passed through to the method implementation.

Listing 4.13 Interface with fixed array parameters

```
[
  uuid(81BAEA9A-46EB-44fe-99E8-9922B77691E7),
  object
]
interface IFixedArray : IUnknown {
  HRESULT TakeMyLongs ( [in] long rgl[50] );
  HRESULT TakeMyStrings ( [in] BSTR bstrData[8] );
}
```

Listing 4.14 Passing fixed-size arrays as input parameters

```
long lData[50];
BSTR bstrData[10];
// Fill arrays with data
HR(pObj->TakeMyLongs ( lData ));
HR(pObj->TakeMyStrings ( bstrData ));
```

The method implementation of `TakeMyLongs` is shown in Listing 4.15. Note the parameter check at the beginning of the function; despite the fact that `rgl` is a top-level parameter, it is treated as a pass-by-value parameter rather than as a pass-by-reference parameter. Consequently, reference pointer semantics do not apply, and null is a valid parameter value.

Listing 4.15 Implementation of IFixedArray::TakeMyLongs

```
STDMETHODIMP TakeMyLongs ( short rgl[50] ) {
  if ( rgl )
  {
    long lTotal = 0;
    for(int i=0;i<20;i++)
    {
      lTotal += rgl[i];
    }
  }
  else
    return E_POINTER;

  return S_OK;
}
```

Fixed arrays may also be used as [in,out] and [out] parameters. Listing 4.16 shows an interface that deals with arrays of BSTRs, while Listing 4.17 shows the C++ client-side call sequence for the [in,out] case.

Listing 4.16   Fixed arrays as [in,out] and [out] parameters

```
[
  uuid(F558C100-5D04-4713-BCF3-C83374FFC6B2),
  object
]
interface IDoStrings : IUnknown {
  HRESULT TakeAndReturnBSTRS ( [in,out] BSTR str[4] );
  HRESULT ReturnBSTRS ( [out] BSTR str[6] );
}
```

Listing 4.17   7 Client-side call sequence for IDoStrings::TakeAndReturnBSTRs

```
BSTR strings[4];
// Initialize array
strings[0] = SysAllocString ( L"XML" );
strings[1] = SysAllocString ( L"is" );
strings[2] = SysAllocString ( L"very" );
strings[3] = SysAllocString ( L"cool" );
HR(pObj->TakeAndReturnBSTRS ( strings ));
// Do something with returned strings...
// Free returned strings
SysFreeString ( strings[0] );
SysFreeString ( strings[1] );
SysFreeString ( strings[2] );
SysFreeString ( strings[3] );
```

The server-side implementation may need to make copies of the strings passed as input. It may also need to free the input strings and allocate new strings for output. Such an implementation is shown in Listing 4.18.

Listing 4.18   Reallocating strings in IDoStrings::TakeAndReturnBSTRs

```
STDMETHODIMP TakeAndReturnBSTRS ( BSTR str[4] ) {
  if ( str ) {
    // Copy and free input strings
    for(int i=0;i<4;i++) {
      m_bstrs[i] =
      SysAllocStringLen ( str[i],
            SysStringLen ( str[i] ));
      SysFreeString ( str[i] );
    }
```

```
      // Allocate output strings
      str[0] = SysAllocString ( L"XSL" );
      str[1] = SysAllocString ( L"is" );
      str[2] = SysAllocString ( L"cool" );
      str[3] = SysAllocString ( L"too" );
   }
   else
      return E_POINTER;

   return S_OK
}
```

Note that ownership of the strings transfers from the client to the object and back again because the strings are embedded resources and must follow the memory management rules for such elements. If the object is able to modify the input strings in place, perhaps it converts to uppercase, and then it need not reallocate the strings, as shown in Listing 4.19.

Listing 4.19 Modifying strings in place in IDoStrings::TakeAndReturnBSTRs

```
STDMETHODIMP TakeAndReturnBSTRS ( BSTR str[4] ) {
   if ( str ) {
      // Convert input strings
      for(int i=0;i<4;i++)
         CharUpperBuffW ( str[i],
            SysStringLen ( str[i] ));
   }
   else
      return E_POINTER;

   return S_OK
}
```

The client-side calling code would not change; the client would still free the strings after the call completes. In this case, where the client calls the implementation shown in Listing 4.19, the client is just freeing the strings it previously allocated, whereas in the case where the call is made to the implementation shown in Listing 4.18, it frees strings allocated by the server.

The code for [out] only arrays is similar, only the client does not allocate any initial resource beyond the top-level array. An example call sequence is shown in Listing 4.20, while the method implementation is shown in Listing 4.21. In this case, the embedded resources are allocated by the object during the method call and released by the client after the call completes.

Listing 4.20   Client-side call sequence for IDoStrings::ReturnBSTRs

```
BSTR strings[6];
HR(pObj->ReturnBSTRS ( strings ));
// Do something with returned strings...
// Free returned strings
::SysFreeString ( strings[0] );
::SysFreeString ( strings[1] );
::SysFreeString ( strings[2] );
::SysFreeString ( strings[3] );
::SysFreeString ( strings[4] );
::SysFreeString ( strings[5] );
```

Listing 4.21   Implementation of IDoStrings::ReturnBSTRs

```
STDMETHODIMP ReturnBSTRS ( BSTR str[6] ) {
  if ( str ) {
    str[0] = SysAllocString ( L"Elvis" );
    str[1] = SysAllocString ( L"is" );
    str[2] = SysAllocString ( L"dead" );
    str[3] = SysAllocString ( L"deal" );
    str[4] = SysAllocString ( L"with" );
    str[5] = SysAllocString ( L"it" );
    return S_OK;
  }
  else
    return E_POINTER;
}
```

Fixed-size arrays are supported only for C++ clients and servers; Visual Basic does not support calling or implementation of methods with fixed-size arrays as parameters. This limitation is a language level problem rather than a problem with type libraries. Fixed array types appear correctly in type libraries, and interceptors built from either Oicf or standard type information may be used.

Multidimensional Fixed-Size Arrays

Fixed-size arrays may have multiple dimensions. For example:

```
HRESULT Take2DArrayOfLongs ( [in] long rgl[3][3] );
```

Arrays in C++ are just blocks of memory, so a 3-by-3 two-dimensional array is very similar to a single-dimension array with nine elements. The only difference is the shape of the array; the size of the memory block is the same. The memory layout of the array passed to `Take2DArrayOfLongs` is shown in

Index	0,0	0,1	0,2	1,0	1,1	1,2	2,0	2,1	2,2
Offset	1	2	3	4	5	6	7	8	9

Figure 4.14 **Layout of two-dimensional array in memory**

Figure 4.14. The top row shows the array index, while the bottom row shows the offset of each element in memory.

IDL uses the same ordering scheme as C++ uses—row-major ordering—so the client-side call sequence is straightforward:

```
long data[3][3];
// Initialize all 9 array elements
HR(pObj->Take2DArrayOfLongs ( data ));
```

The server-side implementation is no more complicated, as shown in Listing 4.22.

Listing 4.22 Implementation of Take2DArrayOfLongs

```
HRESULT Take2DArrayOfLongs ( long rgl[3][3] ) {
  if ( rgl ) {
    m_lTotal = 0;
    for(int i =0;i<3;i++)
      for(int j=0;j<3;j++)
        m_lTotal+=rgl[i][j];
  }
  else
    return E_POINTER;
}
```

Conformant Arrays

The fixed array syntax is fine for data sets whose maximum size is known in advance and whose runtime size does not vary dramatically. For some data sets, the size may not be known in advance, and if the size of the data set varies, the maximum size must be specified in the IDL and the transmission size of the data will always be that maximum size, often resulting in unnecessary transmission overhead. Also, the caller will always have to allocate an array of the required size, or the interception code will end up referring to invalid memory locations. For example, given the IDL shown earlier in Listing 4.13, the following method call will not work correctly because the interception code will try to copy `50* sizeof ( long )`, or 200 bytes, into the network buffer when only 100 bytes are available in the array. At best, the result will be an access violation and the error can be caught. At worst, the interception code will copy other, random data farther down the stack frame into the call.

```
long lData[25];
// Fill array with data
HR(pObj->TakeMyLongs ( lData ));
```

Fortunately, IDL supports another array type, known as a conformant array, which allows the size, or conformance, of an array to be determined at runtime, which can be used to work around these problems. Rather than sizing the array explicitly in the IDL, an additional parameter is specified whose sole purpose is to store the size of the array at runtime. In addition, an extra attribute, `[size_is]`, is attached to the array parameter. An example interface definition is shown in Listing 4.23. The array operator syntax, [], is still used, but with no explicit size.[4] The method parameter `cElems` is being used to store the array size, and the `[size_is]` attribute tells the interception code that `cElems` holds the current array size. The interception code will use the value of the `cElems` parameter to determine how large an array is being passed into the call and marshal accordingly.

Listing 4.23   IDL for a conformant array
```
[
  uuid(E4D21D03-E47B-42c6-ACC7-F78B0741175B),
  object
]
interface ITakeConformantArrays : IUnknown {
  HRESULT TakeMyShorts ( [in] short cElems,
       [in, size_is(cElems)] short Data[] );
}
```

Whenever the client makes a call to the `TakeMyShorts` method described in Listing 4.23, the conformance must be specified. Each call may specify a different conformance if required, as shown in the following example.

---

[4] A second syntax, HRESULT TakeMyShorts ([in] long cElems, [in,size_is (cElems)] short Data[*]);, is also supported by the MIDL compiler. This generates type information identical to the syntax shown here.

```
short Data[50]; // Array on the stack
// Initialize array with some data
pObj->TakeMyShorts ( 50, Data ); // Pass 50 elements
short*pData = new short[30]; // Array on heap
// Initialize array with data
HR(pObj->TakeMyShorts ( 30, pData )); // Pass 30 elements
```

Conformant arrays, like fixed arrays, are treated as pass-by-value parameters with respect to the top level, so null is a valid parameter. The method implementation is shown in Listing 4.24.

Listing 4.24   Implementation of ITakeConformantArrays::TakeMyShorts
```
STDMETHODIMP TakeMyShorts ( short cElems,
                                short Data[] ) {
  if ( Data ) {
    m_lTotal = 0;

    for(short i=0;i<cElems;i++)
      m_lTotal +=Data[i];

    return S_OK
  }
  else
    return E_POINTER;
}
```

It is also possible to use conformant arrays as [in,out] parameters:

```
HRESULT TakeAndReturnMyShorts ( [in,out] short* pcElems,
              [in,out,size_is(*pcElems)] short Data[] );
```

with a client-side call sequence of:

```
short n = 25;
short Data[25];
// Initialize array data
HR(pObj->TakeAndReturnMyShorts ( &n, Data ));
```

Note that the client passes the address of the size variable, n, so that the server can pass back a different value.

The main problem with this syntax is that the server must never return more items than were originally passed in by the client. This is because there is no way for the server to reallocate the array. The client allocated the memory for the array. This may have been on the heap or on the stack; either way, the server has no way of knowing where the memory is and also has no way of resizing it.

At first glance, it would appear that if the client passed in an array with dimensions larger than the conformance specified in the call, the server could safely pass back more data than the client passed in. There are two problems with this picture. First, how does the server know how large the array really is? Typically, the only information the server has about the size of the array is the parameter passed in by the client. Even if the server does have extra knowledge about the size of the array, the interception code provided by the system will defeat any attempt to use more array elements than were actually specified by the caller, because the stub will allocate only enough memory to hold the transmitted data. The stub, like the object, knows nothing about the actual size of the client-side array. Figure 4.15 shows how the call would look.

In step 1 the proxy copies ten elements from the input array. It transmits them to the stub in step 2, and the stub allocates space for the ten elements. In step 3 the stub calls the method that accesses the data, modifies it, and returns in step 4. In step 5 the stub transmits the modified data back to the proxy, and in step 6 the proxy copies the returned data into the client-side array.

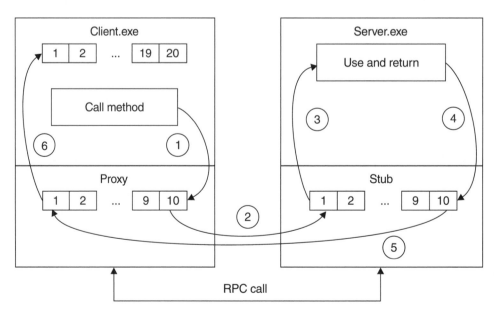

Figure 4.15 Passing a conformant array

Note that the stub allocates memory for only ten array items because the caller specified a conformance of 10 when making the call. This means that the server can return no more than the same amount of data that the client passed in. If the client and server were in direct communication—that is, if they were not separated by a context boundary—the server could safely pass back more data if the client array was large enough. However, any interface implementation that assumes it will never be called across context is inherently fragile, because even though the interface may be used only locally today, in the future it may be used remotely, and the implementation would break at that point.

One limitation of conformant arrays is that they cannot be used as pure [out] parameters, because nothing is passed from client to server for [out] only parameters. Consequently, the stub has no way of knowing how big an array to allocate for the call. The server cannot allocate the memory for the array, because there is no embedded pointer in the method signature.

```
// This signature will not compile
HRESULT ReturnMyLongs ( [out] short*pcElems,
        [out,size_is(*pcElems)] long rgl[] );
```

The lack of the extra level of indirection on the second parameter means that the server has no way to return any allocated memory to the stub or client. One way around this problem is to make the conformance an [in] parameter, which causes the stub to allocate an array of the correct size.

```
// This will compile correctly
HRESULT ReturnMyLongs ( [in] short cElems,
        [out,size_is(cElems)] long rgl[] );
```

However, this version is not much better than the [in,out] case, the only advantage being that no array data is transmitted from client to server. The client is still determining the maximum amount of data the server can return.

Multidimensional Conformant Arrays

Just like fixed arrays, conformant arrays may be multidimensional. However, only a single dimension may be sized at runtime. This variable dimension must always be the first dimension; all other dimensions must be of a fixed size, using the syntax described under Fixed-Size Arrays. The following IDL describes an array that has cElems rows, with each row containing ten columns.

```
HRESULT Take2DArrayOfLongs ( [in] short cElems,
                 [in,size_is(cElems)] long rgl[][10] );
```

The client call sequence would be

```
long rgl1[10][10];
HR(pObj->Take2DArrayOfLongs ( 10, rgl1 ));
long rgl2[5][10];
HR(pObj->Take2DArraySomeLongs ( 5, rgl2 ));
```

Note that in both calls the second dimension is the same because the size is fixed at 10. If the array had more than two dimensions, all dimensions after the first would be of a fixed size.

One way around the problem of a single variable dimension is always to use a single dimension and use some other technique to describe the shape of the array. Consider the following IDL.

```
HRESULT Take2DData ( [in] short nRows,
                      [in] short nCols,
        [in,size_is(nRows*nCols)] short rgs[] );
```

Note that the [size_is] clause is the product of the first two parameters, which may at first glance appear a little odd. It is, however, perfectly legal IDL. The [size_is] clause is in fact an expression and can contain any combination of arithmetic operators, constants, and method parameters. Function calls are not permitted in [size_is] expressions. The client-side call sequence is shown in Listing 4.25.

Listing 4.25   Client-side call sequence for Take2DData
```
short Data[10][25];
// Initialize array data
HR(pObj->Take2DData ( 10, 25, (short*)Data ));
short OtherData[50][50];
// Initialize other array data
HR(pObj->Take2DData ( 50, 50, (short*)OtherData ));
```

Because pointers and arrays are often used interchangeably in C++ and at the end of the day they both just refer to a block of memory somewhere, the IDL syntax for Take2DData and the client call sequence shown in Listing 4.25 work perfectly well. The interception code knows nothing about the shape of the array; it sees it as a contiguous block of memory, which it is, because of the way the C++ compiler lays out the array. In the case of the first call, the size of the memory block is 500 bytes, and for the second call it is 5000 bytes. The reason that two input parameters are used to generate the conformance is to tell the server what the shape of the array is. The server can then treat the array correctly using pointer arithmetic or array indexing.

For example, the method implementation shown in Listing 4.26 uses array indexing to iterate through both array dimensions. Note, however, that the array indexing is not typical C++ array indexing, which would use a pair of square brackets for each dimension, but is rather a combination of array indexing and pointer arithmetic. This is necessary because the C++ compiler "knows" that the array has only a single dimension and so generates an error if two indices are used.

Listing 4.26 Implementation of Take2DData

```
HRESULT Take2DData ( short nRows, short nCols,
                     short rgs[] ) {
  if ( rgs ) {
    m_lTotal = 0;
    for ( short i=0;i<nRows;i++)
      for(short j=0;j<nCols;j++)
          m_lTotal += rgs[(i * nCols ) + j];

    return S_OK;
  }
  else
    return E_POINTER;
}
```

Conformant Pointers

Because of the limitations of conformant arrays—namely, a lack of [out] parameter support and limited usefulness with regard to multiple dimensions—interface designers often use conformant pointers where array types are needed. Conformant pointers, also known as sized pointers, have a conformance associated with them through the [size_is] attribute just as conformant arrays do. They are more flexible than arrays, supporting server-allocated [out] parameters and server resizing of [in,out] parameters, in addition to being more flexible with respect to arrays with multiple dimensions.

The IDL syntax for conformant pointers uses the pointer operator, *, instead of the array operator, []. The IDL shown in Listing 4.27 contains a method that takes a conformant pointer as input.

Listing 4.27   Conformant pointer as [in] parameter

```
[
  uuid(E4E59BB2-520D-4b30-88F3-5844CD44CAD),
  object
]
interface ITakeConformantPointers : IUnknown {
  HRESULT TakeMyFloats ( [in] short cElems,
         [in,size_is(cElems)] float*pData );
}
```

The [size_is] attribute is actually sizing the pointer, pData. Pointers in IDL are assumed to point to a single instance by default. This is different from C++, where the number of instances a pointer points to is largely arbitrary. The [size_is] attribute defines the number of instances a pointer points to, allowing the interception code to marshal the correct amount of data. In the method signature above, the cElems parameter specifies how many elements pData points to. Given a client-side call sequence of:

```
short nElems = 25;
float* p = new float[nElems];
// Initialize array data
HR(pObj->TakeMyFloats ( nElems, p ));
```

the interception code would attempt to marshal 25 floats, as specified by the nElems parameter, rather than just a single float, which would be the case if the [size_is] attribute were not specified. Note also that, because the second parameter is a top-level pointer, and is by default a reference pointer, null values are not allowed. This makes conformant pointers slightly different from conformant arrays in this regard. The conformant pointer could be forced to exhibit the same behavior as a conformant array by annotating the reference parameter with the [unique] attribute.

Note also that the client call style for conformant arrays can still be used with conformant pointers.

```
short Data[25];
HR(pObj->TakeMyShorts ( 25, Data ));
```

This works because of the way C++ treats pointers and arrays.

Visual Basic is also able to call methods that take conformant pointers as input parameters. The call sequence is shown below. Note that the first element of the array must be passed as the array parameter rather than the array itself.

```
Dim data(24) As Integer
' Initialize array data
obj.TakeMyShorts 25, data(0)
```

Conformant Pointers as Output Parameters

When conformant pointers are used as output parameters, the same pointer sizing is necessary. However, a double level of indirection is needed for the array parameter so that the server can allocate the memory and return it to the caller. Unfortunately, the obvious IDL syntax, shown below in the `ReturnSomeShorts` method signature, is incorrect, because it sizes `pData` rather than `*pData`. This tells the interception code to expect a pointer to an array of pointers each pointing to a single short, as shown in Figure 4.16. This

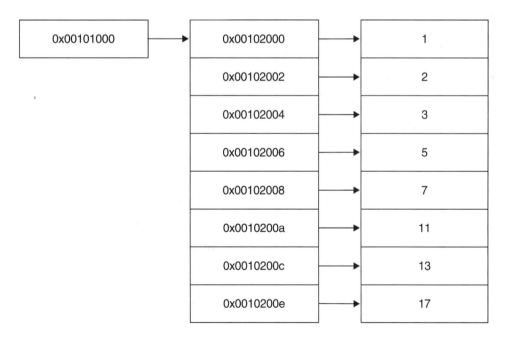

Figure 4.16   Incorrect memory layout for [out] conformant pointer

is not usually what is required. What is required is a pointer to a pointer to an array of shorts, as shown in Figure 4.17.

```
HRESULT ReturnSomeShorts ( [out] short*pcElems,
        [out, size_is(*pcElems)] short**pData );
```

The second level of indirection needs to be sized, rather than the first. To tell the MIDL compiler to size the second level of indirection, the comma operator must be used in the [size_is] expression. For example,

```
HRESULT ReturnSomeShorts ( [out] short*pcElems,
        [out, size_is(1,*pcElems)] short**ppData );
```

generates Oicf type information that expects the correct memory layout. The client-side call sequence for such a method is shown in Listing 4.28.[5] The address of nElems is passed as the first parameter, allowing the object to pass

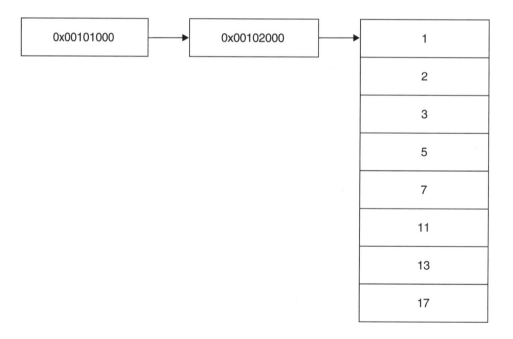

Figure 4.17   Correct memory layout for [out] conformant pointer

---

[5] Visual Basic is unable to call ReturnMyShorts because of the double level of indirection in the method signature.

the size of the array back to the client. Note also that the address of `p` is passed as the second parameter. This allows the object to pass the address of the array back to the client. Lastly, because `p` is an embedded pointer, the client must free the memory using `CoTaskMemFree`.

Listing 4.28 Client-side call sequence for ReturnSomeShorts

```
short nElems = 0;
short*p = 0;
HR(pObj->ReturnSomeShorts ( &nElems, &p ));
for(short i=0;i<nElems;i++)
{
    // Do something with each element
}
// Free server allocated memory
CoTaskMemFree ( p );
```

The method implementation is shown in Listing 4.29, where `m_nElems` is a member variable that contains the number of elements the server currently has stored. Note that the server allocates the memory using the COM memory allocator. Having the server allocate the array in this fashion avoids the client having to guess how much storage to allocate for the data.

Listing 4.29 Implementation of ReturnSomeShorts

```
STDMETHODIMP ReturnSomeShorts ( short*pcElems,
                                short**ppData ) {
    if ( pcElems && ppData ) {
        *ppData = (short*)CoTaskMemAlloc (
            m_nElems * sizeof ( short ));
        if ( *ppData ) {
            for(short i=0;i<*pcElems;i++) {
                // Copy server data into allocated memory
            }
            *pcElems = m_nElems;
            return S_OK;
        }
        else
            return E_OUTOFMEMORY;
    }
    else
        return E_POINTER;
}
```

The IDL syntax shown earlier for `ReturnSomeShorts` is not often seen, because typically an optimization is used.

```
HRESULT ReturnSomeShorts ( [out] short*pcElems,
     [out, size_is(,*pcElems)] short**ppData );
```

Note the lack of an expression before the comma operator. While this is semantically equivalent to the previous IDL and thus supports the same client-side call sequence and method implementation, it does not use the same wire representation. This first form will transmit the value 1 on the wire along with the rest of the data, whereas the second version will not.

Simulating Fixed-Size Arrays Using Conformance

The `size_is` clause is actually an expression, and therefore, fixed-size arrays can be expressed using `size_is` with a constant.

```
HRESULT TakeMyFixedShorts (
   [in,size_is(20)] short*pData );
```

At first glance, this syntax appears to be redundant, and is in fact less efficient on the wire than the standard fixed array syntax, because the conformance is sent along with the array data, wasting 4 bytes per call. However, it allows Visual Basic to use fixed-size arrays as input parameters, which it cannot do with the standard fixed-size array syntax.[6] The Visual Basic call sequence looks like this:

```
Dim x(19) As Integer ' 20 element array
' Initialize array with data
obj.TakeMyFixedShorts x(0) ' Pass first element
```

Output parameters also work. Given the following IDL:

```
HRESULT ReturnFixedShorts (
   [out,size_is(20)] short* pData );
```

the method implementation would be as shown in Listing 4.30.

---

[6] Conformant arrays work the same way in this case; `HRESULT TakeMyFixedShorts ( [in,size_is(20) short rgs[] );` can be called from Visual Basic. However, conformant arrays do not work from Visual Basic when the conformance is specified at runtime. So, `HRESULT TakeMyShorts ( [in] short cElems, [in,size_is(cElems)] short rgs[] );` cannot be called from Visual Basic.

Listing 4.30 Implementation of ReturnFixedShorts

```
STDMETHODIMP ReturnFixedShorts ( short* pData ) {
  if ( pData ) {
    for(int i=0;i<20;i++)
      pData[i] = i * i;
  }

  return S_OK;
}
```

The client-side call would look very similar to that for the input parameter.

```
Dim x(19) As Integer ' 20 element array
Obj.ReturnFixedShorts x(0)
' Do something with array data
```

Although Visual Basic can call methods that take conformant arrays as parameters, because the `[size_is]` attribute is not present in the generated type library, it cannot implement such methods. Note also that only Oicf information may be used to build interceptors for conformant arrays and pointers for the same reason.

Multidimensional Conformant Pointers

Multidimensional arrays can be passed using conformant pointers. The technique used with conformant arrays, using a single dimension and describing the shape of the array in the `[size_is]` clause, also works for conformant pointers. Consider the following IDL syntax.

```
HRESULT Take2DData2 ( [in] short nRows,
                      [in] short nCols,
   [in, size_is(nRows * nCols )] short*pData );
```

The client-side call sequence would be identical to that for conformant arrays.

```
short Data[10][25];
// Initialize array data
HR(pObj->Take2DData2 ( 10, 25, (short*)Data ));
short OtherData[50][50];
// Initialize other array data
HR(pObj->Take2DData2 ( 50, 50, (short*)OtherData ));
```

The method implementation would also be pretty much the same as shown in Listing 4.31.

Listing 4.31 Implementation of Take2DData2

```
HRESULT Take2DData2 ( short nRows, short nCols,
                        short*pData ) {
  if ( pData ) {
    m_lTotal = 0;
    for ( short i=0;i<nRows;i++)
      for(short j=0;j<nCols;j++)
          m_lTotal += pData[(i * nCols) + j];
  }
  else
    return E_POINTER;
}
```

The same technique can be used with conformant pointers for output parameters. For example, for the IDL

```
HRESULT Return2DData ( [out] short* pRows,
                        [out] short* pCols,
     [out, size_is(,(*prows) * (*pCols))] short** pprgs );
```

the method implementation would be as shown in Listing 4.32. Note that, just
as in the case of an input array, the first two parameters describe the shape of
the array and the product defines the number of elements. The client-side call
sequence is shown in Listing 4.33.

Listing 4.32 Implementation of Return2DData

```
STDMETHODIMP Return2DData ( short*pRows,
                             short*pCols,
                             short**pprgs ) {
  if ( pRows && pCols && pprgs ) {
    *pprgs = (short*)CoTaskMemAlloc (
      m_nRows * m_nCols * sizeof ( short ));
    if ( *pprgs ) {
      for(short i=0;i<m_nRows;i++){
        for(short j=0;j<m_nCols;j++)
          (*pprgs)[(i * m_nCols) + j] = i * j;
      }
      *pRows = m_nRows;
      *pCols = m_nCols;
      return S_OK;
    }
    else
      return E_OUTOFMEMORY;
  }
}
```

```
     else
       return E_POINTER;
}
```

Listing 4.33   Client-side call sequence for Return2DData
```
short nRows = 0, nCols = 0;
short*pData = 0;
HR(pObj->Return2DArray ( &nRows, &nCols, &pData ));
long lTotal = 0;
for(i=0;i<nRows;i++)
  for(j=0;j<nCols;j++)
    lTotal += pData[(i * nCols )+ j];
CoTaskMemFree ( pData );
```

The problem with this approach is that it does not map very naturally to C++ array indexing and relies on the fact that C++ compilers lay out multidimensional arrays as contiguous blocks of memory. There is another IDL technique that provides a more natural language mapping at the expense of some tortuous IDL syntax. Specifically, multiple levels of indirection along with multiple comma operators can be used. For example:

```
HRESULT TakeFixed2DPointer (
   [in,size_is(1,10)] short**ppData );
HRESULT TakeFixed3DPointer (
   [in,size_is(1,10,20] short***pppData );
```

The first method signature, `TakeFixed2DPointer`, is similar to:

```
HRESULT Take2DPointer ( [in] short cElems,
        [in,size_is(,cElems)] short**ppData );
```

The second example, `TakeFixed3DPointer`, is more complex, describing a pointer to an array of ten pointers each pointing to an array of 20 shorts. This is very different from the `Take2DData2` example, given above, of a multidimensional array using the product of multiple parameters as the [size_is] expression. Note that with both `TakeFixed2DPointer` and `TakeFixed3D Pointer` the number of commas in the [size_is] expression is always 1 less than the number of * operators in the parameter declaration. The client-side call sequence for `TakeFixed3DPointer` is shown in Listing 4.34.

Listing 4.34   Client-side call sequence for TakeFixed3DPointer
```
short***pppData = new short**;
*pppData = new short*[10];
```

```
for(int j=0;j<10;j++) {
  pppData[i][j] = new short[20];
  for(int k=0;k<20;k++) {
    (*pppData)[j][k] = j + k;
  }
}
HR(pObj->TakeFixed3DPointer ( pppData ));
```

Note that multiple comma operators can also be used in variable [size_is] expressions.

```
HRESULT TakeVariable3DPointer ( [in] short n1,
                                [in] short n2,
                                [in] short n3,
                [in, size_is(n1,n2,n3)] short***pppData );
```

Note that in this case the first level of indirection is being sized in addition to the subsequent levels. The client-side call sequence is shown in Listing 4.35, and Listing 4.36 shows the corresponding method implementation. As in the case of TakeFixed3Dpointer, the array indexing is natural C++ array indexing with no arithmetic expressions.

Listing 4.35   Client-side call sequence for TakeVariable3DPointer
```
short i = 0, j=0, k=0;
short n1 = 2, n2 = 3, n3 = 3;
short***pppData = new short**[n1];
for(i=0;i<n1;i++) {
  pppData[i] = new short*[n2];
  for(j=0;j<n2;j++) {
    pppData[i][j] = new short[n3];
    for(k=0;k<n3;k++) {
      pppData[i][j][k] = i + j + k;
    }
  }
}
HR(pObj->TakeVariable3DPointer ( n1, n2, n3,
                                 pppData ));
// Free up memory after the call
```

Listing 4.36   Implementation of TakeVariable3DPointer
```
STDMETHODIMP
TakeVariable3DPointer ( short n1, short n2,
                        short n3, short***pppData ) {
    long lTotal = 0;
    short i,j,k;
```

```
for(i=0;i<n1;i++) {
    for(j=0;j<n2;j++) {
        for(k=0;k<n3;k++) {
            lTotal + = pppData[i][j][k];
        }
    }
}

return S_OK;
}
```

The memory layout is very different from that of a single dimensional array.
Figure 4.18 shows the layout of the data in memory.

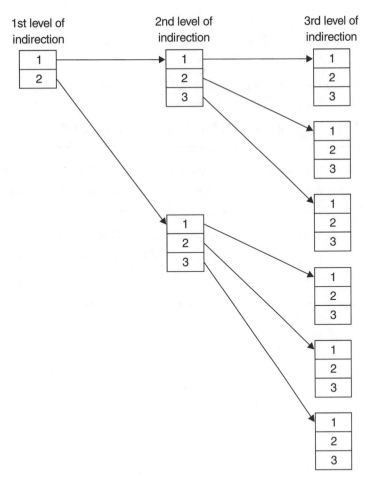

Figure 4.18 Layout of multiple-sized pointers

The same IDL construct can also be used for output parameters.

```
HRESULT ReturnVariable3DPointer (
    [out] short*pn1, [out] short*pn2, [out] short*pn3,
    [out,size_is(,*pn1,*pn2,*pn3)] short****ppppData );
```

In the output case, the first dimension is sized as 1, indicated by the lack of an expression before the first comma. This is done to make the client-side call easier: the client does not need to guess the number of elements at the first level of indirection—it is always one, and only subsequent levels are dynamic. Note that this is the exact opposite of multidimensional conformant arrays, where only the first dimension is dynamic. To understand why the first dimension is fixed, consider what would happen with the following method signature.

```
HRESULT Bad ( [out] short*pn1,
    [out] short*pn2, [out] short*pn3,
    [out,size_is(*pn1,*pn2,*pn3)] short***pppData );
```

The client would have no way to make the call, because it would not know how many pointers to allocate for the first level of indirection. Fortunately, MIDL deals with this, generating an error for such a method signature. Whenever the comma operator is used with output parameters, MIDL requires that the first level of indirection be sized using a constant expression or an input parameter. The method ReturnVariable3DPointer above uses an implicit constant expression, giving the client-side call sequence shown in Listing 4.37. Note the multiple calls to CoTaskMemFree, because of the structure of the data. The method implementation would make multiple calls to CoTaskMemAlloc, as shown in Listing 4.38.

Listing 4.37   Client-side call sequence for ReturnVariable3DPointer
```
short n1, n2, n3;
short***pppData = 0;
HR(pObj->ReturnVariable3DPointer ( &n1, &n2, &n3,
                                    &pppData ));

long lTotal = 0;
short i, j, k;
for(i=0;i<n1;i++) {
  for(j=0;j<n2;j++) {
    for(k=0;k<n3;k++) {
      lTotal += pppData[i][j][k];
    }
```

```
      CoTaskMemFree ( pppData[i][j] );
    }
    CoTaskMemFree ( pppData[i] );
  }
CoTaskMemFree ( pppData );
```

Listing 4.38   Implementation of ReturnA3DPointer

```
STDMETHODIMP
ReturnVariable3DPointer ( short*pn1, short*pn2,
                    short*pn3, short****ppppData ) {
  *pn1 = 5;
  *pn2 = 10;
  *pn3 = 15;
  short i, j, k;
  *ppppData = (short***)CoTaskMemAlloc (
    sizeof ( short** ) * *pn1 );

  for(i=0;i<*pn1;i++) {
    (*ppppData)[i] = (short**)CoTaskMemAlloc (
      sizeof ( short * ) * *pn2 );

    for(j=0;j<*pn2;j++) {
      (*ppppData)[i][j] = (short*)CoTaskMemAlloc (
        sizeof ( short ) * *pn3 );
      for(k=0;k<*pn3;k++){
        (*ppppData)[i][j][k] = i * j * k;
      }
    }
  }
  return S_OK;
}
```

The method `ReturnA3DPointer` uses an implicit constant, 1, to size the first dimension of the array. As mentioned above, the first dimension can be sized dynamically, but only by the client. The following example uses an input parameter to size the first dimension.

```
HRESULT
ReturnMultiple3DPointers ( [in] short n1,
                          [out] short*pn2,
                          [out] short*pn3,
                          [out] short*pn4,
[out,size_is(n1,*pn2,*pn3,*pn4)] short****ppppData );
```

The client-side call sequence is shown in Listing 4.39 while the method implementation is shown in Listing 4.40. Both the client-side call sequence and the method implementation have an extra loop compared with the `ReturnA3DPointer` example.

Listing 4.39 Client-side call sequence for ReturnMultiple3DPointers

```
short n1, n2, n3, n4;
short ***pppData[5];
n1 = 5;
HR(pObj->ReturnMultiple3DPointers ( n1, &n2, &n3, &n4,
                                          pppData );

int i, j, k, l;
for(i=0;i<n1;i++) {
  for(j=0;j<n2;j++) {
    for(k=0;k<n3;k++) {
      for(l=0;l<n4;l++) {
        lTotal += pppData[i][j][k][l];
      }
      CoTaskMemFree ( pppData[i][j][k] );
    }
    CoTaskMemFree ( pppData[i][j] );
  }
  CoTaskMemFree ( pppData[i] );
}
```

Listing 4.40 Implementation of ReturnMultiple3DPointers

```
STDMETHODIMP
ReturnMultiple3DPointers ( short n1, short*pn2,
                           short*pn3, short*pn4,
                           short****ppppData ) {
  *pn2 = 5;
  *pn3 = 10;
  *pn4 = 15;

  for(short i=0;i<n1;i++) {
    short j, k, l;
    ppppData[i] = (short***)CoTaskMemAlloc (
      sizeof ( short** ) * *pn2 );

    for(j=0;j<*pn2;j++) {
      ppppData[i][j] = (short**)CoTaskMemAlloc (
        sizeof ( short * ) * *pn2 );
```

```
      for(k=0;k<*pn3;k++) {
        ppppData[i][j][k] = (short*)CoTaskMemAlloc (
        sizeof ( short ) * *pn4 );

        for(l=0;l<*pn4;l++) {
          ppppData[i][j][k][l] = i * j * k * l;
        }
      }
    }
  }
}
  return S_OK;
}
```

Arrays as Structure Members

All the array types in IDL can also be used as structure members. Fixed arrays can appear anywhere in a structure. A structure can contain multiple fixed arrays. Fixed arrays are allocated inline with the rest of the structure members, so no pointers are involved. For example:

```
struct StructWithFixedArrays {
  long l,m;
  short rgs[10];
  double lf;
  float rgf[25];
};
```

The use of conformant arrays inside structures is more restricted than the use of fixed arrays. A structure can contain only a single conformant array, and that array must be the last structure member. For example:

```
struct StructWithConformantArray {
  long l,m;
  double lf;
  short nElems;
  [size_is(nElems)] float rgf[];
};
```

The reason that the conformant array must be the last structure member is that, as with fixed arrays, the memory is allocated inline with the rest of the structure. Because the size is not known until runtime, the array has to be the last member. If this were not the case, the compiler would be unable to lay out the structure members correctly in memory. The structure actually maps to the following in C++.

```
struct StructWithConformantArray {
  long l;
  long m;
  double lf;
  short nElems;
  float rgf[ 1 ];
};
```

Given the following method signature in IDL:

```
HRESULT CreateStruct (
  [out] struct StructWithConformantArray** pp );
```

the client-side call sequence would be

```
struct StructWithConformantArray*ps = 0;
HR(pObj->CreateStruct ( &ps ));
// Do something with struct
CoTaskMemFree ( ps );
```

The method implementation is shown in Listing 4.41. Note that the memory allocation call creates a block of memory large enough to hold all the members of the structure and the required number of array elements as a contiguous block. This means that using structures with conformant arrays as [out] parameters always requires a double level of indirection, because the entire structure must be embedded, including the array. Passing such structures as input parameters requires only a single level of indirection.

Listing 4.41 Implementation of CreateStruct

```
HRESULT CreateStruct (
  struct StructWithConformantArray**pps ) {
  short nElems = 50;
  struct StructWithConformantArray*ps = 0;
  ps =
  (struct StructWithConformantArray*)CoTaskMemAlloc (
  sizeof ( ConformantStruct ) +
  (( nElems - 1 ) * sizeof ( float )));

  // Initialize structure with data
  ps->m = 10;
  ps->n = 20;
  ps->lf = 3.14;
  ps->nElems = nElems;
  for(short i=0;i<nElems;i++)
    ps->rgf[i] = i/1.5;
```

```
  *pps = ps;
  return S_OK;
}
```

In contrast to conformant arrays, conformant pointers are more flexible and can appear anywhere within a structure. They can also appear multiple times. For example:

```
struct StructWithConformantPointers {
  long l,m;
  short nShortElems;
  [size_is(nShortElems)] short*prgs;
  double lf;
  short nFloatElems;
  [size_is(nFloatElems)] float* prgf;
};
```

Such a structure can be used as an [out] parameter with only a single level of indirection.

```
HRESULT CreateAnotherStruct (
  [out] struct StructWithConformantPointers* ps );
```

In this case, only the conformant pointers inside the structure would be embedded, resulting in the following call sequence.

```
struct StructWithConformantPointers s;
HR(pObj->CreateAnotherStruct ( &s ));
// Do something with struct
CoTaskMemFree ( s.prgs );
CoTaskMemFree ( s.prgf );
```

The method implementation is shown in Listing 4.42.

Listing 4.42 Implementation of CreateAnotherStruct

```
HRESULT CreateAnotherStruct (
  struct StructWithConformantPointers* ps ) {
  ps->l = 10;
  ps->m = 20;
  ps->nShortElems = 40;
  ps->prgs = (short*)CoTaskMemAlloc (
    sizeof ( short ) * ps->nShortElems );
  // Initialize short array
  ps->lf = 3.14;
  ps->nFloatElems = 100;
  ps->prgf = (float*)CoTaskMemAlloc (
    sizeof ( float ) * ps->nFloatElems );
```

```
// Initialize float array
return S_OK;
}
```

For both conformant arrays and conformant pointers, the field used as the argument to the [size_is] clause must be of the same scope as the array/pointer. The following IDL would be illegal, because the array, rgf, is inside struct Inner, whereas the conformance field, nElems, is in struct Outer. The MIDL compiler will generate the error MIDL2058 : attribute expression cannot be resolved : [Field 'rgf' of Struct 'Inner' (Struct 'Outer')].

```
struct Outer {
  long nElems;
  struct Inner {
    long l,m;
    BSTR* pbstrDescription;
    [size_is(nElems)] float rgf[];
  };
};
```

Jagged Arrays

Developers sometimes need to pass jagged arrays into method calls. Jagged arrays are arrays in which the number of elements in a given dimension varies as another dimension is traversed. For example, a two-dimensional jagged array would have rows with varying numbers of columns, as shown in Figure 4.19.

Unfortunately, IDL has no specific support for describing such an array as a method parameter. All is not lost however, because using conformant pointers as structure members can achieve the same result. For example, the IDL shown in Listing 4.43 allows a jagged two-dimensional array of bytes to be passed as an input parameter. The client-side call sequence is shown in Listing 4.44.

Listing 4.43 IDL for method TakeAJaggedArray
```
typedef struct Blob {
  short cElems;
  [size_is(cElems)] byte*pb;
} BLOB, *PBLOB;
HRESULT TakeAJaggedArray ( [in] short cRows,
          [in, size_is(cRows)] PBLOB pArray );
```

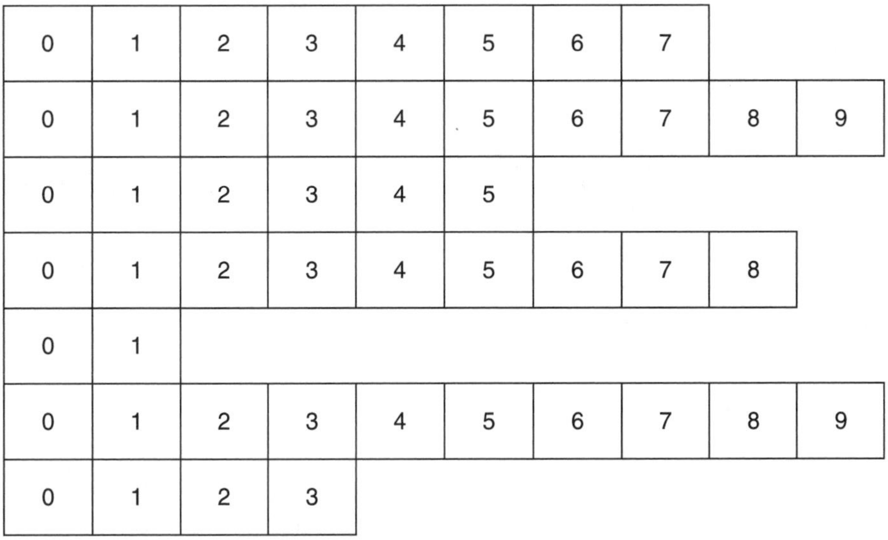

0	1	2	3	4	5	6	7		
0	1	2	3	4	5	6	7	8	9
0	1	2	3	4	5				
0	1	2	3	4	5	6	7	8	
0	1								
0	1	2	3	4	5	6	7	8	9
0	1	2	3						

Figure 4.19   Two-dimensional jagged array

Listing 4.44   Client-side call sequence for TakeAJaggedArray
```
short colcount[] = { 5, 50, 15 };
PBLOB*pData = new BLOB[3];
for(int i = 0;i<3;i++) {
  pData[i].cElems = colcount[i];
  pData[i].pb = new byte[colcount[i]];
}
HR(pObj->TakeAJaggedArray ( 3, pData ));
```

Such a technique can be applied successfully to any data type, and while the syntax for accessing the array data is not as seamless as it is for regular arrays, the wire format is very efficient.

SAFEARRAYs

C++ developers are able to use all the IDL array types described thus far. Visual Basic, however, is unable to use fixed arrays and is limited with respect to conformant arrays and pointers. Fortunately, there is another array type supported by IDL—the SAFEARRAY. The SAFEARRAY is a multidimensional array capable of dealing with any data type that can fit in a VARIANT. Given that the VARIANT type is able to describe complex structures and typed object references in addition to primitive types, this is not much of a limitation.

SAFEARRAYs map directly to a Visual Basic array and in C++ map to a structure called the SAFEARRAY descriptor, which is described in IDL as shown in Listing 4.45.

Listing 4.45   SAFEARRAY descriptor in IDL

```
typedef struct tagSAFEARRAY {
  USHORT cDims;       // Number of dimensions
  USHORT fFeatures;   // Flags
  ULONG  cbElements;  // Size of an element
  ULONG  cLocks;      // Number of locks
  PVOID  pvData;      // Pointer to array data
  [size_is(cDims)] SAFEARRAYBOUND rgsabound[];
} SAFEARRAY;
```

The actual array data is stored in the memory location aliased by pvData. The number of elements is stored in the conformant array of SAFEARRAYBOUND structures; there is an entry in this array for each dimension, with the number of dimensions being defined by the cDims field. The IDL description of the SAFEARRAYBOUND structure is shown in Listing 4.46.

Listing 4.46   SAFEARRAYBOUND in IDL

```
typedef struct tagSAFEARRAYBOUND {
    ULONG cElements; // Number of elements
    LONG  lLbound;   // Lower bound
} SAFEARRAYBOUND, * LPSAFEARRAYBOUND;
```

Note that the lower bound is a signed 32-bit value and hence could be negative. This is the case for arrays in Visual Basic: for example, the following Visual Basic statement declares an array with a negative lower bound.

```
Dim x(-10 to 10) As Integer
```

Such an array would have cDims set to 1, while the single entry in rgsabound would have the value 21 in cElements and −10 in lBound.

The in-memory representation of a SAFEARRAY is shown in Figure 4.20. Note that the descriptor and the array of bounds are contiguous in memory, while the actual array data, while being a contiguous block of memory itself, is not typically contiguous with the descriptor.

The fFeatures field is used to store hints about how the SAFEARRAY should be managed. These hints include information about where the array is allocated, whether or not it is embedded in a structure, and whether it is an

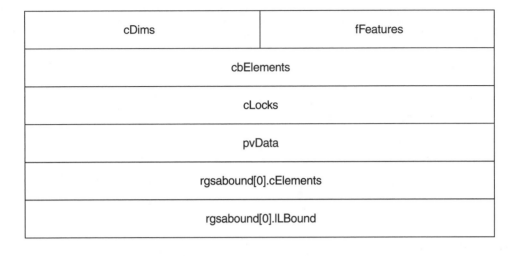

cDims	fFeatures
cbElements	
cLocks	
pvData	
rgsabound[0].cElements	
rgsabound[0].ILBound	

...

rgsabound[cDims-1].cElements
rgsabound[cDims-1].ILBound

Figure 4.20   In-memory representation of a SAFEARRAY

array of structures or typed object references. Hints about specific types such as strings, `IUnknown*`, `IDispatch*`, and `VARIANT` are also defined. These flags are summarized in Table 4.5.

There are actually three forms of IDL syntax for describing SAFEARRAYs, but two of them are of only limited use. The more common syntax takes the form `SAFEARRAY(type)`. The IDL shown in Listing 4.47 uses this form.

Listing 4.47   Use of SAFEARRAY(type) in IDL

```
[
  uuid(2CAD137D-40A7-4c18-B58D-03135C5CC84A)
]
struct Complex {
  float real;
  float imaginary;
};
[
  uuid(6B8401AD-6A92-4c88-9A3D-73E6DB0D720A)
]
```

Table 4.5 SAFEARRAY flags for fFeatures*

Flag	Value	Description
FADF_AUTO	0x0001	Array is allocated on the stack
FADF_STATIC	0x0002	Array is statically allocated
FADF_EMBEDDED	0x0004	Array is embedded in a structure
FADF_FIXEDSIZE	0x0010	Array cannot be resized
FADF_RECORD	0x0020	Array of structures
FADF_HAVEIID	0x0040	Array of typed object references
FADF_HAVEVARTYPE	0x0080	SafeArrayGetVarType can be used
FADF_BSTR	0x0100	Array of BSTRs
FADF_UNKNOWN	0x0200	Array of IUnknown*s
FADF_DISPATCH	0x0400	Array of IDispatch*s
FADF_VARIANT	0x0800	Array of VARIANTs

* There is an undocumented flag, 0x02000, which is set when the descriptor and the array memory are contiguous.

```
struct ComplexStuff {
  long lFlags;
  BSTR bstrDescription;
  SAFEARRAY(struct Complex) psa;
};

[
  uuid(5E1C2D25-AE9D-4a5f-B70C-7508E063CBE4),
  version(1.0)
]
library ArrayLib {
  importlib("stdole2.tlb");
  importlib("msado15.dll");

  typedef struct Complex* PCOMPLEX;
  typedef struct ComplexStuff* PCOMPLEXSTUFF;

  [
    uuid(911BFD7A-91C5-4d29-A6DC-D0AA4680535C),
    object,
    oleautomation
  ]
  interface IDoSafearrays : IUnknown {
    HRESULT TakeShorts ( [in] SAFEARRAY(short)* ppsa );
```

```
    HRESULT TakeStrings ( [in] SAFEARRAY(BSTR)* ppsa );
    HRESULT TakeRecordsets (
      [in] SAFEARRAY(_Recordset*)* ppsa );
    HRESULT ReturnVariants (
       [out,retval] SAFEARRAY(VARIANT)* ppsa );
    HRESULT ReturnStructs (
       [out,retval] SAFEARRAY(struct Complex)* ppsa );
  }
}
```

The C++ mapping for SAFEARRAY(type) is SAFEARRAY*, so the structure
has a single level of indirection whereas the interface methods have two levels.
Listing 4.48 shows the C++ mapping for the IDL shown in Listing 4.47. Note
that the C++ mapping loses the data type of the SAFEARRAY. Listing 4.49
shows the Visual Basic mapping.

Listing 4.48   C++ mapping for SAFEARRAY(type)

```
struct
DECLSPEC_UUID("E1799786-ED65-4A85-8909-07D97628BC3E")
Complex {
  float real;
  float imaginary;
};
struct
DECLSPEC_UUID("664A09B1-5570-4D0C-BC06-EA9524D17D10")
ComplexStuff {
  long lFlags;
  BSTR bstrDesc;
  SAFEARRAY * psa;
};
MIDL_INTERFACE("E1799786-ED65-4A85-8909-07D97628BC3E")
IDoSafearrays : public IUnknown {
public:
  virtual HRESULT STDMETHODCALLTYPE TakeShorts (
    /* [in] */ SAFEARRAY ** psa) = 0;
  virtual HRESULT STDMETHODCALLTYPE TakeStrings (
    /* [in] */ SAFEARRAY ** psa) = 0;
  virtual HRESULT STDMETHODCALLTYPE TakeRecordsets (
    /* [in] */ SAFEARRAY ** psa) = 0;
  virtual HRESULT STDMETHODCALLTYPE ReturnVariants (
    /* [out,retval] */ SAFEARRAY ** psa) = 0;
  virtual HRESULT STDMETHODCALLTYPE ReturnStructs (
    /* [out,retval] */ SAFEARRAY ** psa) = 0;
};
```

Listing 4.49 Visual Basic mapping of SAFEARRAY(type)

```
' Complex structure
Public Type Complex
    real As Single
    imaginary As Single
End Type
' ComplexStuff structure
Public Type ComplexStuff
    bstrDesc As String
    lFlags As Long
    psa() As Complex
End Type
' IDoSafearrays
Private Sub IDoSafearrays_TakeShorts(ppsa() As Integer)
End Sub
Private Sub IDoSafearrays_TakeStrings(ppsa() As String)
End Sub
Private Sub IDoSafearrays_TakeRecordsets(ppsa() As
ADODB.Recordset)
End Sub
Private Function IDoSafearrays_ReturnStructs() As
ArrayLib.Complex()
End Function
Private Function IDoSafearrays_ReturnVariants() As Variant()
End Function
```

The two levels of indirection at the method level are not, strictly speaking, required for input parameters, but if only a single level of indirection is used, Visual Basic will be unable to call or implement the methods. This is because Visual Basic requires that arrays be passed by reference and not by value, and as far as Visual Basic is concerned, SAFEARRAY* in IDL equates to pass-by-value.

While standard type information records the type of the array, the universal marshaler does not check the data type in the SAFEARRAY at method call time.[7] Thus, it is perfectly possible to pass an array of VARIANTs to a method expecting an array of strings. It may seem that putting the type into the parameter declaration is therefore useless, and, certainly from a C++ perspective, there is no runtime or compile time value. However, specifying the type makes

---

[7] Oicf type information does not record the array type and hence cannot check the data type at call time either.

the method definition more explicit and forms part of the interface contract. Also, Visual Basic performs compile time checking on the array type, enforcing the contract specified in the IDL. So the Visual Basic call sequence shown in Listing 4.50 generates a type mismatch at compile time, because an array of type Variant is being passed where an array of type Integer is expected. This checking occurs only at compile time, and there is still nothing to stop a C++ caller from passing a SAFEARRAY of BSTRs to a Visual Basic implementation of the TakeShorts method.

Listing 4.50 Compile time type checking of arrays in Visual Basic

```
Public Sub Foo ( obj As IDoSafearrays )
Dim x(50,5) As Integer
Dim v(10,10) As Variant
obj.TakeShorts x      ' This line is OK
obj.TakeShorts v      ' This line is not
End Sub
```

There may be situations in which the type of the array cannot be specified in the IDL because it is not known until runtime. In this case, use the second syntax, SAFEARRAY, without a type specification. For example, the IDL shown in Listing 4.51 describes methods that can take and return arrays containing any data type. Note the double * in the method signature; SAFEARRAY in IDL without a specified type maps directly to SAFEARRAY in C++, so to maintain the same number of levels of indirection as in the typed examples, two * operators are needed.

Listing 4.51 Use of untyped SAFEARRAY in IDL

```
[
  uuid(A21816F6-E6F0-4845-94B2-12A7506D1644),
  object
]
interface IDoSafearraysToo : IUnknown {
  HRESULT TakeSomething ( [in] SAFEARRAY** ppsa );
  HRESULT ReturnSomething (
    [out,retval] SAFEARRAY**ppsa );
}
```

Note that using this IDL syntax makes the interface contract ambiguous; the caller can pass an array containing anything it likes. It is unlikely that a given implementation of IDoSafearraysToo could handle all possible data types a caller could pass. This syntax should be used only where absolutely necessary; if the type of the array is known in advance, then specify it in the IDL. Another issue with this syntax is that Visual Basic is unable to implement or call interface methods that use it. The only way to describe a "typeless" array that is usable from Visual Basic is to use SAFEARRAY(VARIANT) in the IDL. This is not quite the same thing semantically, although it allows the same effect—namely, the type of the contents of the VARIANTs can be determined at runtime. In fact, SAFEARRAY(VARIANT) is even more flexible than SAFEARRAY, because it allows an array containing several different types to be passed; each VARIANT could be of a different type, whereas with the untyped SAFEARRAY construct all the elements in the array must be of the same type. It could be argued that all the elements in SAFEARRAY(VARIANT) are of the same type, but the extra level of indirection that the VARIANT provides allows the extra flexibility during programming. Hence, given the IDL shown in Listing 4.52, the client-side call sequence shown in Listing 4.53 could be used. Any method implementation would have to be coded to deal correctly with array elements of varying types.

Listing 4.52 Use of SAFEARRAY(VARIANT) in IDL

```
[
  uuid(0555309C-4650-4f7a-87EC-FBB63F4C9DEB),
  object,
  pointer_default(unique)
]
interface IDoSafearraysAswell : IUnknown {
  HRESULT TakeSomething (
    [in] SAFEARRAY(VARIANT)* ppsa );
  HRESULT ReturnSomething (
    [out,retval] SAFEARRAY(VARIANT)* ppsa );
}
```

Listing 4.53 Passing multiple types through SAFEARRAY(VARIANT)

```
Public Sub Bar ( obj as IDoSafearraysAswell )
  Dim v(2) As Variant
  v(0) = "Hello World" ' String
  v(1) = 1234 ' Integer
  v(2) = 0.023 ' Single
  obj.TakeSomething v
End Sub
```

The third IDL syntax uses the type definition LPSAFEARRAY. There is no data type specified for the array when this syntax is used, again making the interface ambiguous. Reworking IDoSafearrays to use LPSAFEARRAY would result in the IDL shown in Listing 4.54.

Listing 4.54 Use of LPSAFEARRAY in IDL

```
[
  uuid(6B8401AD-6A92-4c88-9A3D-73E6DB0D720A),
  object
]
struct ComplexStuff {
long lFlags;
BSTR bstrDescription;
LPSAFEARRAY psa;
};
[
  uuid(911BFD7A-91C5-4d29-A6DC-D0AA4680535C),
  object
]
interface IDoSafearrays2 : IUnknown {
  HRESULT TakeShorts ( [in] LPSAFEARRAY* ppsa );
  HRESULT TakeStrings ( [in] LPSAFEARRAY* ppsa );
  HRESULT TakeRecordsets ( [in] LPSAFEARRAY* ppsa );
  HRESULT ReturnVariants (
    [out,retval] LPSAFEARRAY* ppsa );
  HRESULT ReturnStructs (
    [out,retval] LPSAFEARRAY* ppsa );
}
```

The C++ mapping looks very similar to that for SAFEARRAY(type); LPSAFEARRAY* in IDL maps directly to LPSAFEARRAY* in the generated header file and LPSAFEARRAY is an alias for SAFEARRAY*, so the net effect is the same as for SAFEARRAY(type). Visual Basic is unable to interpret the LPSAFEARRAY type and so is unable to implement or call interfaces that use it. Consequently, LPSAFEARRAY, like the untyped SAFEARRAY construct, should be used only when both client and object will be written in C++. Even in this case, LPSAFEARRAY should be avoided unless there is some compelling reason to describe a typeless array. Interfaces that use LPSAFEARRAY must use Oicf type information to built interception code, because the universal marshaler cannot handle the type, resulting in an error at QueryInterface time.

Managing SAFEARRAYs

To make SAFEARRAYs easier to deal with in C++, there is a dedicated API for allocating, locking, and freeing them. Creation of a SAFEARRAY is a two-step process. The descriptor is allocated first, using either of the following APIs.

```
HRESULT
SafeArrayAllocDescriptor ( /* [in] */ UINT cDims,
   /* [out] */ SAFEARRAY ** ppsaOut);
HRESULT
SafeArrayAllocDescriptorEx ( /* [in] */ VARTYPE vt,
                             /* [in] */ UINT cDims,
   /* [out] */ SAFEARRAY ** ppsaOut);
```

The first API creates a descriptor with the specified number of SAFEARRAYBOUND entries. SafeArrayAllocDescriptorEx allows the type to be specified using a subset of the VT_ constants that the VARIANT data type supports: specifically, VT_BYREF and VT_ARRAY cannot be used. It also sets the FADF_HAVEVARTYPE flag and puts the specified VT_ constant before the descriptor in memory. SafeArrayAllocDescriptorEx should be preferred, because it allows the recipient of the array to determine the contained data type at runtime. It must be used when passing arrays of structures or typed object references, because other data preceding the descriptor needs to be initialized for these data types—specifically, an IRecordInfo* and an interface ID, respectively.

Once the descriptor has been allocated, the size of an individual element must be specified in the cbElements field. There are then two choices. The first is to set pvData to point to an existing block of data in the application. This allows existing data to be passed in a SAFEARRAY without having the overhead of copying the data from the current location into a newly allocated block of memory. Listing 4.55 shows an example of this technique. The second option is to use the following API to allocate space for the data.

```
HRESULT SafeArrayAllocData (
   /* [in] */ SAFEARRAY * psa );
```

This API allocates the required amount of memory, based on the content of the array of SAFEARRAYBOUND structures in the descriptor. It stores the pointer to the newly allocated memory block in the pvData field of the descriptor. Use of

`SafeArrayAllocData` to allocate a two-dimensional array of 16-bit integers is shown in Listing 4.56.[8]

Listing 4.55 Building a SAFEARRAY from stack-based data

```
// First 10 primes
long nData[10] = { 1, 2, 3, 5, 7, 11, 13, 17, 19, 23 };
SAFEARRAY* psa = 0;
// Single dimension
HR(SafeArrayAllocDescriptor ( 1, &psa ));
psa->cbElements = sizeof ( nData[0] );
psa->rgsabound[0].cElements = sizeof ( nData ) /
                                   sizeof ( nData[0] );
psa->rgsabound[0].lLbound = 0;
psa->pvData = &nData;
psa->fFeatures = FADF_AUTO |      // Allocated on stack
                 FADF_FIXEDSIZE; // Cannot be resized
```

Listing 4.56 Building a SAFEARRAY using SafeArrayAllocData

```
SAFEARRAY* psa = 0;
// 2 dimensions
HR(SafeArrayAllocDescriptor ( 2, &psa ));
psa->cbElements = sizeof ( short );
psa->rgsabound[0].lLbound = 0;
psa->rgsabound[0].cElements = 3;
psa->rgsabound[1].lLbound = 0;
psa->rgsabound[1].cElements = 3;
HR(SafeArrayAllocData ( psa ));
```

Such two-stage construction is unnecessary in Visual Basic, where the following line would suffice.

```
Dim sa(2,2) As Integer
```

One thing to note about SAFEARRAYs is that multidimensional SAFEARRAYs, such as the array allocated in Listing 4.56, use column-major ordering of elements rather than row-major ordering of elements. This ordering is the natural ordering used by Visual Basic but is the exact opposite of a standard C++ array. In C++, a 3-by-3 element array is arranged in memory, as shown earlier in Figure 4.14, whereas the memory layout of a SAFEARRAY is as shown in Figure 4.22.

---

[8] When returning SAFEARRAYs from a method implementation to a Visual Basic client, the second technique (or one of the wrapper APIs described later in this chapter) must be used.

Index	0,0	0,1	0,2	1,0	1,1	1,2	2,0	2,1	2,2
Offset	1	2	3	4	5	6	7	8	9

Figure 4.21 Memory layout of a 3-by-3 C++ array

Index	0,0	1,0	2,0	0,1	1,1	2,1	0,2	1,2	2,2
Offset	1	2	3	4	5	6	7	8	9

Figure 4.22 Memory layout of a 3-by-3 SAFEARRAY

As in Figure 4.14, the top row shows the array index and the bottom row shows the offset of each element in memory.

For example, the element that Visual Basic would refer to as `sa(2,1)` is what C++ would see as array element `[1,2]`. Viewed from another perspective, if a C++ program used the same indices as Visual Basic, it would retrieve the value 8 instead of the value 6. This means that standard C++ array indexing cannot be used when accessing elements in a multidimensional SAFEARRAY, and C++ developers must either translate between the two indexing schemes or use the APIs `SafeArrayGetElement` and `SafeArrayPutElement`.

Allocating the descriptor and array memory separately is tedious and seldom necessary. Fortunately, there are four wrapper APIs that allocate the descriptor and the array memory in a single call, as shown in Listing 4.57.

Listing 4.57 SAFEARRAY creation APIs

```
SAFEARRAY *
SafeArrayCreate ( VARTYPE vt, UINT cDims,
                  SAFEARRAYBOUND * rgsabound );
SAFEARRAY *
SafeArrayCreateEx ( VARTYPE vt,
                  UINT cDims,
                  SAFEARRAYBOUND * rgsabound,
                  PVOID pvExtra );
SAFEARRAY *
SafeArrayCreateVector ( VARTYPE vt,
                  LONG lLbound,
                  ULONG cElements );
SAFEARRAY *
```

```
SafeArrayCreateVectorEx ( VARTYPE vt,
                          LONG lLbound,
                          ULONG cElements,
                          PVOID pvExtra );
```

Each of the APIs returns a pointer to a SAFEARRAY descriptor, complete with the requisite number of SAFEARRAYBOUND elements. The vector versions create SAFEARRAYs with a single dimension and allocate the descriptor and the array data contiguously, setting an undocumented FADF flag, 0x2000. The nonvector versions take an array of SAFEARRAYBOUND structures as input and can be used to create single and multidimensional arrays, the memory for which is not contiguous with the descriptor. All four APIs also initialize the fFeatures field with the relevant flags such as FADF_BSTR, FADF_VARIANT, and FADF _HAVEVARTYPE.[9] Creating a two-dimensional array of 32-bit integers using SafeArrayCreate would look like this in C++:

```
SAFEARRAY*psa = 0;
SAFEARRAYBOUND rgbound[2] = { 10, 0, 20, 0 };
psa =
  SafeArrayCreate ( VT_I4, sizeof ( rgbound ) /
    sizeof ( SAFEARRAYBOUND), rgbound );
```

In Visual Basic, this can be done in a single line.

```
Dim sa(10,20) As Long
```

The extended versions of the APIs allow arrays of structures or typed object references to be created, because they have an extra parameter that can be used to pass an IRecordInfo* in the former case and the address of the IID in the latter case. For example, the C++ code shown below creates a vector of ADO Recordset pointers.

```
#include "msado15.h"
SAFEARRAY*psa = 0;
psa = SafeArrayCreateVectorEx (
  VT_DISPATCH | FADF_HAVEIID, 0, 20,
  &_uuidof ( _Recordset ));
```

---

[9] SafeArrayCreateVector does not set up FADF_HAVEVARTYPE and should be avoided. The author assumes that this is a bug in the API.

The following Visual Basic code is equivalent.

```
Dim sa(19) As ADODB.Recordset
```

Constructing SAFEARRAYs of structures involves acquiring the `IRecordInfo*` for the structure from the type library and passing it into either `SafeArray CreateEx` or `SafeArrayCreateVectorEx`. As described in Chapter 3, there are two APIs that can be used to retrieve an `IRecordInfo*`: `GetRecord InfoFromGuids` and `GetRecordInfoFromTypeInfo`. Given the IDL shown earlier in Listing 4.47, the C++ code shown in Listing 4.58 could be used to create a SAFEARRAY of `Complex` structures.

Listing 4.58 Creating a SAFEARRAY of structures in C++

```
CComPtr<ITypeLib> sptl;
HR(LoadRegTypeLib ( LIBID_ArrayLib, 1, 0, 0, &sptl ));
CComPtr<ITypeInfo> spti;
HR(sptl->GetTypeInfoOfGuid (
    __uuidof ( struct Complex ), &spti ));
IRecordInfo* pri = 0;
HR(GetRecordInfoFromTypeInfo ( spti, &pri ));
SAFEARRAY*psa = 0;
psa = SafeArrayCreateVectorEx ( VT_RECORD, 0, 20, pri );
```

Note the `IRecordInfo*` being passed as the last parameter to `Safe ArrayCreateEx`. This code will allocate memory for the structures, so the `cbElements` field of the descriptor will be set to the size of a single structure.

Again, life is much simpler in Visual Basic; the runtime does all the hard work.

```
Dim x(19) As Complex
```

Because the memory for the descriptor and the array is allocated by the creation API, a corresponding API must be used to destroy the SAFEARRAY once it is no longer needed. There are three such APIs, the third being a wrapper around the previous two.

```
HRESULT SafeArrayDestroyDescriptor ( SAFEARRAY * psa );
HRESULT SafeArrayDestroyData ( SAFEARRAY * psa );
HRESULT SafeArrayDestroy ( SAFEARRAY * psa );
```

For embedded resources, `SafeArrayDestroyData` and `SafeArrayDestroy` will release the resources. For example, `IUnknown::Release()` will be called for object references, `SysFreeString` will be called for BSTRs, and `IRecord Info::RecordClear` will be called for structures. In Visual Basic, nothing needs to be done; the descriptor and data block will be released when the array goes out of scope, and any embedded resources will be cleaned up correctly.

Given the IDL shown earlier in Listing 4.47, a possible C++ client-side call sequence is shown in Listing 4.59, while the Visual Basic equivalent is shown in Listing 4.60.

Listing 4.59 Creating, using, and destroying SAFEARRAYs in C++

```
SAFEARRAY* psashort=
  SafeArrayCreateVector ( VT_I2, 0, 100 );
// Initialize array with data...
HR(pObj->TakeShorts ( &psashort ));
SafeArrayDestroy ( psashort );
SAFEARRAY* psabstr =
  SafeArrayCreateVector ( VT_BSTR, 0, 25 );
// Initialize array with data...
HR(pObj->TakeStrings ( psabstr ));
SafeArrayDestroy ( psabstr );
```

Listing 4.60 Creating, using, and destroying SAFEARRAYs in Visual Basic

```
Dim psashort(100) As Integer
' Initialize array with data
pObj.TakeShorts psashort
Dim psavariant(100) As Variant
' Initialize array with data
pObj.TakeVariants psavariant
```

Inside a method implementation, the dimensions must be examined before the data is accessed. This information can be extracted directly from the descriptor or, alternatively, several APIs are provided to access it.

```
UINT SafeArrayGetDim ( SAFEARRAY * psa );
HRESULT SafeArrayGetUBound ( SAFEARRAY * psa,
                             UINT nDim,
                             LONG * plUbound );
HRESULT SafeArrayGetLBound ( SAFEARRAY * psa,
                             UINT nDim,
                             LONG * plLbound );
```

The SafeArrayGetDim API returns the number of dimensions, while SafeArrayGetUBound and SafeArrayGetLBound return the upper and lower bounds, respectively, of a specific dimension. Having extracted the information about the dimensions, the data type would normally be examined. Again, several APIs are provided.

```
HRESULT
SafeArrayGetRecordInfo ( SAFEARRAY * psa,
                         IRecordInfo ** prinfo );
HRESULT SafeArrayGetIID ( SAFEARRAY * psa,
                          GUID * pguid );
HRESULT SafeArrayGetVartype ( SAFEARRAY * psa,
                              VARTYPE * pvt );
```

These APIs must be used to retrieve the information about the datatype, because it is not stored in the descriptor. The most commonly used API of the three is SafeArrayGetVartype, which returns the VT_ constant for the array. If the constant evaluates to VT_RECORD or VT_UNKNOWN/VT_DISPATCH, then SafeArrayGetRecordInfo or SafeArrayGetIID, respectively, should be called for further qualification of the data type.

An implementation of the TakeShorts method that uses the SAFEARRAY APIs is shown in Listing 4.61. Note the use of the dimension APIs and SafeArrayGetVartype before the array data is accessed. This is good practice, because there is no way of knowing in advance how many dimensions an array will have or what data type the array will contain. The corresponding Visual Basic code is shown in Listing 4.62.[10]

Listing 4.61 Implementation of IDoSafearrays::TakeShorts in C++

```
STDMETHODIMP TakeShorts ( SAFEARRAY**ppsa ) {
  if ( !ppsa ) return E_POINTER;
  SAFEARRAY* psa = *ppsa;
  UINT nDims = SafeArrayGetDim ( psa );

  if ( nDims != 1 )        // We don't deal with
    return E_INVALIDARG;  // multidimensional arrays

  long lUBound = 0, lLBound = 0;
```

---

[10] The function GetDims does not actually exist in Visual Basic, and there is no function provided to retrieve the dimensions of an array. The implementation of GetDims repeatedly calls Ubound, incrementing the second parameter until an error is generated. It then returns the number of dimensions.

```
    SafeArrayGetUBound ( psa, 1, &lUBound );
    SafeArrayGetLBound ( psa, 1, &lLBound );
    long lElements = 1 + lUBound - lLBound;

    VARTYPE vt = 0;
    SafeArrayGetVarType ( psa, &vt );
    if (VT_I2 != vt ) // If it's not shorts we can't handle it
      return E_INVALIDARG;

    short*pDa            ta = 0;
    SafeArrayAccessData ( psa, (void*)&pData );

    for(long i=0;i<lElements;i++)
      m_lTotal += pData[i];

    SafeArrayUnaccessData ( psa );
    return S_OK;
}
```

Listing 4.62   Implementation of IDoSafearrays::TakeShorts in Visual Basic

```
Private Sub IDoSafearrays_TakeShorts(ppsa() As Integer)
  Dim nDims As Long
  nDims = GetDims ( ppsa );

  If nDims <> 1 Then
    Err.Raise H&80070057
    Exit Sub
  End If
  Dim lUBound As Long
  Dim lLBound As Long
  lUBound = UBound ( ppsa, 1 )
  lLBound = LBound ( ppsa, 1 );

  If TypeName(ppsa) <> "Integer()" Then
    Err.Raise H&80070057
    Exit Sub
  End If

  Dim i as Long
  For i = lLBound To lUBound
    M_lTotal = ppsa(i)
  Next i
End Sub
```

It is worth noting that, in both C++ and Visual Basic, if the position of
the elements is unimportant, the array can be treated as a single dimension,

regardless of the number of actual dimensions. This would result in a C++ method implementation such as that shown in Listing 4.63; Listing 4.64 shows the Visual Basic version. Note the flattening of the dimension information into a single count of the total number of elements in the array in the C++ version and the use of `For Each` in Visual Basic. The `For Each` construct causes the Visual Basic runtime to determine the dimension information and then iterates through each array element in turn.

Listing 4.63 Treating a multidimensional SAFEARRAY as single-dimensional in C++

```
STDMETHODIMP TakeShorts ( SAFEARRAY**ppsa ) {
  if ( !ppsa ) return E_POINTER;
  SAFEARRAY* psa = *ppsa;
  long lElements = 1;
  UINT nDims = psa->cDims;
  for(UINT n = 0;n<nDims;n++) // Flatten dimensions
    lElements *= psa->rgsabound[n].cElements;

  VARTYPE vt = 0;
  SafeArrayGetVarType ( psa, &vt );
  if (VT_I2 != vt ) // If it's not shorts we can't handle it
    return E_INVALIDARG;

  short*pData = 0;
  SafeArrayAccessData ( psa, (void*)&pData );

  for(long i=0;i<lElements;i++)
  // Treat as single dimension
    m_lTotal += pData[i];

  SafeArrayUnaccessData ( psa );
  return S_OK;
}
```

Listing 4.64 Treating a multidimensional SAFEARRAY as single-dimensional in Visual Basic

```
Private Sub IDoSafearrays_TakeShorts(ppsa() As Integer)
  For Each x In ppsa()
    m_lTotal = m_lTotal + x
  Next
End Sub
```

Conclusions

Few developers can perform their daily tasks without reference types or arrays. IDL provides flexible and comprehensive options for describing both. C++ developers have access to the entire gamut of array types in IDL, while Visual Basic developers are able to use conformant arrays and pointers along with SAFEARRAYs. Listed below are some guidelines for using pointers and arrays in IDL.

1. If top-level pointer semantics other than `[ref]` are required, Oicf type information must be used to build interception code.
2. If embedded pointer semantics other than `[unique]` are required, Oicf type information must be used to build interception code.
3. If integration with Visual Basic is required, use `SAFEARRAY(type)` for array types.
4. Try to avoid passing multidimensional SAFEARRAYs between Visual Basic and C++.
5. If integration with Visual Basic is *not* required, use conformant pointers (`[size_is]`) for passing arrays of data.
6. Favor conformant pointers over conformant arrays, because the former are more flexible.
7. Remember to use the comma operator in the `[size_is]` clause for `[out]` conformant pointers.
8. Remember the rules for memory management, especially for `[out]` parameters.
9. Remember that `[pointer_default]` applies only to embedded pointers that are not explicitly qualified with `[ref]`, `[unique]`, or `[ptr]`.
10. Do not use self-referential structures with the universal marshaler.
11. Do not define structures with embedded pointers if calls will be made by Visual Basic clients.

Chapter 5

Aliasing

Method Aliasing

IDL provides a mechanism for associating a remote method with a local method, perhaps with a different signature. Clients call and objects implement the local method while the remote method is used on the wire. This technique, known as "method aliasing," allows interface designers a greater degree of flexibility with respect to method signatures. This is attributable to the fact that there are few, if any, restrictions on the signatures of local methods. This flexibility allows for parameter types that are not remoteable, modification of pointer semantics, and hand-optimized marshaling of types.

The remote method is associated with its local counterpart through use of the `[call_as()]` attribute, which takes the name of the local method in parentheses. The local method must be annotated with the `[local]` attribute. This suppresses generation of interception code. The MIDL compiler expects code to be provided by the interface designer to perform the local-remote mapping. This code takes the form of two functions that are compiled and linked into the proxy-stub DLL. The first function maps the local method onto the remote method and resides in the proxy. The second function, contained in the stub, maps the remote method back onto the local method as implemented by the object. So method aliasing provides a hook, allowing the interface designer to insert extra code into the standard interception layer. The call sequence for the general case is shown in Figure 5.1.

The client call to the local method proxy occurs in step 1. The local method proxy, provided by the interface designer, performs the required mapping and then calls the remote proxy in step 2. The remote proxy calls the remote stub in step 3, using the wire representation defined by the remote method signature. The remote proxy and the remote stub are machine-generated. The remote stub

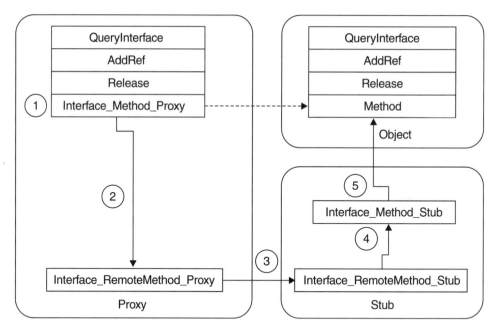

Figure 5.1 Call sequence for an aliased method

calls the local method stub in step 4. The local method stub, also provided by the interface designer, performs any necessary mapping and calls the actual method in step 5. Further mapping may be performed before the local method stub returns to the remote stub and before the local method proxy returns to the client. The dashed arrow shows the logical call between the local method proxy and the actual method.

A common example of method aliasing is found in the `IEnumXXXX` family of interfaces. The IDL for `IEnumUnknown::Next` is shown below.

```
HRESULT Next ( [in] ULONG celt,
               [out] IUnknown** rgelt,
               [out] ULONG* pceltFetched);
```

The first parameter, `celt`, is use by the caller to specify the number of elements—in this case, the number of `IUnknown` pointers—that the method call should return. The object indicates how many elements it actually returned in the last parameter, `pceltFetched`. The documentation for `IEnumXXXX::Next` states that the last parameter may be null if the first parameter has a value of one. However, the last parameter is annotated with the `[out]` attribute, as shown in the definition of `IEnumUnknown::Next` above.[1] Because `[out]` parameters always have `[ref]` semantics, calling the `IEnumXXX::Next` method across a context boundary with a null value for the last parameter would cause an error. The system IDL files use method aliasing to work around this problem, defining local and remote versions of the `Next` method. So `IEnumUnknown::Next` is actually defined as shown in Listing 5.1. Note that the `[call_as()]` attribute takes the name of the local method, `Next`, in parentheses. This allows the MIDL compiler to determine which local method the remote method is aliasing. The two mapping functions provide code to deal with the specific parameter values that cannot be remoted, as shown in Listing 5.2.

Listing 5.1 IDL definition of IEnumUnknown::Next

```
[local]
HRESULT Next ( [in] ULONG celt,
               [out] IUnknown** rgelt,
               [out] ULONG* pceltFetched);


[call_as(Next)]
HRESULT RemoteNext ( [in] ULONG celt,
                     [out, size_is(celt),
length_is(*pceltFetched)] IUnknown** rgelt,
                     [out] ULONG* pceltFetched);
```

Listing 5.2 Implementation of IEnumUnknown_Next_Proxy and IEnumUnknown_Next_Stub

```
HRESULT
IEnumUnknown_Next_Proxy ( IEnumUnknown *This,
                          ULONG celt,
                          IUnknown** rgelt,
                          ULONG* pceltFetched) {
  // catch bad parameter combination
  if (celt > 1 && pceltFetched == 0)
    return E_INVALIDARG;
  // declare dummy variable for the
  // case pceltFetched == 0
  ULONG celtFetched;
  return IEnumUnknown_RemNext_Proxy ( This, celt,
                                      rgelt,
       pceltFetched ? pceltFetched : &celtFetched);
}
```

---

[1] The documentation for `IEnumXXX::Next` in the Platform SDK shows the last parameter as being marked `[in,out]`. However, all instances in system IDL files are marked `[out]` only.

```
HRESULT
IEnumUnknown_Next_Stub ( IEnumUnknown *This,
                         ULONG celt,
                         IUnknown** rgelt,
                         ULONG* pceltFetched) {
  HRESULT hr = This->lpVtbl->Next ( This, celt,
                                    rgelt,
                                    pceltFetched);
  if (hr == S_OK && celt == 1)
    *pceltFetched = 1;
  return hr;
}
```

Method aliasing can also be used to optimize marshaling code. For example, consider a doubly linked list of points and an interface method that operates on such a list, as shown in Listing 5.3.

Listing 5.3 A doubly linked list of points and associated interface method
```
typedef struct Point {
  long x, y;
} Point;

typedef struct PointNode {
  Point pt;
  // Next node in list
  [ptr] struct PointNode* pNext;
  // Previous node in list
  [ptr] struct PointNode* pPrev;
} PointNode;

[
  uuid(D5932C4A-6A48-431c-9E0E-B1F03337D401),
  object,
  pointer_default(unique)
]
interface IPlot : IUnknown {
  HRESULT Curve ( [in] PointNode* pNode );
}
```

Although the PointNode type could be successfully transmitted as is, such transmission would be inefficient in terms of both size and speed. A more efficient transmission format would be a conformant array of points.[2] Method alias-

---

[2] This and subsequent examples assume a true doubly linked list—that is, there are no cycles in the list of nodes, and each node has pointers to both the next and previous nodes in the list.

ing could be used to insert code to convert a linked list into such an array. The IDL for the aliased version of the `Curve` method is shown in Listing 5.4.

Listing 5.4 Aliased version of the Curve method

```
[local]
HRESULT Curve ( [in] PointNode* pNode );

[call_as(Curve)]
HRESULT RemCurve ( [in] unsigned long nNodeIndex,
                   [in] unsigned long cElems,
      [in,size_is(cElems)] Point*pPointData );
```

Because the node passed into the local method may not always be the head of the list, the remote method has a parameter, `nNodeIndex`, to track the actual node passed by the client. This allows the mapping code on the stub side to pass the correct node into the method implementation.

Compiling the IDL produces type information for the remote method. The MIDL compiler also emits the function prototypes for the following two mapping functions.

```
HRESULT STDMETHODCALLTYPE
IPlot_Curve_Proxy ( IPlot * This,
                    PPOINTNODE pNode);

HRESULT STDMETHODCALLTYPE
IPlot_Curve_Stub ( IPlot * This,
                   unsigned long nNodeIndex,
                   unsigned long cElems,
                   Point* pPointData);
```

Note that an explicit `IPlot*` is the first parameter to do each of the methods. While this parameter is implicit in C++, proxy-stub DLLs are built using the C compiler and so an explicit parameter is needed.

The names of the local functions and their remote counterparts are generated according to a fixed format as shown in Table 5.1.

The code for `IPlot_Curve_Proxy` needs to convert the linked list into a conformant array and then call the remote method, `IPlot_RemCurve_Proxy`. The code is shown in Listing 5.5.

Listing 5.5 Implementation of IPlot_Curve_Proxy

```
HRESULT STDMETHODCALLTYPE
IPlot_Curve_Proxy ( IPlot * This, PPOINTNODE pNode ) {
  HRESULT hr = S_OK;
```

Table 5.1 Formatting of function names for aliased methods

Method Type	Generic Name	Example
Local Proxy	Interface_LocalName_Proxy	IPlot_Curve_Proxy
Remote Proxy	Interface_RemoteName_Proxy	IPlot_RemCurve_Proxy
Local Stub	Interface_LocalName_Stub	IPlot_Curve_Stub
Remote Stub	Interface_RemoteName_Stub	IPlot_RemCurve_Stub

```
unsigned long cElems = 0; // Number of nodes in list
unsigned long nNodeIndex = 0; // Index of pNode
Point* pPointData = 0; // Pointer to array of points
PointNode* pHead = 0;  // Pointer to head of list
PointNode* pCurrent = pNode; // Store passed-in node

while ( pCurrent->pPrev != 0 ) {
  // Walk back to front of list
  nNodeIndex++;  // Store index of passed-in node
  pCurrent = pCurrent->pPrev;
}
pHead = pCurrent; // Store head node

while ( pCurrent != 0 )      {
  cElems++; // Count number of nodes
  pCurrent = pCurrent->pNext;
}

// Allocate transmission memory
pPointData = CoTaskMemAlloc (
  sizeof ( Point ) * cElems  );
if ( pPointData ) {
  int i = 0;
  pCurrent = pHead; // Reset to head of list

  // Copy Point data from list nodes into
  // transmission array
  while ( pCurrent != 0 ) {
    pPointData[i++] = pCurrent->pt;
    pCurrent = pCurrent->pNext;
  }
} else return E_OUTOFMEMORY;
```

```
    // Call remote proxy function
    hr = IPlot_RemCurve_Proxy( This, nNodeIndex,
                               cElems, pPointData );
    CoTaskMemFree ( pPointData );
    return hr;
}
```

The method has to determine the index of the passed-in node and the total number of nodes in the list. It then allocates a block of memory and copies the contents of the linked list, without the pointer information, into the memory block. The `This` pointer and the conformant array data are then passed to the remote proxy through the `IPlot_RemCurve_Proxy` function. With method aliasing in general, all allocated resources must be cleaned up, and in this specific case, when the remote proxy method returns, the memory allocated for the conformant array is freed.

On the stub side, the code must work in reverse, taking the conformant array and reconstructing the linked list. It must also ensure that the correct node in the list is passed to the actual method as specified by the client and transmitted in the `nNodeIndex` parameter of the remote method. The implementation of `IPlot_Curve_Stub` is shown in Listing 5.6. The local stub method is responsible for freeing any resources it allocates. In Listing 5.6, after the actual method call completes, `IPlot_Curve_Stub` walks the linked list, freeing each node in turn.

Listing 5.6 Implementation of IPlot_Curve_Stub

```
HRESULT STDMETHODCALLTYPE
IPlot_Curve_Stub ( IPlot* This,
                   unsigned long nNodeIndex,
                   unsigned long cElems,
                   Point *pPointData ) {
    HRESULT hr = S_OK;
    unsigned long i = 0; // Loop counter
    PointNode* pNode = 0;
    // Allocate head node
    PointNode* pHead = CoTaskMemAlloc (
      sizeof ( PointNode ));
    PointNode* pCurrent = pHead; // Scratch pointer
    PointNode* pPrevious = 0;    // Scratch pointer
```

```
          // Iterate through transmission array
          for(i=0;i<cElems;i++) {
            // Copy Point data from transmission array into
            // current node
            pCurrent->pt = pPointData[i];
            pCurrent->pPrev = pPrevious;

            // If we're at the node index then...
            if ( i == nNodeIndex )
              // ... make the current node pointer the
              // returned value
              pNode = pCurrent;

            // If we're at the last array element...
            if ( i+1 == cElems )
              // ...set pNext to null
              pCurrent->pNext = 0;
            else {
              // Allocate memory for next node and iterate
              pCurrent->pNext = CoTaskMemAlloc (
                sizeof ( PointNode ));
              pPrevious = pCurrent;
              pCurrent = pCurrent->pNext;
            }
          }

          // Call method on object
          hr = This->lpVtbl->Curve ( This, pNode );

          // Free up resources
          pCurrent = pHead;
          while ( pCurrent ) {
            PointNode* pNext = pCurrent->pNext;
            CoTaskMemFree ( pCurrent );
            pCurrent = pNext;
          }
          return hr;
        }
```

The [call_as()] attribute is ignored inside the library block, and the MIDL compiler does not emit the function prototypes for the mapping functions. Consequently, interfaces that use method aliasing should always appear outside the library block. Such interfaces may be referenced inside the library block, but rather than the expected local method being present in the type library, the remote method will appear instead. This makes it difficult for environments that rely on type libraries to call the local method. Fortunately, conditional compilation can be used to work around this problem.[3] Both local and remote versions of the method need to be visible to the MIDL compiler when the header file and the Oicf type information are being generated. Only the local version must be visible at type library generation time. The declaration of the local method can be duplicated inside a conditional compilation block, as shown in Listing 5.7.

Listing 5.7 Conditional compilation of local IDL method signature

```
#ifdef BUILDING_PS
[local]
HRESULT Curve ( [in] PointNode* pNode );
[call_as(Curve)]
HRESULT RemCurve ( [in] unsigned long nNodeIndex,
                   [in] unsigned long cElems,
    [in,size_is(cElems)] Point*pPointData );
#else
HRESULT Curve ( [in] PointNode* pNode );
#endif
```

When the proxy stub needs to be generated, the MIDL compiler is run with an extra switch, /DBUILDING_PS. Standard invocations of the MIDL compiler will generate a type library containing the local method signature.

Type Aliasing

Using method aliasing to marshal a parameter type manually can be very tedious, especially when multiple methods have that type as a parameter, because two extra functions must be provided for each method. In such cases, type aliasing should be used instead. Type aliasing allows the IDL author to define a mapping between a presentation type and a transmission type. The presentation type is the programmatic type used at the application level, whereas the transmission type defines the wire format. Whenever the MIDL compiler sees the presentation type, it will use the transmission type on the wire. In the method aliasing example, the presentation type is the PointNode structure and there is no concrete transmission type. Rather, the transmission type is the union of the parameters to the remote method. These parameters

---

[3] Don Box first discovered this workaround.

can be gathered together into a structure that can be used as the transmission type.

```
typedef struct PointListXmit {
  unsigned long nNodeIndex;
  unsigned long cElems;
  [size_is(cElems)] Point PointData[];
} PointListXmit;
```

A mapping can then be defined between the transmission and presentation types using the [transmit_as()] attribute. The attribute forms part of a type definition of an alias for the presentation type. The transmission type appears in the parentheses of the [transmit_as()] attribute.[4] The type definition used to map the PointNode presentation type to the PointListXmit transmission type looks like this:

```
typedef [transmit_as(PointListXmit)] PointNode* PPOINTNODE;
```

The transmission type cannot contain any pointer types, although conformant arrays, as used in PointListXmit, are allowed. This is because the interception code provided by the system requires that the memory for the transmission type be a single contiguous block. An example interface IPlot2 that uses the new type definition is shown in Listing 5.8.

Listing 5.8 IPlot2 interface definition

```
[
  uuid(87EEC0C4-7225-48e3-97DB-E69BC2A29667),
  object,
  pointer_default(unique)
]
interface IPlot2 : IUnknown {
  HRESULT Curve ( [in] PPOINTNODE pNode );
  HRESULT Area ( [in] PPOINTNODE pNode );
  HRESULT Integral ( [in] PPOINTNODE pNode );
}
```

Whenever one of the methods of IPlot2 is called, the interception code will attempt to convert the linked list to the PointListXmit type. It does this by

---

[4] Strictly speaking, the type argument to [transmit_as] is not a transmission type but another presentation type. The marshaling layer will generate a slightly different representation on the wire. However, for the purposes of this discussion, the term will suffice.

calling into four functions provided by the interface designer. These four functions are really two pairs of functions. The first pair is responsible for converting the presentation type into the transmission type. The first function in the pair performs the conversion while the second function frees any resources allocated by the first. The second pair of functions takes the transmission type and converts it back into the presentation type. Again, the first function in the pair does the conversion while the second frees resources. The names of the four functions are based on the name of the alias defined by the type definition. The function names, along with their responsibilities, are shown in Table 5.2.

The MIDL compiler generates the prototypes for the four functions. The prototypes generated for the PPOINTNODE type are shown in Listing 5.9, and the implementation of the presentation-to-transmission type conversion functions is shown in Listing 5.10.

Listing 5.9 Function prototypes for PPOINTNODE conversion functions

```
void _RPC_USER
PPOINTNODE_to_xmit ( PPOINTNODE *,
                     PointListXmit  * * );
void _RPC_USER
PPOINTNODE_free_xmit ( PointListXmit  * );
void _RPC_USER
PPOINTNODE_from_xmit ( PointListXmit  *,
                       PPOINTNODE * );
void _RPC_USER
PPOINTNODE_free_inst( PPOINTNODE * );
```

Table 5.2 Responsibilities and naming of [transmit_as()] conversion functions

Responsibility	Generic Name	Example
Convert from presentation to transmission type	<alias>_to_xmit	PPOINTNODE_to_xmit
Free resources allocated by alias_to_xmi	<alias>_free_xmit	PPOINTNODE_free_xmit
Convert from transmission to presentation type	<alias>_from_xmit	PPOINTNODE_from_xmit
Free resources allocated by alias_from_xmit	<alias>_free_inst	PPOINTNODE_free_inst

Listing 5.10 Implementation of PPOINTNODE_to_xmit and PPOINTNODE_free_xmit

```
void __RPC_USER
PPOINTNODE_to_xmit ( PPOINTNODE* ppPointNode,
               PointListXmit** ppPointListXmit )
{
  unsigned long cElems = 0; // Number of nodes in list
  unsigned long nNodeIndex = 0; // Index of
                                // *ppPointNode
  PointNode* pHead = 0;  // Pointer to head of list
  PointNode* pCurrent = *ppPointNode; // Store passed
                                      // in-node

  while ( pCurrent->pPrev != 0 ) {
    // Walk back to front of list
    nNodeIndex++; // Store index of passed-in node
    pCurrent = pCurrent->pPrev;
  }

  pHead = pCurrent; // Store head node

  while ( pCurrent != 0 )      {
    cElems++;    // Count number of nodes
    pCurrent = pCurrent->pNext;
  }

  // Allocate transmission memory
  *ppPointListXmit = CoTaskMemAlloc (
    sizeof ( PointListXmit ) + ( sizeof ( Point ) *
    (cElems - 1)) );

  if ( * ppPointListXmit ) {
    int i = 0;
    // Set node index
    (*ppPointListXmit)->nNodeIndex = nNodeIndex;
    // Set number of nodes
    (*ppPointListXmit)->cElems = cElems;
    // Reset to head of list
    pCurrent = pHead;
    // Copy Point data from list nodes into
    // transmission array
    while ( pCurrent != 0 ) {
      (*ppPointListXmit)->PointData[i++] =
        pCurrent->pt;
      pCurrent = pCurrent->pNext;
    }
  }
}
```

ESSENTIAL IDL

```
void __RPC_USER
PPOINTNODE_free_xmit ( PointListXmit* pPointListXmit )
{
  // Free transmission memory
  CoTaskMemFree ( pPointListXmit );
}
```

The code for PPOINTNODE_to_xmit looks very similar to the code for Plot _Curve_Proxy in the method aliasing example. The major differences are the use of a structure, PointListXmit, instead of separate method parameters and the fact that memory is freed in a separate function, PPOINTNODE _free_xmit. Note that the memory is allocated as a single contiguous block to satisfy the interception code provided by the system. This allows the interception code to block-copy the data returned by PPOINTNODE_to_xmit into the network buffer for transmission in a single operation. If IDL did not mandate a contiguous memory block for [transmit_as()] types, the interception code might have to dereference pointers in the transmission type, resulting in several copy operations—an unnecessary marshaling overhead.

The corresponding functions to convert from the transmission type back to the presentation type are shown in Listing 5.11.

Listing 5.11 Implementation of PPOINTNODE_from_xmit and PPOINTNODE_free_inst

```
void __RPC_USER
PPOINTNODE_from_xmit ( PointListXmit* pPointListXmit,
                       PPOINTNODE* ppPointNode ) {
  unsigned long i = 0;   // Loop counter
  PointNode* pPrevious = 0; // Scratch pointer
  // Allocate head node
  pCurrent = CoTaskMemAlloc ( sizeof ( PointNode ));
  // Iterate through transmission array
  for(i=0;i< pPointListXmit ->cElems;i++) {
    // Copy Point data from transmission array into
    // current node
    pCurrent->pt = pPointListXmit->PointData[i];
    pCurrent->pPrev = pPrevious;

    // If we're at the node index then...
    if ( i == pPointListXmit->nNodeIndex )
      // ... make the current node pointer the
      // returned value
      *ppPointNode = pCurrent;
```

```
      // If we're at the last array element...
      if ( i+1 == pPointListXmit->cElems )
        pCurrent->pNext = 0; // ...set pNext to null
      else {
        // Allocate memory for next node and iterate
        pCurrent->pNext = CoTaskMemAlloc (
          sizeof ( PointNode ));
        pPrevious = pCurrent;
        pCurrent = pCurrent->pNext;
      }
    }
  }
}
void __RPC_USER
PPOINTNODE_free_inst ( PPOINTNODE * ppPointNode ) {
  PointNode* pCurrent = *ppPointNode;

  // Walk backwards to front of list
  while(pCurrent->pPrev != 0 ) {
    pCurrent = pCurrent->pPrev;
  }

  while ( pCurrent ) { // Free each node
    PointNode* pNext = pCurrent->pNext;
    CoTaskMemFree ( pCurrent );
    pCurrent = pNext;
  }
}
```

Again, the implementation of PPOINTNODE_from_xmit looks very similar to the code found in IPlot_Curve_Stub in the method aliasing example, with the same differences noted for the presentation-to-transmission conversion functions.

The four functions will be called automatically by the interception code whenever type conversion is required. When the client makes a call to IPlot::Curve, PPOINTNODE_to_xmit is called, followed by a call to PPOINTNODE_free_xmit. Then PPOINTNODE_to_xmit is called a second time, followed by another call to PPOINTNODE_free_xmit. At first this seems nonsensical, but an examination of the interaction between the interception code and the channel provides an explanation.

The interceptor interacts with the channel through an interface called IrpcChannelBuffer, the IDL for which is shown in Listing 5.12.

Listing 5.12 IDL for IRpcChannelBuffer

```
[
    local,
    object,
    uuid(D5F56B60-593B-101A-B569-08002B2DBF7A)
]
interface IRpcChannelBuffer : IUnknown {
  typedef unsigned long RPCOLEDATAREP;

  typedef struct tagRPCOLEMESSAGE {
    void* reserved1;
    RPCOLEDATAREP dataRepresentation;
    void* Buffer;
    ULONG cbBuffer;
    ULONG iMethod;
    void* reserved2[5];
    ULONG rpcFlags;
  } RPCOLEMESSAGE;

  HRESULT GetBuffer ( [in] RPCOLEMESSAGE *pMessage,
                      [in] REFIID riid );
  HRESULT
  SendReceive ( [in,out] RPCOLEMESSAGE* pMessage,
                [out] ULONG *pStatus );
  HRESULT FreeBuffer ( [in] RPCOLEMESSAGE *pMessage );
  HRESULT GetDestCtx ( [out] DWORD *pdwDestContext,
                       [out] void **ppvDestContext );
  HRESULT IsConnected ( void );
}
```

First, the interceptor asks the channel to allocate a transmission buffer by calling IRpcChannelBuffer::GetBuffer, having set the cbBuffer field of the RPCOLEMESSAGE to the number of bytes required. The channel allocates a buffer of the required size and returns a pointer to the buffer in the Buffer field of the RPCOLEMESSAGE. The interceptor then marshals all the parameter data into the buffer supplied by the channel and then calls IRpcChannelBuffer::SendReceive, which causes the channel to transmit the marshaled data to the stub. It is this two-step process that results in the two calls to the conversion routines.

Before the interceptor can make the call to GetBuffer, it needs to know how large a buffer to ask for. This is determined by the first call to

PPOINTNODE_to_xmit. The interceptor examines the field values in the returned structure to determine the required buffer size. It then frees the structure with the first call to PPOINTNODE_free_xmit. The interceptor then makes the call to GetBuffer, and the channel returns a memory block of the required size. The interceptor does not maintain any state information about the marshaled data between the call to GetBuffer and the call to SendReceive, so it needs to call the conversion function again before calling SendReceive.[5] Moreover, having called PPOINTNODE_to_xmit for the second time, the interceptor then has to copy the returned data structure into the buffer returned by the GetBuffer call before calling SendReceive. Having copied the data, the interceptor calls PPOINTNODE_free_xmit followed by the call to SendReceive. So there are two inherent inefficiencies associated with [transmit_as()]: the duplicate calls to the presentation-to-transmission type conversion function and the copying of the data into the channel buffer.

On the object side, the interceptor calls PPOINTNODE_from_xmit to convert the transmission type back into the presentation type and then calls the actual method. When the method returns, PPOINTNODE_free_inst is called to free up resources allocated by PPOINTNODE_from_xmit. These two functions are called only once. The call sequence for all four functions is shown in Figure 5.2.

If additional methods are defined that also use the PPOINTNODE type or if the PPOINTNODE type is used as a structure member, the same four functions will be called. No further work is required, unlike the method aliasing case, in which two new functions would need to be provided for each aliased method.

Despite the inherent inefficiencies of [transmit_as()] noted above, it can still provide significant performance gains. Transmitting a 2000-node list using [transmit_as()] is six times faster than using the standard Oicf marshaler. The speed benefits increase as the number of nodes in the list increases, but even for a 100-node list the [transmit_as()] code still provides a fourfold speed increase. Perhaps even more important is the fact that the standard Oicf marshaler can handle lists up to only around 8400 nodes in

---

[5] The runtime could retain the data structure after the call to IRpcChannelBuffer::GetBuffer, but the current implementation does not.

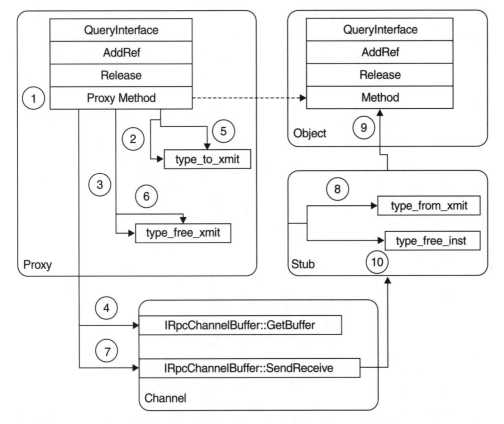

Figure 5.2   Call sequence for a method containing a [transmit_as()] type

size. Larger lists result in a stack overflow. The [transmit_as()] example does not suffer from this limitation.[6]

More Type Aliasing

A search through the system IDL files for examples of [transmit_as()] proves fruitless because IDL provides a more efficient mechanism that does not suffer from the inefficiencies inherent in the [transmit_as()] usage pattern. This mechanism uses the [wire_marshal()] attribute, and the system IDL files all use this attribute rather than [transmit_as()]. This mechanism gives the interface designer direct access to the channel-allocated buffer; data is marshaled directly into the buffer rather than through an intermediate

---

[6] It is worth noting that the standard marshaler can handle more complex data structures such as trees and cyclic graphs. The [transmit_as()] example presented here can deal with only true lists.

memory block. This typically results in performance gains. The down side of using [wire_marshal()] as opposed to [transmit_as()] is that writing the marshaling code to map between presentation and transmission types is considerably harder, requiring knowledge of the underlying marshaling format that IDL uses.

The IDL for [wire_marshal()] is very similar to the IDL for [transmit_as()]. A transmission type is defined and then a typedef is used to associate the presentation type with the transmission type. The IDL for the doubly linked list example used previously, converted to use [wire_marshal()], is shown in Listing 5.13.

Listing 5.13 [wire_marshal()] version of PointNode

```
typedef struct PointListMarshal
{
  unsigned long nNodeIndex;
  unsigned long cElems;
  [size_is(cElems)] Point *pPointData;
} PointListMarshal;

typedef
[wire_marshal(PointListMarshal)] PointNode* PPOINTNODE;
```

All transmission types for [wire_marshal()] must be of a fixed size and so conformant arrays cannot be used. However, pointers, including conformant pointers, are perfectly valid. The PointListMarshal structure above uses a conformant pointer.

As with [transmit_as()], the interface designer is required to implement four functions. The first function returns the size of buffer required to marshal the data. The second function marshals the presentation type into the network buffer, and the third unmarshals it. Finally, the fourth function frees any resources allocated at unmarshal time. As with [transmit_as()], the names of the four functions are based on the name of the type alias. The function names for [wire_marshal()] types, along with their responsibilities, are shown in Table 5.3.

The MIDL compiler generates function prototypes for the four functions. The generated prototypes for the PPOINTNODE type are shown in Listing 5.14.

Table 5.3   Responsibilities and naming of [wire_marshal()] functions

Responsibility	Generic Name	Example
Calculate size of buffer required by <alias>_UserMarshal	<alias>_UserSize	PPOINTNODE_UserSize
Marshal presentation type into network buffer	<alias>_UserMarshal	PPOINTNODE_UserMarshal
Unmarshal presentation type from network buffer	<alias>_UserUnmarshal	PPOINTNODE_UserUnmarshal
Free resources allocated by <alias>_UserUnmarshal	<alias>_UserFree	PPOINTNODE_UserFree

Listing 5.14   Function prototypes for PPOINTNODE marshaling functions

```
unsigned long __RPC_USER
PPOINTNODE_UserSize ( unsigned long *,
                      unsigned long,
                      PPOINTNODE * );
unsigned char* __RPC_USER
PPOINTNODE_UserMarshal ( unsigned long *,
                         unsigned char *,
                         PPOINTNODE * );
unsigned char * __RPC_USER
PPOINTNODE_UserUnmarshal ( unsigned long *,
                           unsigned char *,
                           PPOINTNODE * );
void __RPC_USER
PPOINTNODE_UserFree ( unsigned long *,
                      PPOINTNODE * );
```

When transmitting data types, IDL uses an encoding format known as the Network Data Representation, or NDR. This format specifies how a given data type or IDL construct is represented at the wire level. All [wire_marshal()] types must use NDR encoding. This includes dealing with alignment and conformance issues.[7] It is this requirement that makes writing of [wire

---

[7] For more detail on NDR rules, see *http://www.opengroup.org/onlinepubs/9629399/toc.htm*

`_marshal()]` functions more difficult than writing the equivalent code for `[transmit_as()]`.

The implementation of `PPOINTNODE_UserSize` is shown in Listing 5.15. The function is passed the current size of the buffer in the `Starting Size` parameter. This must be used as the starting point for the size calculation, because as the interception code may have already calculated storage requirements for other method parameters. Note that the function first counts the number of nodes in the list and then calculates the extra buffer space required to transmit the data. The buffer in this case is aligned on a word boundary, hence the modulo division of the `StartingSize` parameter. Having aligned the buffer, space is needed for the `PointListMarshal` structure itself, with an extra `unsigned long` for the conformance. These extra 4 bytes are needed because in NDR the conformance is passed on the wire twice: once as the structure field `cElems` and once as the argument to the `[size_is()]` attribute. The marshaling and unmarshaling code also needs to take this into account. Finally, the space required for the data is calculated by multiplying the size of a `Point` by the number of points being transmitted.

Listing 5.15 Implementation of PPOINTNODE_UserSize

```
unsigned long __RPC_USER
PPOINTNODE_UserSize ( unsigned long * pFlags,
                      unsigned long StartingSize,
                      PPOINTNODE * ppPointNode ) {
  // Scratch pointer
  PointNode* pCurrent = * ppPointNode;
  // Number of nodes in list
  unsigned long cElems = 0;

  // Walk backwards to front of list
  while ( pCurrent->pPrev != 0 ) {
    pCurrent = pCurrent->pPrev;
  }

  while ( pCurrent != 0 )      {
    cElems++; // Count number of nodes
    pCurrent = pCurrent->pNext;
  }
```

```
  // return required memory size
  return StartingSize + StartingSize%2 +
    sizeof ( PointListMarshal ) +
    sizeof ( unsigned long ) +
    ( sizeof ( Point ) * cElems );
}
```

Having calculated the buffer space required for all method parameters, the interception code will ask the channel to allocate a buffer of the required size through `IRpcChannelBuffer::GetBuffer`. It will then marshal the parameters into the buffer, resulting in a call to `PPOINTNODE_UserMarshal`. The code is shown in Listing 5.16.

Listing 5.16 Implementation of PPOINTNODE_UserMarshal

```
unsigned char * __RPC_USER
PPOINTNODE_UserMarshal ( unsigned long * pFlags,
                         unsigned char * Buffer,
                         PPOINTNODE  * ppPointNode ) {
  PointNode* pHead = 0; // Pointer to head of list
  // Scratch pointer
  PointNode* pCurrent = * ppPointNode;
  // Number of nodes in list
  unsigned long cElems = 0;
  // Index of passed-in node
  unsigned long nNodeIndex = 0;

  // Walk backwards to front of list
  while ( pCurrent->pPrev != 0 ) {
    nNodeIndex++; // Store passed-in node index
    pCurrent = pCurrent->pPrev;
  }

  // Store head node
  pHead = pCurrent;

  while ( pCurrent != 0 )      {
    cElems++; // Count number of nodes
    pCurrent = pCurrent->pNext;
  }

  // Add padding for alignment
  Buffer += (unsigned long)(Buffer)%2;
```

```
// Write out node index
*(unsigned long*)(Buffer) = nNodeIndex;
Buffer += sizeof ( unsigned long );
// Write out cElems
*(unsigned long*)(Buffer) = cElems;
Buffer += sizeof ( unsigned long );
// Write out conformance
*(unsigned long*)(Buffer) = cElems;
Buffer += sizeof ( unsigned long );
// Write out pointer to data
*(Point**)(Buffer) = (Point*)(Buffer +
  sizeof ( Point* ));
Buffer += sizeof ( Point* );

// Reset to head of list
pCurrent = pHead;

// Copy Point data from list nodes into
// transmission array
while ( pCurrent != 0 )      {
  *(Point*)(Buffer) = pCurrent->pt;
  Buffer += sizeof ( Point );
  pCurrent = pCurrent->pNext;
}
return Buffer;
}
```

The initial processing performed by PPOINTNODE_UserMarshal is identical to that performed by the corresponding [transmit_as()] function,
PPOINTNODE_to_xmit, storing the current node index and calculating the
number of nodes in the list. The marshaling code is, however, very different.
With [wire_marshal()], data is marshaled into an untyped array of bytes,
supplied to the function through the Buffer parameter, rather than into a typed
buffer as was the case with [transmit_as()]. This means that the marshaling function has to write each data element out in turn and then increment
the Buffer parameter by the correct amount. Notice that the function also has
to add the correct amount of padding at the start of the marshaling operation
and that it marshals the content of the cElems field twice to conform to the
NDR rules. Finally, the marshaling code writes the address of the array and
the array data into the buffer. The function then returns the final value of the

Buffer parameter that now points to the byte after the data the function has marshaled. The layout of the data in the buffer is shown in Figure 5.3.

Having marshaled the method parameters, the client-side interceptor transmits the buffer to the server-side interceptor through a call to `IRpcChannel Buffer::SendReceive`. The server-side interceptor then calls `PPOINT NODE_UserUnmarshal` to re-create the presentation type to pass to the actual method call. The code for the unmarshal function is shown in Listing 5.17.

Listing 5.17   Implementation of PPOINTNODE_UserUnmarshal

```
unsigned char * __RPC_USER
PPOINTNODE_UserUnmarshal ( unsigned long * pFlags,
                           unsigned char * Buffer,
                           PPOINTNODE * ppPointNode ) {
```

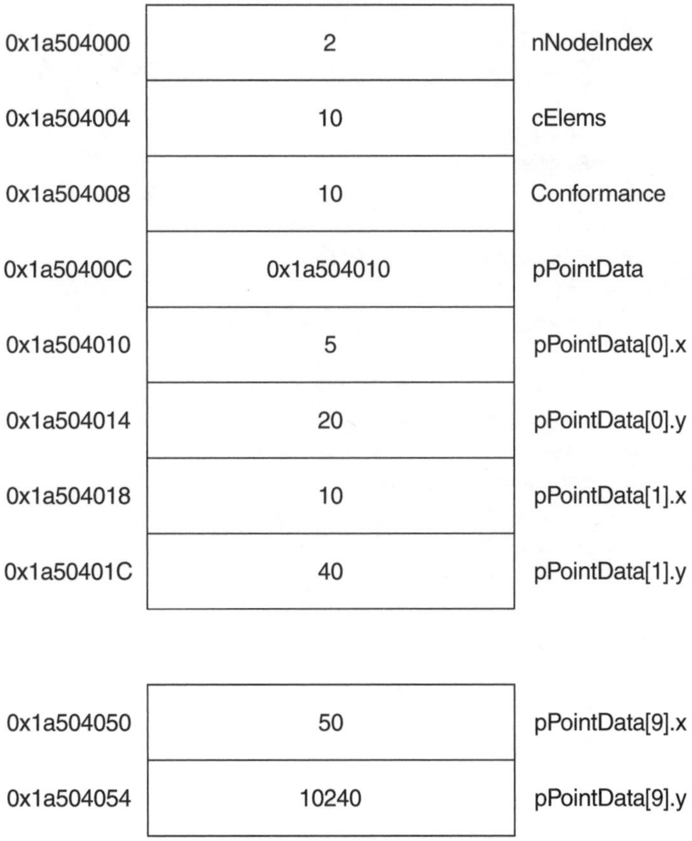

Address	Value	Field
0x1a504000	2	nNodeIndex
0x1a504004	10	cElems
0x1a504008	10	Conformance
0x1a50400C	0x1a504010	pPointData
0x1a504010	5	pPointData[0].x
0x1a504014	20	pPointData[0].y
0x1a504018	10	pPointData[1].x
0x1a50401C	40	pPointData[1].y
0x1a504050	50	pPointData[9].x
0x1a504054	10240	pPointData[9].y

Figure 5.3   Buffer layout for [wire_marshal()] of PPOINTNODE

```
unsigned long i = 0;            // Loop counter
PointNode* pCurrent = 0;        // Scratch pointer
PointNode* pPrevious = 0;       // Scratch pointer
unsigned long cElems = 0; // Number of nodes in list
// Index of passed-in node
unsigned long nNodeIndex = 0;
// Align buffer pointer
Buffer += (unsigned long)(Buffer)%2;
// Get node index and number of nodes
nNodeIndex = *(unsigned long*)(Buffer);
Buffer += sizeof ( unsigned long );
cElems = *(unsigned long*)(Buffer);
Buffer += sizeof ( unsigned long );

// Skip conformance and data pointer
Buffer += sizeof ( unsigned long ) +
  sizeof ( Point* );

// Allocate head node
pCurrent = CoTaskMemAlloc ( sizeof ( PointNode ));

// Iterate through transmission array
for(i=0;i<cElems;i++) {
  // Copy Point data from transmission array into
  // current node
  pCurrent->pt = *(Point*)(Buffer);
  Buffer += sizeof ( Point );
  pCurrent->pPrev = pPrevious;

  // If we're at the node index then...
  if ( i == nNodeIndex )
    // ... pass out the current node pointer
    *ppPointNode = pCurrent;

  // If we're at the last array element...
  if ( i+1 == cElems )
    // ...set pNext to null
    pCurrent->pNext = 0;
  else {
    // Allocate memory for next node
    pCurrent->pNext = CoTaskMemAlloc (
      sizeof ( PointNode ));
    // store current node in pPrevious,
    pPrevious = pCurrent;
```

```
      // store next node in pCurrent
      pCurrent = pCurrent->pNext;
    }
  }
  return Buffer;
}
```

For the most part, PPOINTNODE_UserUnmarshal works like PPOINT
NODE_UserMarshal, only in reverse. It reads the data from the transmission
buffer and re-creates the list of nodes. At the same time, the function determines which node should be passed out from the function. As it reads each
piece of data from the buffer, the function increments the Buffer parameter,
returning the final value after all data has been read. The unmarshaling function is able to ignore the extra conformance field, because the value was stored
in the cElems field of the structure. The pointer to the array of Point structures, pPointData, can and should be ignored, becauses the value is not
converted by the NDR layer when crossing process boundaries. Because the
data pPointData points to is always stored immediately after the pointer itself
by PPOINTNODE_UserMarshal, there is no need for the unmarshaling function to look at the value.

After PPOINTNODE_UserUnmarshal returns, the stub calls the method on the
object. When the method call completes, the stub calls PPOINTNODE_UserFree
to release all resources allocated by PPOINTNODE_UserUnmarshal. The code
for PPOINTNODE_UserFree is shown in Listing 5.18.

Listing 5.18 Implementation of PPOINTNODE_UserFree

```
void __RPC_USER
PPOINTNODE_UserFree ( unsigned long * pFlags,
                      PPOINTNODE * ppPointNode ) {
  PointNode* pCurrent = *ppPointNode;
  // Walk backwards to front of list
  while(pCurrent->pPrev != 0 ) {
    pCurrent = pCurrent->pPrev;
  }

  while ( pCurrent ) { // Free each node
    PointNode* pNext = pCurrent->pNext;
    CoTaskMemFree ( pCurrent );
    pCurrent = pNext;
  }
}
```

Note that the implementation is exactly the same as that of the corresponding `[transmit_as()]` function, `PPOINTNODE_free_inst`. The call sequence for the four functions is shown in Figure 5.4.

No treatment of `[wire_marshal()]` would be complete without mentioning the `pFlags` parameter that is passed by the interception layer to each of the four functions. This parameter is a bit mask that informs the `[wire_marshal()]` functions of the NDR format flags and the marshaling context. The format flags specify the floating point representation, byte ordering, and character encoding. The `[wire_marshal()]` functions do not need to take the format flags into account, because the NDR engine will convert the data as necessary. It is because of this potential for conversion that the wire format must conform to the NDR rules. The encoding formats are stored in the upper 16 bits of the pFlags parameter, as shown in Table 5.4.

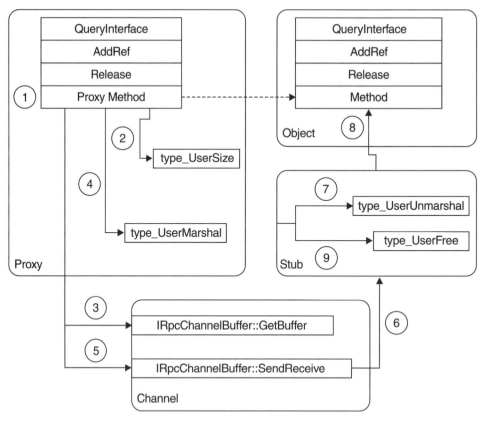

Figure 5.4 Call sequence for a method containing a [wire_marshal()] type

ESSENTIAL IDL

Table 5.4 Layout of NDR format flags in the pFlags parameter

Bits	Format Flag	Values
31-24	Floating point format	0 = IEEE
		1 = VAX
		2 = Cray
		3 = IBM
23-20	Byte ordering	0 = Big-endian
		1 = Little-endian
19-16	Character encoding	0 = ASCII1
		1 = EBCDIC

The upper 16 bits are valid only in calls to `<alias>_UserUnmarshal` functions. In calls to the other three functions, they are always set to zero. On Windows 2000 running on an x86 family processor, the upper 16 bits are set to 0x0010, denoting IEEE floating point format stored in little-endian byte order with ASCII character encoding.

The more interesting part of the `pFlags` parameter is the lower 16 bits which denote the marshaling context for the current call. The possible values are shown in Table 5.5.[8]

One reason that the marshaling context is so interesting is that it opens up additional optimization possibilities. For instance, the list of `Point` nodes in the examples above only needs to be marshaled in full if the call is cross-process or cross-host. If the call is cross-thread or cross-context, the `[wire_marshal()]` functions could pass the pointer to the input node directly, resulting in a serious performance gain for large lists. Because of the NDR requirements, the `[wire _marshal()]` functions cannot merely serialize the 4-byte pointer to the input node into the transmission buffer. The buffer format must conform to the layout defined in the IDL description of the `[wire_marshal()]` type. If the buffer does not conform to the expected layout, the interception layer generates the

---

[8] A fifth constant, `MSHCTX_NOSHAREDMEM`, is also defined by the system but was relevant only when calling 32-bit code from 16-bit code, or vice versa.

Table 5.5   Marshaling context constants and values

Constant	Meaning	Value
MSHCTX_DIFFERENTMACHINE	Cross host call	2
MSHCTX_LOCAL	Same host, cross process call	0
MSHCTX_INPROC	Same process, cross thread call	3
MSHCTX_CROSSCTX	Same thread, cross context call	4

error 0x800706f8, `The supplied user buffer is not valid for the requested operation'. Consequently, ensuring that any optimized code provides the correct buffer layout is critical. Versions of the four PPOINTNODE functions optimized for cross-thread and cross-context calls are shown in Listing 5.19.

Listing 5.19   Optimized version of PPOINTNODE [wire_marshal()] functions

```
unsigned long __RPC_USER
PPOINTNODE_UserSize ( unsigned long * pFlags,
                      unsigned long StartingSize,
                      PPOINTNODE * ppPointNode ) {
  if ( *pFlags & 0x7 ) {
    // If cross-thread/context call
    // return required memory size
    return StartingSize + StartingSize%2 +
      sizeof ( PointListMarshal ) +
      sizeof ( unsigned long );
  }
  else { // .. as previous implementation
  }
}

unsigned char * __RPC_USER
PPOINTNODE_UserMarshal ( unsigned long * pFlags,
                         unsigned char * Buffer,
                         PPOINTNODE  * ppPointNode ) {
  if ( *pFlags & 0x7 ) {
    // If cross-thread/context call
    // Set node index to zero
    *(unsigned long*)(Buffer) = 0;
    Buffer += sizeof ( unsigned long );
    // Set number of nodes to zero
    *(unsigned long*)(Buffer) = 0;
```

```c
    Buffer += sizeof ( unsigned long );
    // Set conformance to zero
    *(unsigned long*)(Buffer) = 0;
    Buffer += sizeof ( unsigned long );

    // Store the address of the input node
    // in pPointData
    *(Point**)(Buffer) = (Point*)(*ppPointNode);
    Buffer += sizeof ( Point* );
    return Buffer;
  }
  else     { // .. as previous implementation
  }
}


unsigned char * __RPC_USER
PPOINTNODE_UserUnmarshal ( unsigned long * pFlags,
                           unsigned char * Buffer,
                           PPOINTNODE * ppPointNode ) {
  if ( *pFlags & 0x7 ) {
    // If cross-thread/context call
    // Skip node index and number of nodes
    Buffer += sizeof ( unsigned long );
    Buffer += sizeof ( unsigned long );
    // Skip conformance
    Buffer += sizeof ( unsigned long );

    // Extract address of input node
    *ppPointNode = *((PPOINTNODE*)Buffer);
    Buffer += sizeof ( PPOINTNODE* );
    return Buffer;
  }
  else     { // .. as previous implementation
  }
}


void __RPC_USER
PPOINTNODE_UserFree ( unsigned long * pFlags,
                      PPOINTNODE * ppptnd ) {
  if ( *pFlags & 0x7 )  {
    // If cross-thread/context call
    return; // Do nothing
  }
  else     { // .. as previous implementation
  }
}
```

Note that the optimized code still works in terms of the `PointListMarshal` type, serializing all the required fields, including the conformance. However, rather than serializing the address of a `Point` into the `pPointData` field, the code serializes the address of the input node stored in the `ppPointNode` parameter instead. No array data is written to the buffer, because the number of nodes being transmitted is zero. The node index is also set to zero. The optimized versions of the functions are about ten times faster than the standard implementations when calling across a thread or context boundary. Call speed across process or host boundaries is unchanged.

The examples above illustrate how aliasing can be used to outperform the standard interception layer. This is typically possible whenever the interface designer has extra knowledge about the types being transmitted and that knowledge is not available to the MIDL compiler.

Both `[transmit_as()]` and `[wire_marshal()]` allow the interface designer to inject code into the interception layer on a type-by-type basis just as `[local]\[call_as()]` allows insertion of code on a method-by-method basis. While the typical purpose of the injected code is to perform optimized marshaling, other processing tasks may also be useful. For example, certain data types may be able to be compressed to a fraction of their normal size. Injecting compression/decompression code into the standard interception layer would allow the interface designer to take advantage of that characteristic. There would, of course, be a balance between saving bytes on the wire and incurring extra processing overhead to compress and decompress data on each call. Another possible purpose for the inserted code could be logging of specific method calls or method calls containing specific parameter types. In addition to marshaling the data types, the functions could log information about the call to a file or database. Note that method aliasing would have to be used in order to log information about a specific method. If information was required for all methods that took a particular type as a parameter, then type aliasing would be used.

Note that none of the aliasing techniques shown will work with type library marshaling. Also, the IDL alone no longer provides enough information to build the proxy-stub DLL; the C source files containing the aliasing functions are also needed. Any assumptions that the aliasing functions make, such as the fact that the examples above work only with true lists and will fail if passed a cyclic or tree-style graph should be clearly documented.

One final note about aliasing: while the examples shown all use the `CoTaskMemAlloc/CoTaskMemFree`, other memory management APIs can be used also. However, using APIs other than the standard COM APIs for type aliasing should be carefully documented, because any method that returns an aliased parameter type must use the same memory management API as the aliasing code.

Conclusions

IDL provides several aliasing techniques that an interface designer can use to increase performance, perform logging operations, or indeed inject arbitrary code into the standard interception layer. Of these techniques, method aliasing is the easiest to implement, while the type aliasing mechanisms provide greater flexibility and reusability of code. Listed below are some guidelines for using the IDL aliasing techniques described in this chapter.

1. Favor type aliasing over method aliasing. Type aliasing code is reusable purely through IDL, whereas method aliasing requires that new C functions be written for every aliased method.
2. Use [wire_marshal] only where the performance gain outweighs the extra coding complexity. Writing [transmit_as] aliasing code is significantly easier than writing [wire_marshal] aliasing code.
3. Remember that [transmit_as] types must be contiguous; think conformant arrays.
4. Remember that [wire_marshal] types must be of a fixed size; think conformant pointers.

Chapter 6

Asynchronous COM

Asynchronous Calls

Windows 2000 supports asynchronous COM calls from both a client and a server perspective. Making an asynchronous call on the client side allows the client to do useful work while the server executes the method. Using asynchrony on the server side frees up the RPC thread that initially serviced the method request, resulting in a smaller RPC thread pool. The asynchronous behavior is built into the COM channel, and in order to take advantage of it a method definition must be modeled as two separate signatures. Fortunately, the MIDL compiler will split standard interface methods in two whenever it sees the `[async_uuid()]` attribute on an interface definition. This attribute is supported only on Windows 2000, and the resulting output files must be compiled with the `_WIN32_WINNT` constant set to `0x0500` or higher. An example interface annotated with the `[async_uuid]` attribute is shown in Listing 6.1.

Listing 6.1   IDL definition of an asynchronous interface

```
[
  uuid(74241B75-264B-4f60-8420-33AE876BB619),
  async_uuid(7BE7E5B7-774A-45dd-9583-6B3F8811B297),
  object,
  pointer_default(unique)
]
interface IMath : IUnknown {
HRESULT CalculatePrimes ( [in] long nMaxNumber,
                          [out] long* pnPrimes,
     [out,size_is(,*pnPrimes)] long** ppResults );
}
```

Note that the `[async_uuid()]` is distinct from the standard `[uuid()]` attribute. When the interface definition is compiled, the MIDL compiler outputs two definitions: one for IMath and one for AsyncIMath. The IMath definition contains no surprises; the definition of AsyncIMath is shown in Listing 6.2.

Listing 6.2 C++ mapping of AsyncIMath

```
interface AsyncIMath : public IUnknown {
public:
  virtual HRESULT STDMETHODCALLTYPE
  Begin_CalculatePrimes ( long nMaxNumber) = 0;
  virtual HRESULT STDMETHODCALLTYPE
  Finish_CalculatePrimes ( long* pnPrimes,
                           long** ppResults) = 0;
};
```

Each method in the interface has been split into two separate methods, the first containing all parameters annotated with the [in] attribute and the second containing all the parameters marked with the [out] attribute. It is this interface that the client calls to get asynchronous behavior from the underlying COM channel. The server may optionally implement AsyncIMath in order to free threads in the RPC thread pool.

Client-Side Asynchrony

In the client context, it is typically the client-side interceptor that provides an implementation of the asynchronous version of a given interface. Such interface implementations are acquired through a call to ICallFactory::Create Call, which creates a call object that implements the specified asynchronous interface. The IDL for ICallFactory is shown in Listing 6.3. The riid parameter denotes the asynchronous interface that the client wishes to call. The riid2 parameter denotes the interface on the call object that the client wishes to be returned. This is typically the asynchronous interface, but the client could request IUnknown or ISynchronize.

Listing 6.3 IDL for ICallFactory

```
[
  local,
  object,
  uuid(1c733a30-2a1c-11ce-ade5-00aa0044773d),
  pointer_default(unique)
]
```

```
interface ICallFactory : IUnknown {
  HRESULT CreateCall( [in] REFIID riid,
                      [in] IUnknown* pCtrlUnk,
                      [in] REFIID riid2,
       [out, iid_is(riid2)] IUnknown** ppv );
}
```

Having acquired the call object, the client then calls the `Begin_` method that marshals the method parameters into the network buffer and then returns control to the client. The client-side call sequence for `Begin_CalculatePrimes` is shown in Listing 6.4.

Listing 6.4   Client-side call sequence for AsyncIMath::Begin_CalculatePrimes
```
CComPtr<IUnknown> spObj;
HR(spObj.CoCreateInstance ( __uuidof ( MathObj )));
CComPtr<ICallFactory> spcf;
HR(spObj->QueryInterface ( &spcf ));

CComPtr<AsyncIMath> spAsyncMath;
HR(spcf->CreateCall ( __uuidof ( spAsyncMath ), 0,
                      __uuidof ( spAsyncMath ),
                      (IUnknown**)&spAsyncMath));
HR(spAsyncMath->Begin_CalculatePrimes ( 25000 ));
```

Note that in this case the client requests a call object for `AsyncIMath` and also requests the `AsyncIMath` interface on that call object. Figure 6.1 shows the client-side object model; note that the proxy and the call object are distinct from one another. The call object can be used repeatedly to make asynchronous calls, but it can be used to make only one call at a time. If multiple parallel calls are required, then multiple call objects must be used.

Having called `Begin_CalculatePrimes`, the client can continue processing while the server performs the calculation. The implementation of `CalculatePrimes` is shown in Listing 6.5. Because of the brute force approach, the method can take a long time to execute—especially when the client passes in values of 20,000 or more.[1]

---

[1] Obviously, this is an inefficient algorithm for computing prime numbers, and much faster algorithms exist. But if the method executes quickly, there is little reason for the client to want asynchronous execution.

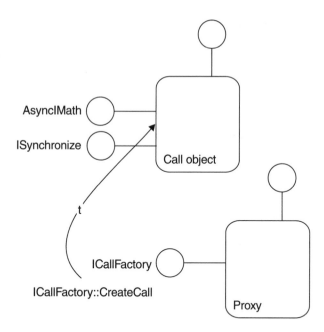

AsyncIMath

ISynchronize

Call object

ICallFactory

ICallFactory::CreateCall

Proxy

t

Figure 6.1   Client-side object model for AsyncIMath

Listing 6.5   Implementation of IMath::CalculatePrimes

```
STDMETHODIMP CalculatePrimes ( long nMaxNumber,
                               long* pnPrimes,
                               long** ppResults ){
  HR( pnPrimes && ppResults ? S_OK : E_POINTER );
  long lCount=1;
  // Count number of primes
  for(long i=1;i<=nMaxNumber;i++) {
    for(long j=2;j<i;j++)
      if ( i % j == 0 )
        break;

    if ( j == i )
    lCount++;
  }

  *pnPrimes = lCount;
  *ppResults = (long*)CoTaskMemAlloc (
    sizeof ( long ) * lCount );

  lCount = 0;
  (*ppResults)[lCount++]=1;
```

```
    for(i=1;i<=nMaxNumber;i++) {
      for(long j=2;j<i;j++)
        if ( i % j == 0 )
          break;

      if ( j == i )
        (*ppResults)[lCount++]=i;
    }
    return S_OK;
  }
```

Note that the server implements the standard, synchronous version of the interface. It does not implement Begin_CalculatePrimes or Finish _CalculatePrimes, which instead are implemented on the client side by the call object. The call object makes calls to an asynchronous implementation of the channel. This asynchronous channel behavior is modeled by the IAsyncRpcChannelBuffer interface, the IDL for which is shown in Listing 6.6.

Listing 6.6 IDL for IAsyncRpcChannelBuffer

```
[
  local,
  object,
  uuid(a5029fb6-3c34-11d1-9c99-00c04fb998aa),
  pointer_default(unique)
]
interface IAsyncRpcChannelBuffer : IRpcChannelBuffer2 {
  HRESULT Send ( [in,out] RPCOLEMESSAGE *pMsg,
                      [in] ISynchronize *pSync,
                      [out] ULONG *pulStatus );
  HRESULT Receive ( [in,out] RPCOLEMESSAGE *pMsg,
                      [out] ULONG *pulStatus );
  HRESULT GetDestCtxEx ( [in] RPCOLEMESSAGE *pMsg,
                      [out] DWORD *pdwDestContext,
                      [out] void **ppvDestContext );
};
```

The interesting methods are Send and Receive, which break the synchronous nature of the standard SendReceive method found in IRpcChannel Buffer, enabling asynchronous communication. When the client calls Begin_CalculatePrimes, the call object makes a call to Send, passing in an implementation of ISynchronize. The IDL for ISynchronize is shown in Listing 6.7.

Listing 6.7   IDL for ISynchronize

```
[
    object,
    uuid(00000030-0000-0000-C000-000000000046)
]
interface ISynchronize : IUnknown {
    HRESULT Wait ( [in] DWORD dwFlags,
                   [in] DWORD dwMilliseconds);
    HRESULT Signal();
    HRESULT Reset();
}
```

By default, the implementation of ISynchronize is provided by the call object and is merely a COM wrapper around a Win32 manual reset event object. The Reset method puts the event object into the unsignaled state. The channel implementation of IAsyncRpcChannelBuffer::Send calls ISynchronize::Reset. When the remote method call completes, the channel calls ISynchronize::Signal, which puts the event object into the signaled state.

At any point after the call to Begin_CalculatePrimes, the client can call ISynchronize::Wait to determine whether the method call has completed. If the method call has completed, then Wait returns S_OK; otherwise, assuming that no errors have occurred, it returns RPC_S_CALLPENDING.[2] The typical implementation of Wait simply calls CoWaitForMultipleHandles to wait on the event object. If the method call has not yet completed, then Wait blocks until the event object is signaled or the timeout period specified in the dwMilliseconds parameter expires. Once a call to Wait signals that the method call has completed, the client can call Finish_CalculatePrimes to harvest the output parameters.

Certain clients may not wish to call the Wait method periodically in order to determine whether the method has completed. Such clients can provide an implementation of ISynchronize that aggregates the call object returned by CreateCall. To achieve this aggregation, the ISynchronize implementation passes its IUnknown as the second parameter to the CreateCall method. The object diagram is shown in Figure 6.2.

---

[2] Although this constant looks like a success code, its hex value is 0x80010115, and so it is clearly a failure code.

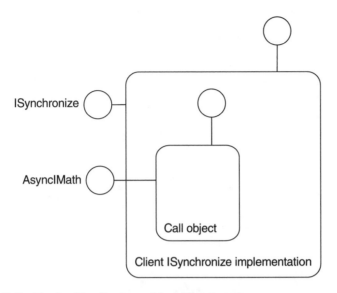

Figure 6.2   Call object with client provided ISynchronize

Now, when the asynchronous call completes, it will call the client imple-mentation of `ISynchronize::Signal`. Typically, the implementation of `Signal` harvests the `out` parameters, either directly or indirectly. A simple implementation of `ISynchronize` (that does not harvest `[out]` parameters) is shown in Listing 6.8, and client-side code that uses the implementation is shown in Listing 6.9. The client code creates an instance of the `CSync` class, passing the `ICallFactory` of the proxy as the constructor parameter. The `CSync` class calls `CreateCall`, passing its own `IUnknown` as the second parameter and asking for the `IUnknown` of the call object as required by the rules of aggregation.

Listing 6.8   Simple implementation of ISynchronize

```
class CSync : public ISynchronize {
private: // Member variables
HANDLE m_hEvent;
DWORD m_dwRef;
IUnknown* m_pUnkCallObj;
public:
CSync( ICallFactory* pcf ) : m_hEvent ( 0 ),
                             m_dwRef ( 0 ),
                             m_pUnkCallObj ( 0 ) {
  m_hEvent = ::CreateEvent ( 0, TRUE, FALSE, 0 );
```

```
          pcf->CreateCall ( __uuidof ( AsyncIMath ),
                            static_cast<IUnknown*>(this),
                            IID_IUnknown,
                            (IUnknown**)&m_pUnkCallObj);
        }

        virtual ~CSync() {
          CloseHandle ( m_hEvent );
          if (m_pUnkCallObj  ) m_pUnkCallObj->Release();
        }

        // IUnknown
        STDMETHODIMP
        QueryInterface ( REFIID riid, void** ppv ) {
          if ( !ppv ) return E_POINTER;
          if ( IID_IUnknown == riid ||
               IID_ISynchronize == riid ) {
            *ppv = static_cast<ISynchronize*>(this);
            reinterpret_cast<IUnknown*>(*ppv)->AddRef();
            return S_OK;
          }
          else
            return m_pUnkCallObj->QueryInterface ( riid, ppv );
        }

        STDMETHODIMP_(ULONG) AddRef() {
          return ++m_dwRef;
        }

        STDMETHODIMP_(ULONG) Release() {
          ULONG u = --m_dwRef;
          if ( !u )
            delete this;
          return u;
        }

        // ISynchronize
        STDMETHODIMP
        Wait(DWORD dwFlags, DWORD dwMilliseconds ) {
          DWORD dw;
          return CoWaitForMultipleHandles ( dwFlags,
                                            dwMilliseconds,
                                            1, &m_hEvent,
                                            &dw );
        }
```

```
STDMETHODIMP Signal() {
  return SetEvent ( m_hEvent ) ? S_OK :
        HRESULT_FROM_WIN32(::GetLastError());
}

STDMETHODIMP Reset() {
  return ResetEvent ( m_hEvent ) ? S_OK :
        HRESULT_FROM_WIN32(::GetLastError());
}
};
```

Listing 6.9 Client usage of ISynchronize implementation

```
CComPtr<IUnknown> spObj;
HR(spObj.CoCreateInstance ( __uuidof ( MathObj )));
CComPtr<ICallFactory> spcf;
HR(spObj->QueryInterface ( &spcf ));

// Create the (aggregated) call object
CSync* pSyncObj = new CSync ( spcf );
HR ( pSyncObj ? S_OK : E_OUTOFMEMORY );
pSyncObj->AddRef();
CComPtr<IUnknown> spSyncObj;
HR(pSyncObj->QueryInterface ( __uuidof ( spSyncObj ),
                              (void*)(&spSyncObj)));
pSyncObj->Release();
CComPtr<AsyncIMath> spAsyncMath;
HR(spSyncObj->QueryInterface ( &spAsyncMath ));
HR(spAsyncMath->Begin_CalculatePrimes ( 25000 ));
```

Server-Side Asynchrony

The examples so far have concentrated on client-side code, and the server implementation has not been aware that it was being used asynchronously. The server side of the call can also benefit from an asynchronous implementation. In this case the server implements `ICallFactory` and creates a call object that implements the asynchronous version of the interface, `AsyncI Math`. This call object is aggregated by a system-provided implementation of `ISynchronize`. The object diagram for the server side is shown in Figure 6.3.

The COM channel calls `QueryInterface` on the object, asking for `Icall Factory`, and then calls `CreateCall`, passing the `IUnknown*` of the system `ISynchronize` implementation as the second parameter. The implementation of `CreateCall` creates a call object that is aggregated by the system

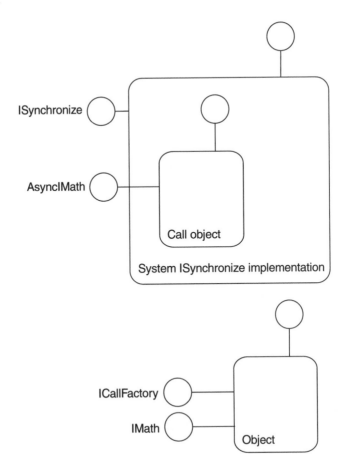

Figure 6.3   Server-side object model for AsyncIMath

`ISynchronize` implementation. The channel then calls `Begin_Calculate Primes`, the implementation of which asynchronously executes `Calculate Primes`, perhaps by posting a Windows message or maybe by starting a new thread to perform the operation. When the method call completes, the object calls `ISynchronize::Signal`, which then calls `Finish_Calculate Primes` to harvest the output parameters. The benefit of server-side asynchrony is the freeing up of the RPC thread that initially handled the call. In synchronous COM, this thread is blocked while the method executes.

A possible implementation of the asynchronous parts of the `AsyncIMath` call object is shown in Listing 6.10, and Listing 6.11 shows the implementation of `ICallFactory`. This particular implementation of `AsyncIMath::Begin`

`_CalculatePrimes` starts a thread to process each call and as such is not terribly efficient. In reality, a pool of threads would be used in order to limit the total number of threads executing within the server address space. The thread function, `_CalcPrimes/CalcPrimes`, started by `Begin _CalculatePrimes` calls back into the standard, synchronous implementation of `CalculatePrimes`. Note that the `Begin_CalculatePrimes` function calls `ISynchronize::Reset` before calling `CreateThread` and that the thread function calls `ISynchronize::Signal` when the method call completes. The runtime implementation of signal then calls `Finish_Calculate Primes` to harvest the output parameters.

Listing 6.10 Server-side implementation of AsyncIMath

```
class CallObject : public AsyncIMath {
private: // Member variables
IUnknown* m_pOuterUnk;
IMath* m_pMath;
DWORD m_dwRef;
long m_lMaxNumber, m_lCount, *m_pPrimes;


public:
CallObject ( IUnknown* pOuterUnk, IMath* pMath ) :
  m_pOuterUnk ( pOuterUnk ), m_pMath ( pMath ),
  m_dwRef ( 0 ), m_lMaxNumber ( 0 ),  m_lCount ( 0 ),
  m_pPrimes ( 0 ) {
    if ( m_pMath ) m_pMath->AddRef();
}


~CallObject(){
  if ( m_pMath ) m_pMath->Release();
}


HRESULT CalcPrimes() {
  HR(m_pMath->CalculatePrimes ( m_lMaxNumber,
                                &m_lCount,
                                &m_pPrimes ));
  CComPtr<ISynchronize> spSync = 0;
  HR(m_pOuterUnk->QueryInterface ( __uuidof ( spSync ),
                                   (void**)&spSync));
  HR(spSync->Signal());
  return S_OK;
}
```

```
static DWORD WINAPI _CalcPrimes ( void* pv ) {
  CoInitializeEx (0, COINIT_MULTITHREADED);
  CallObject* pThis = (CallObject*)pv;
  HRESULT hRet = pThis->CalcPrimes();
  CoUninitialize();
  return hRet;
}


// ASyncIMath
STDMETHODIMP
Begin_CalculatePrimes ( long nMaxNumber ) {
  CComPtr<ISynchronize> spSync;
  HR(m_pOuterUnk->QueryInterface ( __uuidof ( spSync ),
                                   (void**)&spSync));
  HR(spSync->Reset());
  m_lMaxNumber = nMaxNumber;
  DWORD dwid;
  HANDLE h = CreateThread ( 0, 0, _CalcPrimes, this,
                            0, &dwid );
  HR(h ? S_OK : HRESULT_FROM_WIN32(GetLastError()));
  CloseHandle ( h );
  return S_OK;
}


STDMETHODIMP
Finish_CalculatePrimes ( long* pnPrimes,
                         long** ppResults ) {
  HR ( pnPrimes && ppResults ? S_OK : E_POINTER );
  *pnPrimes = m_lCount;
  *ppResults = m_pPrimes;
  return S_OK;
}
// Delegating and non-delegating IUnknown implementation elided
for brevity
};
```

Listing 6.11 Server-side implementation of ICallFactory

```
// ICallFactory
STDMETHODIMP CreateCall ( REFIID riid,
                          IUnknown* pUnkOuter,
                          REFIID riid2,
                          IUnknown**ppUnk ) {
  HR ( __uuidof ( AsyncIMath ) == riid ?
    S_OK : E_INVALIDARG );
  HR ( pUnkOuter ? S_OK : E_INVALIDARG );
```

```
CallObject* pCallObj =
  new CallObject ( pUnkOuter,
                   static_cast<IMath*>(this));
HR( pCallObj ? S_OK : E_OUTOFMEMORY );
return
  pCallObj->InternalQueryInterface ( riid2,
                                     (void**)ppUnk );
}
```

It is worth noting that asynchronous calls do not work with type library mar-shaled interfaces, so Oicf proxy-stub DLLs must be used instead. Also, COM+ configured components do not support asynchronous calls. The proxy to such a component does not implement ICallFactory. To work around this limitation, an asynchronous call could be made to a nonconfigured component that would then call the configured component synchronously.

Conclusions

Windows 2000 supports asynchrony of execution on both the client and server sides of a given call. Listed below are some guidelines related to that asynchronous support.

1. When designing interfaces, think about asynchrony. If a given interface could sensibly be called asynchronously, provide an [async_uuid] attribute at design time. Having to amend the IDL later to provide an [async_uuid] attribute will necessitate rebuilding and subsequent redeployment of the proxy-stub DLL.
2. If designing an asynchronous interface, use Oicf type information.
3. Remember that providing an asynchronous version of an interface does not force objects to implement it but does allow clients to call it.

Chapter 7

IDL Types

This chapter provides a reference for each of the built-in IDL types. The information for each type is divided into several sections. The *Description* and *Notes* fields immediately below the type name provide a general description of the data type along with any notable features. Range information is also provided for numeric types. Both unsigned and signed ranges are listed for integer types.

The IDL section lists the size of the data type in bits or bytes along with the standard type library and Oicf constants used to represent the data type. The *Sign* field provides information about whether the signed and unsigned modifiers can be applied to the data type. Example IDL statements are also provided.

The C++ and Visual Basic sections provide the language mapping for the IDL type, followed by the underlying type definition in the C++ case. Any notable features about the language mapping are shown in the *Notes* field. Finally, examples are provided in each language where appropriate.

■ boolean

Description: The `boolean` data type is used where only the values true and false are required. True equates to the value 1, and false equates to the value 0.
Notes: Represented internally as a small.

■ IDL

Size: 8 bits
TLB Type: VT_I1
Oicf String: 0x03
Sign: Not applicable

Notes: If a boolean type is required for an oleautomation or scripting interface, `VARIANT_BOOL` should be used, because these environments treat true as -1.

Examples

- `HRESULT Up ( [in] boolean b );`
- `HRESULT Down ( [out,retval] boolean* pb );`
- `HRESULT Truth ( [in] boolean* pb );`
- `HRESULT Strange ( [in, out] boolean* pb );`
- `HRESULT Beauty( [out] boolean* pb );`

■ C++

Language Mapping: Boolean

Underlying Typedef: unsigned char

Notes: Because of the underlying type definition, any character is a valid value.

Examples

- `HRESULT Up ( boolean b );`
- `HRESULT Down ( boolean *pb );`
- `HRESULT Truth( boolean *pb );`
- `HRESULT Strange ( boolean *pb );`
- `HRESULT Beauty ( boolean *pb );`

■ Visual Basic

Language Mapping: None

■ byte

Description: An 8-bit integer type

Notes: No transmission time conversion occurs for byte types, and therefore arrays of byte type can be used to transfer binary data. The `char` data type may be converted from one character representation to another at transmission time. Consequently, arrays of `char` type should not be used when transferring binary data.

Unsigned Range: 0 to 255

■ IDL

Size: 8 bits

TLB Type: VT_UI1

Oicf String: 0x01

Sign: unsigned

Examples

- HRESULT Up ([in] byte b);
- HRESULT Down ([out,retval] byte* pb);
- HRESULT Truth ([in] byte* pb);
- HRESULT Strange ([in, out] byte* pb);
- HRESULT Beauty([out] byte* pb);

■ C++

Language Mapping: Byte

Underlying Typedef: unsigned char

Examples

- HRESULT Up (byte b);
- HRESULT Down (byte *pb);
- HRESULT Truth (byte *pb);
- HRESULT Strange (byte *pb);
- HRESULT Beauty (byte *pb);

■ Visual Basic

Language Mapping: Byte

Examples

- Private Sub IQuark_Up (ByVal b As Byte)
- Private Function IQuark_Down() As Byte
- Private Sub IQuark_Truth (b As Byte)
- Private Sub IQuark_Strange (b As Byte)

■ char

Description: The `char` data type is used to represent 8-bit characters.

Notes: Conversion from one character representation to another—for example, from ASCII to EBCDIC—may occur at transmission time. Consequently, arrays of `char` type should not be used when transferring binary data; use arrays of `byte` type instead. Using `char` as a COM data type is considered bad style. `wchar_t` should be used instead.

■ IDL

Size: 8 bits

TLB Type: VT_I1 / VT_UI1

Oicf String: 0x02

Sign: Either

Automation Compatible: Yes

Notes: By default, the char type is unsigned, so char and unsigned char are synonymous. This can be changed using the /char command line switch, q.v. The fact that the char type is unsigned by default is not reflected in the type library. In the type library, both char and signed char translate to VT_I1; unsigned char translates to VT_UI1. Owing to the differences between the type library mapping and the internal IDL representation, the char data type should be explicitly qualified with either signed or unsigned whenever it is used.

Examples

- HRESULT Up ([in] char c);
- HRESULT Down ([out,retval] char* pc);
- HRESULT Truth ([in] char* pc);
- HRESULT Strange ([in, out] char* pc);
- HRESULT Beauty ([out] char* pc);

■ C++

Language Mapping: Unsigned char

Examples

- HRESULT Up (unsigned char c);
- HRESULT Down (unsigned char *pc);
- HRESULT Truth (unsigned char *pc);
- HRESULT Strange (unsigned char *pc);
- HRESULT Beauty (unsigned char *pc);

Visual Basic

Language Mapping: None

Notes: No mapping is available for the IDL char or signed char type; unsigned char provides the same mapping as byte, q.v.

■ double

Description: The double data type is used to represent double precision floating point numbers.

Notes: double values have at least 15 digits of precision.

Signed Range: $-1.7 * 10 \char`^ 308$ to $1.7 * 10 \char`^ 308$

■ IDL

Size: 64 bits

TLB Type: VT_R8

Oicf String: 0x0c

Sign: signed

Examples

- HRESULT Up ([in] double lf);
- HRESULT Down ([out,retval] double *plf);
- HRESULT Truth ([in] double *plf);
- HRESULT Strange ([in,out] double *plf);
- HRESULT Beauty ([out] double *plf);

■ C++

Language Mapping: Double

Notes: There is no IDL equivalent to the 80-bit C++ type, long double.

Examples

- HRESULT Up (double lf);
- HRESULT Down (double *plf);
- HRESULT Truth (double *plf);
- HRESULT Strange (double *plf);
- HRESULT Beauty (double *plf);

■ Visual Basic

Language Mapping: Double

Examples

- Private Sub IQuark_Up (ByVal lf As Double)
- Private Function IQuark_Down() As Double
- Private Sub IQuark_Truth (lf As Double)
- Private Sub IQuark_Strange (lf As Double)

■ float

Description: The float data type is used to represent single-precision floating point numbers.

Notes: float values have at least 8 digits of precision.

Signed Range: $-3.4 * 10 ^ 38$ to $3.4 * 10 ^ 38$

■ IDL

Size: 32 bits

TLB Type: VT_R4

Oicf String: 0x0a

Sign: Signed

Automation Compatible: Yes

Examples

- HRESULT Up ([in] float f);
- HRESULT Down ([out,retval] float *pf);
- HRESULT Truth ([in] float *pf);
- HRESULT Strange ([in,out] float *pf);
- HRESULT Beauty ([out] float *pf);

C++

Language Mapping: Float

Examples

- HRESULT Up (float f);
- HRESULT Down (float *pf);
- HRESULT Truth (float *pf);
- HRESULT Strange (float *pf);
- HRESULT Beauty (float *pf);

Visual Basic

Language Mapping: Single

Examples

- Private Sub IQuark_Up (ByVal f As Single)
- Private Function IQuark_Down() As Single
- Private Sub IQuark_Truth (f As Single)
- Private Sub IQuark_Strange (f As Single)

hyper

Description: A 64-bit integer type

Unsigned Range: 0 to 18,446,744,073,709,551,616

Signed Range: -9,223,372,036,854,775,808 to 9,223,372,036,854,775,807

IDL

Size: 64 bits

TLB Type: VT_I8 / VT_UI8

Oicf String: 0x0b

Sign: Either

Notes: hyper and __int64 are synonymous. hyper and signed hyper are synonymous.

Examples

- HRESULT Up ([in] hyper h);
- HRESULT Down ([out,retval] hyper *ph);

- HRESULT Truth ([in] hyper *ph);
- HRESULT Strange ([in,out] hyper *ph);
- HRESULT Beauty ([out] hyper *ph);

■ C++

Language Mapping: Hyper
Underlying Typedef: __int64

Examples

- HRESULT Up (hyper h);
- HRESULT Down (hyper *ph);
- HRESULT Truth (hyper *ph);
- HRESULT Strange (hyper *ph);
- HRESULT Beauty (hyper *ph);

■ Visual Basic

Language Mapping: None

■ int

Description: An integer type whose size is fixed in IDL but whose size in C++ is platform dependent

Notes: Because of the change in size across platforms, int data types should be avoided. Specific sized types such as small, short, long, or hyper should be used instead.

■ IDL

Size: 32 bits
TLB Type: VT_INT / VT_UINT
Oicf String: 0x08
Sign: Either
Automation Compatible: Yes
Notes: int and signed int are synonymous. The Oicf string for IDL int and long are the same.

Examples

- HRESULT Up ([in] int i);
- HRESULT Down ([out,retval] int *pi);
- HRESULT Truth ([in] int *pi);
- HRESULT Strange ([in,out] int *pi);
- HRESULT Beauty ([out] int *pi);

■ C++

Language Mapping: Int

Notes: The int data type does not have a fixed size in C++ and may change from platform to platform.

Examples

- `HRESULT Up ( int i );`
- `HRESULT Down ( int *pi );`
- `HRESULT Truth ( int *pi );`
- `HRESULT Strange ( int *pi );`
- `HRESULT Beauty ( int *pi );`

■ Visual Basic

Language Mapping: Long

Notes: No mapping is available for the unsigned int type.

Examples

- `Private Sub IQuark_Up ( ByVal f As Long )`
- `Private Function IQuark_Down() As Long`
- `Private Sub IQuark_Truth ( f As Long )`
- `Private Sub IQuark_Strange ( f As Long )`

■ __int64

Description: A 64-bit integer type

Unsigned Range: 0 to 18,446,744,073,709,551,616

Signed Range: -9,223,372,036,854,775,808
to 9,223,372,036,854,775,807

■ IDL

Size: 64 bits

TLB Type: VT_I8 / VT_UI8

Oicf String: 0x0b

Sign: Either

Automation Compatible: Yes

Notes: __int64 and hyper are synonymous. __int64 and signed __int64 are synonymous.

Examples

- `HRESULT Up ( [in] __int64 i );`
- `HRESULT Down ( [out,retval] __int64 *pi );`
- `HRESULT Truth ( [in] __int64 *pi );`
- `HRESULT Strange ( [in,out] __int64 *pi );`
- `HRESULT Beauty ( [out] __int64 *pi );`

■ C++

Language Mapping: __int64

Examples

- `HRESULT Up ( __int64 i );`
- `HRESULT Down ( __int64 *pi );`
- `HRESULT Truth ( __int64 *pi );`
- `HRESULT Strange ( __int64 *pi );`
- `HRESULT Beauty ( __int64 *pi );`

■ Visual Basic

Language Mapping: None

■ long

Description: A 32-bit integer type

Unsigned Range: 0 to 4,294,967,295

Signed Range: -2,147,483,648 to 2,147,483,647

■ IDL

Size: 32 bits

TLB Type: VT_I4 / VT_UI4

Oicf String: 0x08

Sign: Either

Notes: `long` and `signed long` are synonymous.

Examples

- `HRESULT Up ( [in] long l );`
- `HRESULT Down ( [out,retval] long *pl );`
- `HRESULT Truth ( [in] long *pl );`
- `HRESULT Strange ( [in,out] long *pl );`
- `HRESULT Beauty ( [out] long *pl );`

■ C++

Language Mapping: Long

Examples

- `HRESULT Up ( long l );`
- `HRESULT Down ( long *pl );`
- `HRESULT Truth ( long *pl );`
- `HRESULT Strange ( long *pl );`
- `HRESULT Beauty ( long *pl );`

■ Visual Basic

Language Mapping: Long

Notes: The IDL `long` and `signed long` types produce the same mapping. No mapping is available for the `unsigned long` type.

Examples
- `Private Sub IQuark_Up ( ByVal f As Long )`
- `Private Function IQuark_Down() As Long`
- `Private Sub IQuark_Truth ( f As Long )`
- `Private Sub IQuark_Strange ( f As Long )`

■ short

Description: A 16-bit integer type
Unsigned Range: 0 to 65,535
Signed Range: -32,768 to 32,767

■ IDL

Size: 16 bits
TLB Type: VT_I2 / VT_UI2
Oicf String: 0x06
Sign: Either
Automation Compatible: Yes
Notes: `short` and `signed short` are synonymous.

Examples
- `HRESULT Up ( [in] short s );`
- `HRESULT Down ( [out,retval] short *ps );`
- `HRESULT Truth ( [in] short *ps );`
- `HRESULT Strange ( [in,out] short *ps );`
- `HRESULT Beauty ( [out] short *ps );`

■ C++

Language Mapping: Short

Examples
- `HRESULT Up ( short s );`
- `HRESULT Down ( short *ps );`
- `HRESULT Truth ( short *ps );`
- `HRESULT Strange ( short *ps );`
- `HRESULT Beauty ( short *ps );`

■ Visual Basic

Language Mapping:　Integer

Notes:　The IDL `short` and `signed` `short` types produce the same mapping. No mapping is available for the `unsigned` `short` type.

Examples

- `Private Sub IQuark_Up ( ByVal s As Integer )`
- `Private Function IQuark_Down() As Integer`
- `Private Sub IQuark_Truth ( s As Integer )`
- `Private Sub IQuark_Strange ( s As Integer )`

■ small

Description:　An 8-bit integer type

Unsigned Range:　0 to 255

Signed Range:　-128 to 127

■ IDL

Size:　8 bits

TLB Type:　VT_I1 / VT_UI1

Oicf String:　0x03

Sign:　Either

Automation Compatible:　Yes

Notes:　`small` and `signed` `small` are synonymous.

Examples

- `HRESULT Up ( [in] small s );`
- `HRESULT Down ( [out,retval] small *ps );`
- `HRESULT Truth ( [in] small *ps );`
- `HRESULT Strange ( [in,out] small *ps );`
- `HRESULT Beauty ( [out] small *ps );`

■ C++

Language Mapping:　Small

Underlying Typedef:　Char

Examples

- `HRESULT Up ( small s );`
- `HRESULT Down ( small *ps );`
- `HRESULT Truth ( small *ps );`
- `HRESULT Strange ( small *ps );`
- `HRESULT Beauty ( small *ps );`

■ Visual Basic

Language Mapping: Byte

Notes: No mapping is available for the IDL `small` or `signed small` types. `unsigned small` produces the same mapping as `byte`, q.v.

■ void

Description: The `void` data type is used as a return type when a method returns no value. It is also used as a pointer type to data of unknown type.

■ IDL

Size: None

TLB Type: VT_VOID

Oicf String: None

Sign: Not applicable

Automation Compatible: Yes

Notes: The `void` type, in both return type and pointer form, can be used only in interfaces marked with the `[local]` attribute, q.v.

Examples

- `void Up();`
- `HRESULT Truth ( [in] void* pv );`
- `HRESULT Strange ( [in,out] void* pv );`
- `HRESULT Beauty ( [out] void* pv );`

■ C++

Language Mapping: Void

Examples

- `void Up();`
- `HRESULT Truth ( void* pv );`
- `HRESULT Strange ( void* pv );`
- `HRESULT Beauty ( void* pv );`

■ Visual Basic

Language Mapping: None

■ wchar_t

Description: The `wchar_t` data type is used to represent 16-bit characters.

Notes: Conversion from one character representation to another may occur at transmission time. `wchar_t` is the preferred character type for COM interfaces.

■ IDL

Size: 16 bits
TLB Type: VT_UI2
Oicf String: 0x05
Sign: unsigned
Automation Compatible: Yes
Notes: The wchar_t data type is usually used for passing character strings where it is qualified with the [string] attribute, q.v. When passing character strings through oleautomation or script interfaces or for compatiblity with Java or Visual Basic, use BSTR.

Examples

- HRESULT Up ([in] wchar_t wc);
- HRESULT Down ([out,retval] wchar_t *pwc);
- HRESULT Truth ([in] wchar_t *pwc);
- HRESULT Strange ([in,out] wchar_t *pwc);
- HRESULT Beauty ([out] wchar_t *pwc);

■ C++

Language Mapping: Wchar_t
Underlying Typedef: Unsigned short

Examples

- HRESULT Up (wchar_t wc);
- HRESULT Down (wchar_t *pwc);
- HRESULT Truth (wchar_t *pwc);
- HRESULT Strange (wchar_t *pwc);
- HRESULT Beauty (wchar_t *pwc);

■ Visual Basic

Language Mapping: None

■ BSTR

Description: A 16-bit character string type
Notes: The length of a BSTR, in bytes, is stored immediately before the character data in memory. BSTRs are null terminated and may contain embedded null characters.

■ IDL

Size: 4 bytes
TLB Type: VT_BSTR

Oicf String: 0xb4 0x83 0x00 0x04 0x00 0x12/0x13 0x00 0x17 0x03 0x08 0x1b 0x01 0x01 0x09 0x00 0xfffc 0x06 0x5b 0x08 0x08 0x5c 0x5b 0x00

Sign: Not applicable

Automation Compatible: Yes

Examples

- `HRESULT Up ( [in] BSTR bstr );`
- `HRESULT Down ( [out,retval] BSTR* pbstr );`
- `HRESULT Truth ( [in] BSTR* pbstr );`
- `HRESULT Strange ( [in, out] BSTR* pbstr );`
- `HRESULT Beauty ( [out] BSTR* pbstr );`

■ C++

Language Mapping: BSTR

Underlying Typedef: Wchar_t*

Notes: The typedef to `wchar_t*` is unfortunate, because it means that any wide character string can be passed where a BSTR is expected. Because wide character strings are not length prefixed, the odds of the 4 bytes immediately preceding the string containing the correct value are 1 in 2^{32}.

Examples

- `HRESULT Up ( BSTR bstr );`
- `HRESULT Down ( BSTR* pbstr );`
- `HRESULT Truth ( BSTR* pbstr );`
- `HRESULT Strange ( BSTR* pbstr );`
- `HRESULT Beauty ( BSTR* pbstr );`

■ Visual Basic

Language Mapping: String

Examples

- `Private Sub IQuark_Up ( ByVal s As String )`
- `Private Function IQuark_Down() As String`
- `Private Sub IQuark_Truth ( s As String )`
- `Private Sub IQuark_Strange ( s As String )`

■ SAFEARRAY

Description: An `array` type used to describe arrays with an arbitrary number of dimensions

■ IDL

Size: 16 bytes + 8 bytes per dimension

TLB Type: VT_SAFEARRAY

Oicf String: Complex

Sign: Not applicable

Automation Compatible: Yes

Notes: IDL provides three separate ways of declaring a SAFEARRAY. See Chapter 4 for more information on the syntax.

Examples

- `HRESULT Up ( [in] SAFEARRAY(long) sa );`
- `HRESULT Down ( [out,retval] SAFEARRAY(long)* psa );`
- `HRESULT Truth ( [in] SAFEARRAY(long)* psa );`
- `HRESULT Strange ( [in, out] SAFEARRAY(long)* psa );`
- `HRESULT Beauty ( [out] SAFEARRAY(long)* psa );`

■ C++

Language Mapping: SAFEARRAY*

Notes: SAFEARRAY is a structure describing the array and its dimensions. Note that the C++ method signatures have an extra level of indirection and lose the type information.

Examples

- `HRESULT Up ( SAFEARRAY* sa );`
- `HRESULT Down ( SAFEARRAY** psa );`
- `HRESULT Truth ( SAFEARRAY** psa );`
- `HRESULT Strange ( SAFEARRAY** psa );`
- `HRESULT Beauty ( SAFEARRAY** psa );`

■ Visual Basic

Language Mapping: ()

Notes: All array types must be passed by reference.

Examples

- `Private Function IQuark_Down() As Long()`
- `Private Sub IQuark_Truth ( s() As Long )`
- `Private Sub IQuark_Strange ( s() As Long )`

■ VARIANT

Description: A data type capable of representing various different types

Notes: The VARIANT is a discriminated union—that is, a union that knows its own type.

■ IDL

Size: 16 bytes

TLB Type: VT_VARIANT

Oicf String: complex

Sign: Not applicable

Automation Compatible: Yes

Examples

- `HRESULT Up ( [in] VARIANT b );`
- `HRESULT Down ( [out,retval] VARIANT* pb );`
- `HRESULT Truth ( [in] VARIANT* pb );`
- `HRESULT Strange ( [in, out] VARIANT* pb );`
- `HRESULT Beauty ( [out] VARIANT* pb );`

■ C++

Language Mapping: VARIANT

Notes: `VARIANT` is a structure containing a union.

Examples

- `HRESULT Up ( VARIANT b );`
- `HRESULT Down ( VARIANT* pb );`
- `HRESULT Truth ( VARIANT* pb );`
- `HRESULT Strange ( VARIANT* pb );`
- `HRESULT Beauty ( VARIANT* pb );`

■ Visual Basic

Language Mapping: Variant

Examples

- `Private Sub IQuark_Up ( ByVal s As Variant )`
- `Private Function IQuark_Down() As Variant`
- `Private Sub IQuark_Truth ( s As Variant )`
- `Private Sub IQuark_Strange ( s As Variant )`

■ VARIANT_BOOL

Description: The `VARIANT_BOOL` data type is used where only the values true and false are required. True equates to the value -1 and false equates to the value 0.

■ IDL

Size: 16 bits

TLB Type: VT_BOOL

Oicf String: 0x06

Sign: Not applicable

Notes: `VARIANT_BOOL` is the preferred boolean data type for oleautomation interfaces.

Examples

- `HRESULT Up ( [in] VARIANT_BOOL f );`
- `HRESULT Down ( [out,retval] VARIANT_BOOL *pf );`
- `HRESULT Truth ( [in] VARIANT_BOOL *pf );`
- `HRESULT Strange ( [in,out] VARIANT_BOOL *pf );`
- `HRESULT Beauty ( [out] VARIANT_BOOL *pf );`

■ C++

Language Mapping: VARIANT_BOOL

Underlying Typedef: Short

Notes: The constants `VARIANT_TRUE` and `VARIANT_FALSE` should be used when dealing with `VARIANT_BOOL` types.

Examples

- `HRESULT Up ( VARIANT_BOOL f );`
- `HRESULT Down ( VARIANT_BOOL *pf );`
- `HRESULT Truth ( VARIANT_BOOL *pf );`
- `HRESULT Strange ( VARIANT_BOOL *pf );`
- `HRESULT Beauty ( VARIANT_BOOL *pf );`

■ Visual Basic

Language Mapping: Boolean

Examples

- `Private Sub IQuark_Up ( ByVal s As Boolean )`
- `Private Function IQuark_Down() As Boolean`
- `Private Sub IQuark_Truth ( s As Boolean )`
- `Private Sub IQuark_Strange ( s As Boolean )`

Chapter 8

IDL Type Modifiers

This chapter provides a reference for each of the IDL type modifiers. The information for each modifier is divided into several sections. The *Description* and *Notes* fields immediately below the modifier provide a general description of the modifier along with any notable features.

The IDL section includes several fields. The *Type Library* and *Oicf* fields denote whether information about the modifier is present in standard type information and Oicf type information respectively. The *Applies to* field lists the IDL data types and other constructs to which the modifier may be applied. Data types such as `short` or `long` are listed first, followed by other IDL constructs such as `struct`. Example IDL statements are also provided.

The C++ and Visual Basic sections specify in each language whether the modifier is supported. Any notable features about the language support for a modifier are shown in the *Notes* field. Finally, examples are provided in each language where appropriate.

■ const

Description: When applied to a method parameter, the `const` modifier is used to denote that the value of the parameter may not be changed inside the method implementation. For pointer types, the pointer value or the underlying type, or both, may be declared `const`. The `const` modifier may also be used in a typedef statement.

Notes: `[out]` parameters may not be marked `const`, although the pointers to them may be. However, MIDL will not allow `const` pointers for `[out]` parameter declarations, although a typedef can be used as a workaround.

■ IDL

Type Library: No

Oicf: No

Applies to:

boolean	hyper	VARIANT
BSTR	int	VARIANT_BOOL
byte	__int64	wchar_t
char	long	enum
double	short	struct
float	small	union

Examples

- `HRESULT Proton ( [in] const short s );`
  `typedef long * const CPLONG; HRESULT Neutron ( [out] CPLONG pl );`
- `HRESULT Electron ( [in] const VARIANT * const pvt );`
  `typedef const short CSHORT; HRESULT Positron ( [in] CSHORT s );`

■ C++

Supported: Yes

Examples

- `HRESULT Proton ( const short s );`
  `typedef long * const CPLONG; HRESULT Neutron ( CPLONG pl );`
- `HRESULT Electron ( const VARIANT * const pvt );`
  `typedef const short CSHORT; HRESULT Positron ( CSHORT s );`

■ Visual Basic

Supported: No

■ signed

Description: Indicates that an integer data type may contain positive and negative values.

■ IDL

Type Library: Yes

Oicf: No

Automation Compatible: Yes

Applies to:

char	__int64	short
hyper	long	small
int		

Examples

- `HRESULT Proton ( [in] signed char c );`
- `HRESULT Neutron ( [in] signed hyper h );`
- `HRESULT Electron ( [out,retval] signed short* ps );`
- `HRESULT Positron ( [in] signed long l );`

■ C++

Supported: Yes

Examples

- `HRESULT Proton ( signed char c );`
- `HRESULT Neutron ( signed hyper h );`
- `HRESULT Electron ( signed short* ps );`
- `HRESULT Positron ( signed long l );`

■ Visual Basic

Supported: Some

Notes: There is no support for `signed char`, `hyper`, `__int64`, or `small`.

Examples

- `Private Function IParticle_Electron () as Integer`
- `Private Sub IParticle_Positron ( ByVal l as Long )`

■ unsigned

Description: Indicates that an integer data type may contain only positive values.

■ IDL

Type Library: Yes

Oicf: No

Automation Compatible: Yes

Applies to:

char	__int64	short
hyper	long	small
int		

Examples
- `HRESULT Proton ( [in] unsigned __int64 i );`
- `HRESULT Neutron ( [in] unsigned small s );`
- `HRESULT Electron ( [out,retval] unsigned long* pl );`

■ C++

Supported: Yes

Examples
- `HRESULT Proton ( unsigned __int64 i );`
- `HRESULT Neutron ( unsigned small s );`
- `HRESULT Electron ( unsigned long* pl );`

■ Visual Basic

Supported: Some

Notes: There is no support for `unsigned hyper`, `int`, `__int64`, `long`, or `short`. `unsigned char` and `unsigned small` both map to `Byte`.

Example
- `Private Sub IParticle_Neutron ( ByVal s as Byte )`

■ *

Description: `*` indicates that the parameter is a pointer to the specified type.

Notes: `[out]` and `[in,out]` parameters must be pointer types. Unless annotated with the `[size_is]` attribute, q.v., pointer types always point to a single instance of the specified type. Pointer types may have the `[ref]`, `[unique]`, or `[ptr]` attribute, q.v., applied to them.

■ IDL

Type Library: Yes
Oicf: Yes
Automation Compatible: Yes

Applies to:

boolean	hyper	VARIANT
BSTR	int	VARIANT_BOOL
byte	__int64	wchar_t
char	long	enum
double	short	struct
float	small	union

Examples

- `HRESULT Proton ( [in] byte* pb );`
- `HRESULT Neutron ( [in,out] float* pf );`
- `HRESULT Electron ( [out,retval] BSTR* pbstr );`
- `HRESULT Positron ( [in] long lNumElems, [in, size_is`
  `( lNumElems )] long* pData );`

■ C++

Supported: Yes

Examples

- `HRESULT Proton ( byte* pb );`
- `HRESULT Neutron ( float* pf );`
- `HRESULT Electron ( BSTR* pbstr );`
- `HRESULT Positron ( long lNumElems, long* pData );`

■ Visual Basic

Supported: Yes

Notes: Pointer parameters are mapped to `ByRef` parameters.

Examples

- `Private Sub IParticle_Proton ( pb As Byte )`
- `Private Sub IParticle_Neutron ( pf As Single )`
- `Private Function IParticle_Electron() As String`

■ []

Description: Indicates an array of values. When used without a subscript, the array size is defined by another method parameter or structure field through the [`size_is`] attribute, q.v. When a subscript is present, the subscript indicates the number of elements the array can hold.

■ IDL

Type Library: Fixed arrays only

Oicf: Yes

Automation Compatible: Yes

Applies to:

boolean	hyper	VARIANT
BSTR	int	VARIANT_BOOL
byte	__int64	wchar_t
char	long	enum
double	short	struct
float	small	encapsulated union

Examples

- `HRESULT Proton ( [in] double lfElems[128] );`
- `HRESULT Neutron ( [in] hyper hArray[256] );`
- `HRESULT Electron ( [in] VARIANT vtArray[100] );`
- `HRESULT Positron ( [in] long lNumElems, [in, size_is`
  `( lNumElems )] long Data[] );`

▓ C++

Supported: Yes

Examples

- `HRESULT Proton ( double lfElems[128] );`
- `HRESULT Neutron ( hyper hArray[256] );`
- `HRESULT Electron ( VARIANT vtArray[100] );`
- `HRESULT Positron ( long lNumElems, long Data[] );`

▓ Visual Basic

Supported: Some

Notes: Visual Basic can call methods that take conformant arrays but cannot call methods that take fixed arrays.

Chapter 9

IDL Keywords

This chapter provides a reference for each of the IDL keywords. The information for each keyword is divided into several sections. The *Description* and *Notes* fields immediately below the keyword provide a general description of the word along with any notable features.

The IDL section includes several fields. The *Present in TLB* and *Present in Oicf* fields denote whether information about the keyword is present in standard type information and Oicf type information, respectively. The *Notes* field provides further information about using the keyword in IDL. The *Syntax* field shows the outline syntax for using the keyword in IDL. Where the IDL language supports multiple syntaxes, each syntax is shown in a separate *Syntax* field. The *Attributes* field lists the IDL attributes that can be applied to the keyword. Mandatory attributes are listed first in **bold** font. Optional attributes follow in standard typeface. If there are no applicable attributes, the *Attributes* field is omitted. Examples showing IDL usage of the keyword are also provided. Where more than one example is provided, each one is numbered separately.

The C++ and Visual Basic sections provide notes about the mapping of the keyword into the programming language. Finally, examples are provided in each language where appropriate. Where multiple numbered examples are provided in the IDL section, the C++ and Visual Basic examples are numbered accordingly. For instance, a Visual Basic example labeled "Example 2" corresponds to the IDL example labeled "Example 2."

■ coclass

Description: Provides a list of interfaces implemented by a given CLSID, effectively describing the capabilities of the class.

Notes: At least one interface or dispinterface must be listed. One interface or dispinterface may be qualified with the `default` attribute, q.v. Multiple interfaces or dispinterfaces may be qualified with the `source` attribute, q.v. One interface or dispinterface may be qualified with the `default` and `source` attributes. If no interface is qualified with the `default` attribute, the first interface listed is implicitly annotated with the `default` attribute.

■ IDL

Present in TLB: Yes

Present in Oicf: No

Notes: Listing all the interfaces a class implements will provide the most accurate type information to users of the class. Unfortunately, there is no requirement that all interfaces that a class implements be listed in the coclass statement. There is no check performed to ensure that a coclass implements an interface listed in the coclass statement, so it is possible to include interfaces that the class does not implement and leave out interfaces that it does implement.

SYNTAX
```
[
  uuid(...)
  < optional attributes >
]
coclass name
{
  < interface list >
}
```

Attributes:

uuid	helpstring	noncreatable
appobject	helpstringcontext	public
control	hidden	restricted
custom	licensed	version
helpcontext		

Example

```
[
  uuid(A60916EC-BECF-499F-B4C9-4F6C60A6746C)
]
coclass CoParticle
{
  interface IUnknown;
  interface IAtom;
  interface IProton;
  interface INeutron;
}
```

■ C++

Notes: The coclass generates the CLSID constant in the _i.c file and a class with attached UUID in the .h file.

Example

```
// In .h file
class DECLSPEC_UUID
("A60916EC-BECF-499F-B4C9-4F6C60A6746C")
CoParticle;
// In _i.c file
MIDL_DEFINE_GUID
(CLSID, CLSID_CoParticle,
0xA60916EC,0xBECF,0x499F,0xB4,0xC9,0x4F,
0x6C,0x60,0xA6,0x74,0x6C);
```

■ Visual Basic

Notes: No source code is generated from a coclass definition. The coclass may be used as a data type if the type library containing the coclass definition is included in the project references. The default interface will be hidden although still accessible. The name of the coclass may be used in place of the default interface. To prevent the hiding of the default interface, specify IUnknown as the default interface in the coclass.

Example

```
Dim atom as IAtom
Dim proton as IProton
Dim neutron as INeutron
Set atom = New CoParticle
Set neutron = New CoParticle
atom.Split
Set proton = atom
proton.Collide neutron
```

■ const

Description: Declares a constant value that can be referred to elsewhere in the IDL.

■ IDL

Present in TLB: No

Present in Oicf: No

Notes: `const` statements can use any data type. 64-bit `const` values are not supported, so `const` values of type `hyper` or `__int64` must be initialized with 32-, 16-, or 8-bit values. There are no attributes that are applicable to the `const` keyword.

SYNTAX
```
const < type description > < identifier > = < value >
```

Examples

EXAMPLE 1
```
const byte BITE = 240;
```

EXAMPLE 2
```
const char X = 'g';
```

EXAMPLE 3
```
const double InterestRate = 5.25;
```

EXAMPLE 4
```
const wchar_t* Root = L"cdl";
```

EXAMPLE 5
```
const wchar_t LAST = L'Z';
```

■ C++

Notes: IDL `const` statements generate a corresponding `#define` statement in the .h file. The data type is not preserved in the .h file.

Examples

EXAMPLE 1
```
#define BITE ( 240 )
```

EXAMPLE 2
```
#define X ( 0x67 )
```

EXAMPLE 3
```
#define InterestRate ( 5.25 )
```

EXAMPLE 4
```
#define Root ( L"cdl" )
```
EXAMPLE 5
```
#define LAST ( L'Z' )
```

■ Visual Basic

Notes: IDL `const` statements do not appear in the type library and so are not available to Visual Basic.

■ cpp_quote

Description: Inserts a string into the generated header file.

Notes: The string is inserted verbatim; no preprocessor expansion occurs. Use cpp_quote to keep all related definitions together in a single IDL file rather than splitting definitions between an IDL file and a hand-coded header file.

■ IDL

Present in TLB: No

Present in Oicf: No

Notes: `cpp_quote` and `#pragma midl_echo` are equivalent. There are no attributes that are applicable to the `cpp_quote` keyword.

SYNTAX
```
cpp_quote ( "< string >" )
```

Examples

EXAMPLE 1
```
cpp_quote ( "#ifdef __cplusplus" )
cpp_quote ( "typedef const IID& REFIID" )
cpp_quote ( "#else" )
cpp_quote ( "typedef const IID* REFIID" )
cpp_quote ( "#endif // __cplusplus" )
```

EXAMPLE 2
```
cpp_quote ( "STDAPI GetMeAUsefulObject ( /* [out] */
IUnknown**pUnk );" )
```

EXAMPLE 3
```
cpp_quote ( "wchar_t wszPathName[MAX_PATH];" )
```

EXAMPLE 4
```
cpp_quote ( "#define PARTICLE_ERROR_NEGATIVEENERGY 0x80040101" )
cpp_quote ( "#define PARTICLE_ERROR_ANTIMATTER 0x80040102" )
cpp_quote ( "#define PARTICLE_ERROR_COLLISION 0x80040103" )
```

■ C++

Notes: cpp_quote is often used to provide C++ typedefs for IDL data types. It is also used for conditional preprocessing and for providing API definitions that are related to the interfaces being defined. Constants that are needed at the language level but not by the IDL are also defined using cpp_quote.

Examples

EXAMPLE 1
```
#ifdef __cplusplus
typedef const IID& REFIID
#else
typedef const IID* REFIID
#endif // __cplusplus
```

EXAMPLE 2
```
STDAPI GetMeAUsefulObject ( /* [out] */ IUnknown**pUnk );
```

EXAMPLE 3
```
wchar_t wszPathName[MAX_PATH];
```

EXAMPLE 4
```
#define PARTICLE_ERROR_NEGATIVEENERGY 0x80040101
#define PARTICLE_ERROR_ANTIMATTER 0x80040102
#define PARTICLE_ERROR_COLLISION 0x80040103
```

■ Visual Basic

Notes: cpp_quote contributes nothing to the type library, and so anything defined in a cpp_quote is not available to Visual Basic.

■ dispinterface

Description: Defines a dispatch interface, a set of methods and properties that can be called through IDispatch.

IDL

Present in TLB: Yes

Present in Oicf: No

Notes: There are two supported syntaxes for defining dispinterfaces in IDL. The second syntax presented here is a shorthand for the first.

SYNTAX 1
```
[
  uuid(...)
  <optional attributes>
]
```

```
dispinterface name
{
  properties:
    list of properties
  methods:
    list of methods
};
```

SYNTAX 2

```
[
  uuid(...)
  <optional attributes>
]
dispinterface name
{
  interface name;
}
```

Attributes:

uuid	helpstring	public
custom	helpstringcontext	restricted
helpcontext	hidden	version

Examples

EXAMPLE 1

```
[
  uuid(0DF40898-90F6-4b06-9B75-45F4289D9F32)
]
dispinterface _Quark
{
  properties:
    [id(0x00001001)] long Spin;
    [id(0x00001002)] BSTR Name;
  methods:
    [id(0x00002001)] void Collide();
};
```

EXAMPLE 2

```
[
  uuid(C1923E37-1793-4d4f-B74F-2ABC4EF265FB),
  object
]
interface IQuark : IUnknown
{
  [id(0x00001001), propput] HRESULT Spin ( [in] long Spin );
  [id(0x00001001), propget] HRESULT Spin ( [out,retval]
long* pSpin );
```

```
    [id(0x00001002), propput] HRESULT Name ( [in] BSTR Name );
    [id(0x00001002), propget] HRESULT Name ( [out,retval] BSTR*
pName );
    [id(0x00002001)] HRESULT Collide();
  }
  [
    uuid(0DF40898-90F6-4b06-9B75-45F4289D9F32)
  ]
  dispinterface _Quark
  {
    interface IQuark;
  }
```

■ C++

Notes: A pure dispinterface generates only the associated GUID, because there is no v-table to describe. A dispinterface based on a v-table interface generates GUIDs for both the dispinterface and the v-table interface. The v-table layout for the v-table interface is also generated. In both cases, the dispinterface GUID can be used to locate the type information for that interface in the appropriate type library.

Examples

EXAMPLE 1

```
// .h file
MIDL_INTERFACE("0DF40898-90F6-4b06-9B75-45F4289D9F32")
_Quark : public IDispatch
{
};
// _i.c file
MIDL_DEFINE_GUID(IID, DIID__Quark,0x0df40898, 0x90f6, 0x4b06,
0x9b, 0x75, 0x45, 0xf4, 0x28, 0x9d, 0x9f, 0x32);
```

EXAMPLE 2

```
// .h file
MIDL_INTERFACE("C1923E37-1793-4d4f-B74F-2ABC4EF265FB")
IQuark : public IUnknown
{
public:
  virtual HRESULT STDMETHODCALLTYPE put_Spin( long Spin) = 0;
  virtual HRESULT STDMETHODCALLTYPE get_Spin( long *pSpin) = 0;
  virtual HRESULT STDMETHODCALLTYPE put_Name( BSTR Name) = 0;
  virtual HRESULT STDMETHODCALLTYPE get_Name( BSTR *pName) = 0;
  virtual HRESULT STDMETHODCALLTYPE Collide( void) = 0;
};
```

```
// _i.c file
MIDL_DEFINE_GUID
(IID, IID_IQuark,0xC1923E37,0x1793,0x4d4f,
0xB7,0x4F,0x2A,0xBC,0x4E,0xF2,0x65,0xFB);
MIDL_DEFINE_GUID
(IID, DIID__Quark,0x0DF40898,0x90F6,0x4b06,
0x9B,0x75,0x45,0xF4,0x28,0x9D,0x9F,0x32);
```

■ Visual Basic

Notes: A pure dispinterface generates no definitions visible to the Visual Basic IDE. For a dispinterface based on a v-table interface, the v-table interface is visible to the IDE. To use the dispinterface from Visual Basic, use a variable of type `Object` when accessing the COM component that implements the dispinterface.

■ enum

Description: Defines an enumerated type. The enumerated type can be used as a method argument or a field in a structure. Enumerated types can also be part of a typedef.

Notes: Enumerated types are 32-bit values.

■ IDL

Present in TLB: Yes

Present in Oicf: 0x0e

Notes: Unless the `[v1_enum]` attribute is specifed, enumerated types are transmitted on the wire as 16-bit values. Consequently, `[v1_enum]` should usually be specified.

```
SYNTAX
[
  <optional attributes>
]
enum name
{
  <symbol1> = <value1>,
  <symbol2> = <value2>
};
```

Attributes:

custom	helpstringcontext	v1_enum
helpcontext	hidden	
helpstring	uuid	

Examples

EXAMPLE 1

```
[
  uuid(B8B3D81E-65B6-46B5-9885-9487D44133EC),
   v1_enum
]
enum QUARK
{
  UP = -1,
  DOWN = 1,
  STRANGE,
  BEAUTY
};
```

EXAMPLE 2

```
[
  uuid(A758E355-63ED-4FF9-A2F8-EFA40B09A3B6)
]
struct Q1
{
  long l;
  enum QUARK q;
};
```

■ C++

Notes: IDL enumerated types are mapped to C++ enumerated types. The c++ enum is tagged with the uuid if present.

Examples

EXAMPLE 1

```
enum DECLSPEC_UUID("B8B3D81E-65B6-46B5-9885-9487D44133EC") QUARK
{
  UP = -1,
  DOWN = 1,
  STRANGE = DOWN + 1,
  BEAUTY = STRANGE + 1
};
```

EXAMPLE 2

```
struct DECLSPEC_UUID("A758E355-63ED-4FF9-A2F8-EFA40B09A3B6") Q1
{
  long l;
  enum QUARK q;
};
```

■ Visual Basic

Notes: An enumerated type produces no syntax in Visual Basic but may be used as a global variable, a local variable, a method parameter, or a field for a user-defined type.

Example

```
Public Type Q2
l As Long
q As QUARK
End Type
```

■ import

Description: The `import` statement brings in the contents of another IDL file. The interfaces, typedefs, and other definitions in the imported IDL file may then be referenced in the importing IDL file.

Notes: Using `import` will bring in the imported IDL but will not regenerate the marshaling code for the imported IDL. This is the opposite of using `#include`. The `import` statement uses the current directory followed by the `INCLUDE` environment variable to resolve filenames.

■ IDL

Present in TLB: Special

Present in Oicf: Not applicable

Notes: The `import` statement may appear anywhere in an IDL file. Because of the way IDL files are parsed by the compiler, an IDL file need not appear before the use of a type defined within it. Note also that included interfaces referenced in the library block will be redefined in that type library. The `import` statement must be terminated with a semicolon. There are no attributes that are applicable to the `import` keyword.

SYNTAX

```
import "idlfilename";
```

Examples

EXAMPLE 1

```
import "objidl.idl";
```

EXAMPLE 2

```
[
  uuid(682A3DBB-E210-44B3-9D9C-392953836EFF),
  object,
  pointer_default(unique)
]
interface IFoo : IBar
{
  import "bar.idl";
  HRESULT SomeMethod ( [in] short s );
}
```

■ C++

Notes: An `import` statement in an IDL file is translated to a `#include` statement in the corresponding C++ header file. The `.idl` extension is replaced with a `.h` extension.

Examples

EXAMPLE 1
```
#include "objidl.h"
```

EXAMPLE 2
```
/* header files for imported files */
#include "bar.h"
MIDL_INTERFACE("682A3DBB-E210-44B3-9D9C-392953836EFF")
IFoo : public IBar
{
public:
  virtual HRESULT STDMETHODCALLTYPE SomeMethod ( /* [in] */ short
s) = 0;
  };
```

■ Visual Basic

Notes: The `import` keyword has no effect on the Visual Basic mapping, except that imported interface definitions subsequently referenced in a library block will be present in that type library.

■ importlib

Description: The `importlib` statement brings in the contents of another type library. The interfaces, typedefs, and other definitions in the imported type library may then be referenced in the importing type library.

■ IDL

Present in TLB: Yes

Present in Oicf: No

Notes: A library block should always use the `importlib` keyword to bring in the system types defined in `stdole2.tlb`. This type library includes the definitions of `IUnknown` and `IDispatch`, among others. Using `importlib` to bring in type definitions ensures that only references to the imported types appear in the generated type library. There are no attributes that are applicable to the `importlib` keyword.

SYNTAX

```
importlib ( "tlbfilename" );
```

Examples

EXAMPLE 1

```
[
  uuid(14F1DFB9-AE1E-4F83-8A9D-9A4A3EDB50F5)
]
library ParticleLib
{
  importlib ( "stdole2.tlb" );
  [
    object,
    uuid(EACEE091-A173-4ED1-B659-C3E476E38246),
    pointer_default(unique)
  ]
  interface IQuark : IUnknown
  {
    [propput] HRESULT Spin ( [in] long Spin );
    [propget] HRESULT Spin ( [out,retval] long*pSpin);
    [propput] HRESULT Name ( [in] BSTR Name );
    [propget] HRESULT Name ( [out,retval] BSTR*pName );
    HRESULT Collide();
  }
}
```

EXAMPLE 2

```
[
  uuid(38A8FC07-4A92-484C-9B10-074994F20ADE)
]
library ParserLib
{
```

```
      importlib ( "stdole2.tlb" );
      importlib ( "msxml.dll" );
      [
        object,
        uuid(1889F73B-ADC5-4562-BE8A-EAACBBE973F1),
        pointer_default(unique)
      ]
      interface IParser : IUnknown
      {
        HRESULT AddNode ( [in] BSTR bstrName, [in] IXMLDOMNode*
  pNode );
        HRESULT GetNode ( [in] BSTR bstrName, [out,retval]
  IXMLDOMNode** ppNode );
      }
    }
```

■ C++

Notes: `importlib` generates no output in the C++ files.

■ Visual Basic

Notes: The `importlib` keyword has no effect on the Visual Basic mapping.

■ include

Description: The `include` statement brings in the contents of another file, either an IDL file or a C source file.

Notes: Using `#include` to bring in an IDL file will regenerate the marshaling code for the included IDL. This is the opposite of using import. The `#include` statement uses the current directory followed by the INCLUDE environment variable to resolve filenames.

■ IDL

Present in TLB: No

Present in Oicf: No

Notes: The `#include` statement may appear anywhere in an IDL file. Because of the way IDL files are parsed by the compiler, an included IDL file must appear before any references are made to the types defined within it. This is in contrast to using the import keyword to bring in the contents of an IDL file. Note also that included interfaces referenced in the library block will be redefined in that type library. There are no attributes that are applicable to the `include` keyword.

```
#include "filename"
```
Example
```
#include "mtxattr.h"
```

■ C++

Notes: The contents of the included file will be present verbatim in the generated C/C++ header file. Consequently, there will be no corresponding `#include` statement in the generated header file.

■ Visual Basic

Notes: The `include` keyword has no effect on the Visual Basic mapping, except that included interface definitions subsequently referenced in a library block will be present in that type library.

■ interface

Description: Defines an interface, a set of related methods, and/or properties that are callable through a v-table.

■ IDL

Present in TLB: Yes

Present in Oicf: Yes

Notes: An interface must have a base interface from which it derives. This base interface must be `IUnknown` or an interface that has `IUnknown` in its interface hierarchy. All methods in an interface must have unique names. Although the `[object]` and `[pointer_default]` keywords are not mandatory, it is good practice to use both attributes with all interface definitions.

SYNTAX
```
[
  uuid(...)
  <optional attributes>
]
interface name : derivedname
{
  <methods>
}
```

Attributes:

uuid	helpstringcontext	oleautomation
async_uuid	hidden	pointer_default
custom	local	public
dual	nonextensible	restricted
helpcontext	object	version
helpstring		

Examples

EXAMPLE 1

```
[
  uuid(B86E30AF-FDFA-4DA0-855D-6F8AD98D6F0D),
  object,
  pointer_default(unique)
]
interface IAtomSmasher : IUnknown
{
  HRESULT SmashAtom ( [in] IAtom* pAtom );
}
```

EXAMPLE 2

```
[
  uuid(54910FB3-D4E5-4A84-898F-AF7054AC1498),
  object,
  pointer_default(unique)
]
interface IAtomSmasher2 : IAtomSmasher
{
  HRESULT SmashTwoAtoms ( [in] IAtom* pAtom1, [in] IAtom*
pAtom2, [out,retval] IParticle** ppResult );
}
```

■ C++

Notes: IDL interface definitions map to C++ abstract classes. The MIDL_INTERFACE macro expands to struct __declspec(uuid(x)) __declspec (novtable).

Examples

EXAMPLE 1

```
MIDL_INTERFACE("B86E30AF-FDFA-4DA0-855D-6F8AD98D6F0D")
IAtomSmasher : public IUnknown
{
```

```
public:
   virtual HRESULT STDMETHODCALLTYPE SmashAtom ( /* [in] */
IAtom __RPC_FAR *pAtom) = 0;
};
```

EXAMPLE 2
```
MIDL_INTERFACE("54910FB3-D4E5-4A84-898F-AF7054AC1498")
IAtomSmasher2 : public IAtomSmasher
{
public:
   virtual HRESULT STDMETHODCALLTYPE SmashTwoAtoms ( /* [in]
*/ IAtom __RPC_FAR *pAtom1, /* [in] */ IAtom __RPC_FAR
*pAtom2, /* [retval][out] */ IParticle __RPC_FAR *__RPC_FAR
*ppResult) = 0;
};
```

■ Visual Basic

Notes: The interface keyword produces no source code in Visual Basic. However, the Implements keyword can be used to specify that a class implements a particular interface definition. Visual Basic can implement only interfaces that derive directly from IUnknown or IDispatch.

Examples

EXAMPLE 1
```
' .cls file
Implements IAtomSmasher
Private Sub IAtomSmasher_SmashAtom(ByVal pAtom As
NuclearPhysicsLib.IAtom)
   End Sub
```

■ interface (in coclass statement or forward declaration)

Description: Used to specify that a coclass implements a given interface or supports a given interface as an event sink. Also used to forward declare an interface within an IDL file.

■ IDL

Present in TLB: Yes

Present in Oicf: No

Notes: There is no compile time or runtime check to ensure that the class implements the interfaces listed in the coclass statement.

SYNTAX 1

```
[
  uuid(...)
  < optional attributes >
]
coclass name
{
  < optional attributes > interface itfname;
}
```

SYNTAX 2

```
interface itfname;
```

Attributes:

default

source

Examples

EXAMPLE 1

```
[
  uuid(A60916EC-BECF-499F-B4C9-4F6C60A6746C)
]
coclass CoParticle
{
  interface IUnknown;
  interface IAtom;
  interface IProton;
  interface INeutron;
}
```

EXAMPLE 2

```
interface IXMLDOMNode;
```

■ C++

Notes: Use of the `interface` keyword within a coclass generates no extra information over the `coclass` keyword.

Examples

EXAMPLE 1

```
// In .h file
class DECLSPEC_UUID
("A60916EC-BECF-499F-B4C9-4F6C60A6746C")
CoParticle;
// In _i.c file
MIDL_DEFINE_GUID
(CLSID, CLSID_CoParticle,0xA60916EC,0xBECF,0x499F,
0xB4,0xC9,0x4F,0x6C,0x60,0xA6,0x74,0x6C);
```

■ Visual Basic

Notes: Use of the `interface` keyword adds that interface to the type library, making the interface available to Visual Basic. The default interface will be hidden although still accessible. The name of the coclass may be used in place of the default interface. To prevent the hiding of the default interface, specify `IUnknown` as the default interface in the coclass.

Examples

EXAMPLE 1

```
Dim atom as IAtom
Dim proton as IProton
Dim neutron as INeutron
Set atom = New CoParticle
Set neutron = New CoParticle
atom.Split
Set proton = atom
proton.Collide neutron
```

■ library

Description: Declares a library block. The contents of the library block will be output to a type library.

■ IDL

Present in TLB: Yes

Present in Oicf: No

Notes: Only one library block may appear in a given IDL file. While the `[version]` attribute is not mandatory, it is good practice to provide one. If a `[version]` attribute is not provided, a default version of 0.0 will be used. All library blocks should reference `stdole2.tlb` through the `importlib` keyword.

SYNTAX

```
[
  uuid(...)
  <other attributes>
]
library libname
{
  importlib ( "stdole2.tlb" );
}
```

Attributes:

uuid	helpstring	lcid
custom	helpstringcontext	restricted
helpcontext	helpstringdll	version
helpfile	hidden	

Example
```
[
  uuid(BC72343C-9B2C-4CC5-BA6F-02695367F772),
  version(1.0)
]
library ParticleLib
{
  importlib("stdole2.tlb");
}
```

■ C++

Notes: The library block does not produce any C++ code, but only the GUID constant for the uuid.

Example
```
// In .h file
EXTERN_C const IID LIBID_ArrayLib;
// In _i.c file
MIDL_DEFINE_GUID
(IID, LIBID_ArrayLib,0xBC72343C,0x9B2C,0x4CC5,
0xBA,0x6F,0x02,0x69,0x53,0x67,0xF7,0x72);
```

■ Visual Basic

Notes: The library block does not generate any Visual Basic code, but the resulting type library can be brought in using the Project, References dialog. Interfaces, coclasses, and other data types defined in the type library can then be used in Visual Basic, either on the client side or as part of a component implementation.

■ midl_pragma warning

Description: Allows MIDL compiler warnings to be disabled, enabled, or returned to the default state.

■ IDL

Present in TLB: No
Present in Oicf: No

Notes: There are no attributes that apply to `midl_pragma` warning.

SYNTAX
```
midl_pragma warning ( disable | enable | default: msgid1 msgid2 ... )
```

Examples

EXAMPLE 1
```
midl_pragma warning ( disable: 2347 )
```

EXAMPLE 2
```
midl_pragma warning ( disable: 2072 2347 )
```

■ C++

Notes: `midl_pragma` generates no C++ source code.

■ Visual Basic

Notes: `midl_pragma` has no effect on the Visual Basic mapping.

■ module

Description: The `module` statement is used to describe a group of typed constants and functions. The functions are typically those exported from a DLL.

■ IDL

Present in TLB: Yes

Present in Oicf: No

Notes: The `[dllname]` attribute is required if function declarations appear in the module definition. `module` statements containing only constant declarations are not required to have a `[dllname]` attribute.

SYNTAX
```
[
  dllname ( "<filename>" )
  <other attributes>
]
module modulename
{
  <constant declaration>
  <function declaration>
}
```

Attributes:

dllname	helpfile
uuid	helpstring
helpcontext	hidden

Examples

EXAMPLE 1

```
[
  dllname("pca.dll"),
  uuid(75FB8FA8-B87C-44A1-BCAA-2F2CE415F540)
]
module pca
{
  [entry(1)] HRESULT _stdcall
  CoCreateChannelProxy ( [in] BSTR progid,
      [in] BSTR transportProgId,
      [out,retval] IUnknown**ppUnk );
  [entry(2)] HRESULT _stdcall
  CoCreateChannelPlayer ( [in] BSTR transportId,
      [out,retval] IUnknown**ppUnk );
}
```

EXAMPLE 2

```
module atom
{
  unsigned long const SPIN = -1;
  unsigned long const PARTICLE = 1;
  unsigned short const DOWN = -1;
  unsigned short const UP = 1;
  unsigned short const TRUTH = 2;
  unsigned short const BEAUTY = 3;
  unsigned short const STRANGE = 4;
}
```

◼ C++

Notes: Any functions declared in a module statement will have a corresponding function prototype in the generated header file. Module statements also provide a way of declaring typed constants. The resulting constants are present in the generated type library and in any generated header file.

Examples

EXAMPLE 1

```
HRESULT _stdcall
CoCreateChannelProxy ( BSTR progid,
    BSTR transportProgId,
    IUnknown**ppUnk );
HRESULT _stdcall
CoCreateChannelPlayer ( BSTR transportId,
    IUnknown**ppUnk );
```

EXAMPLE 2

```
const unsigned long SPIN = -1;
const unsigned long PARTICLE = 1;
const unsigned short DOWN = -1;
const unsigned short UP = 1;
const unsigned short TRUTH = 2;
const unsigned short BEAUTY = 3;
const unsigned short STRANGE = 4;
```

◾ Visual Basic

Notes: The constants and functions declared in a module statement are available to Visual Basic through the type library.

Examples

EXAMPLE 1

```
Dim prx As IUnknown
Set prx = pca.CoCreateChannelProxy ( "TestBed.Duvet",
"Transport.MSMQ" )
Dim plyr As IUnknown
Set plyr = pca.CoCreateChannelPlayer ( "Transport.MSMQ" )
```

EXAMPLE 2

```
Dim q1 As Integer
q1 = DOWN
Dim q2 As Integer
q2 = STRANGE
Dim s As Long
s = SPIN
```

◾ pragma

Description: The #pragma directive is used to pass the pragma to the C preprocessor. The only exception is #pragma midl_echo, which is identical to the cpp_quote in function.

◾ IDL

Present in TLB: No

Present in Oicf: Yes

Notes: The use of #pragma pack to specify structure alignment is reflected in the compiled proxy-stub DLL. Because no alignment information is present in the type library, use of alignment values other than the default (8) should be avoided. There are no attributes that apply to midl_pragma warning.

```
#pragma <tokens>
```

SYNTAX 2

```
#pragma midl_echo ( "output string" )
```

Examples

EXAMPLE 1

```
// This is passed through to the C preprocessor
#pragma optimize ( "agp", on )
```

EXAMPLE 2

```
// This is equivalent to:
// cpp_quote ( "#define _WIN32_WINNT 0x0500" )
#pragma midl_echo ( "#define _WIN32_WINNT 0x0500" )
```

EXAMPLE 3

```
// Avoid using this
#pragma pack (4)
```

▨ C++

Notes: With the exception of #pragma midl_echo, all pragmas are passed through to the C/C++ preprocessor.

Examples

EXAMPLE 1

```
// This is passed through to the C preprocessor
#pragma optimize ( "agp", on )
```

EXAMPLE 2

```
// This is equivalent to:
// cpp_quote ( "#define _WIN32_WINNT 0x0500" )
#define _WIN32_WINNT 0x0500
```

EXAMPLE 3

```
// Avoid using this
#pragma pack (4)
```

▨ Visual Basic

Notes: #pragma directives are not present in the type library and so are not visible to Visual Basic. Because of this, #pragma pack should be avoided.

■ struct

Description: The struct keyword is used to define a new compound data type. It is also used when referencing a compound type as a parameter or structure field.

▪ IDL

Present in TLB: Yes

Present in Oicf: Yes

SYNTAX

```
[
  attributes
]
struct <structname>
{
  <fields>
}
```

Attributes:

uuid

custom

hidden

restricted

Examples

EXAMPLE 1

```
[
  uuid(8CDDE2C2-48D9-4C65-94D2-E463E65414C6)
]
struct Point
{
  long x;
  long y;
};
```

EXAMPLE 2

```
struct Rect
{
  struct Point topleft;
  struct Point bottomright;
};
```

EXAMPLE 3

```
[
  uuid(5FDB3666-2CBD-468F-8A93-27B2DC83276E),
  object
]
```

```
interface IPlot : IUnknown
{
  HRESULT TakeAPoint ( [in] struct *pPoint );
  HRESULT TakeARect ( [in] struct *pRect );
}
```

■ C++

Notes: The IDL `struct` keyword maps directly to the C/C++ `struct` keyword.

Examples

EXAMPLE 1
```
struct DECLSPEC_UUID("8CDDE2C2-48D9-4C65-94D2-E463E65414C6")
Point
{
  long x;
  long y;
};
```

EXAMPLE 2
```
struct Rect
{
  struct Point topleft;
  struct Point topright;
};
```

EXAMPLE 3
```
MIDL_INTERFACE("5FDB3666-2CBD-468F-8A93-27B2DC83276E")
IPlot : public IUnknown
{
  virtual HRESULT STDMETHODCALLTYPE TakeAPoint ( struct
Point *pPoint ) = 0;
  virtual HRESULT STDMETHODCALLTYPE TakeARect ( struct Rect*
pRect ) = 0;
};
```

EXAMPLE 4
```
Point pt;
pt.x = 10;
pt.y = 20;
pPlot->TakeAPoint ( &pt );
```

EXAMPLE 5
```
Rect* pRect = new Rect();
pRect->topleft.x = 10;
pRect->topleft.y = 20;
pRect->bottomright.x = 50;
pRect->bottomright.y = 70;
pPlot->TakeARect ( pRect );
```

■ Visual Basic

Notes: IDL `struct` definitions are represented as user-defined types in Visual Basic. A `struct` that appears in a type library can be used in Visual Basic. Visual Basic does not support passing of user-defined types by value; all user defined types must be passed by reference.

Examples

EXAMPLE 1
```
Implements IPlot
Private Sub IPlot_TakeAPoint(ByRef pPoint As Point)
End Sub
Private Sub IPlot_TakeARect(ByRef pRect As Rect)
End Sub
```

EXAMPLE 2
```
Dim pt As Point
pt.x = 10
pt.y = 20
pPlot.TakeAPoint pt
```

EXAMPLE 3
```
Dim rt As Rect
rt.topleft.x = 10
rt.topleft.y = 20
rt.bottomright.x = 50
rt.bottomright.y = 70
pPlot.TakeARect rt
```

■ switch

Description: The `switch` keyword is used to specify the type and name of the discriminant for an IDL encapsulated union.

Notes: To define a nonencapsulated union, use the switch-type keyword.

■ IDL

Present in TLB: Yes

Present in Oicf: Yes

Notes: There are no attributes that apply directly to the `switch` keyword. See the `union` keyword for attributes applicable to that keyword.

```
union <structname> switch ( <integertype> <discriminator
name> ) <unionname>
{
  case <value>:
    <integertype> <discriminator name>
};
```

Examples

```
union Salary switch ( short nDiscrim ) _Salary
{
  case 1:
    short nValue;
  case 2:
    long lValue;
};
```

■ C++

Notes: The switch clause becomes a field in the encapsulating structure in the C/C++ mapping.

Examples

```
struct Salary
{
  short nDiscrim;
  union __MIDL___MIDL_itf_keywords2Eunion_0000_0001
  {
    short nValue;
    long lValue;
  } _Salary;
};
```

■ Visual Basic

Notes: User-defined union types are not supported in Visual Basic.

■ typedef

Description: The typedef keyword allows aliases to be defined for both simple and complex types.

■ IDL

Present in TLB: Maybe

Present in Oicf: No

Notes: Type aliases will appear in a type library only if the alias is to a complex type or the typedef is annotated with the [uuid] attribute. There is no special Oicf representation for type aliases. The Oicf strings for a type alias will be identical to those for the aliased type.

SYNTAX

```
[
  optional attributes
]
typedef [ optional attributes ] <aliased type> <alias> <alias>;
```

Attributes:

uuid

custom

Examples

EXAMPLE 1

```
typedef short* PSHORT;
```

EXAMPLE 2

```
typedef [unique] short* UNQPSHORT;
```

EXAMPLE 3

```
typedef struct Point
{
  long x,y;
} POINT, *PPOINT;
```

▇ C++

Notes: IDL typedef declarations translate into C/C++ typedef declarations.

Examples

EXAMPLE 1

```
typedef short* PSHORT;
```

EXAMPLE 2

```
typedef short* UNQPSHORT;
```

EXAMPLE 3

```
typedef struct Point
{
  long x;
  long y;
} POINT;
typedef struct Point *PPOINT;
```

▇ Visual Basic

Notes: Typedefs that appear in a type library will be available to Visual Basic provided they are not aliases to pointer types.

Example

```
Dim pt As Point
```

■ union

Description: The `union` keyword is used to define encapsulated and non-encapsulated union types.

■ IDL

Present in TLB: Yes

Present in Oicf: Yes

Notes: Although union types appear in type libraries, the case statements are lost. The `[uuid]` attribute cannot be applied to a nonencapsulated union.

SYNTAX 1
```
[
  attributes
]
union <structname> switch ( <integertype> <discriminator
name> ) <unionname>
{
  case <value>:
    <type> <field name>
};
```

SYNTAX 2
```
[switch_type(<integertype>)] union <unionname>
{
[case(<integervalue>)]
  <type> <field name>
};
```

Attributes:

uuid

custom

Examples

EXAMPLE 1
```
union Salary switch ( short nDiscrim ) _Salary
{
  case 1:
    short nValue;
  case 2:
    long lValue;
};
```

EXAMPLE 2

```
[switch_type(short)] union U2
{
[case(1)]
  double lf;
[case(2)]
  float(f);
[case(3)]
  long l;
};
```

■ C++

Notes: IDL encapsulated unions map to C/C++ structures. IDL nonencapsulated unions map to C/C++ unions.

Examples

EXAMPLE 1
```
struct Salary
{
  short nDiscrim;
  union __MIDL___MIDL_itf_keywords2Eunion_0000_0001
  {
    short nValue;
    long lValue;
  } _Salary;
};
```

EXAMPLE 2
```
union U2
{
  double lf;
  float f;
  long l;
};
```

■ Visual Basic

Notes: User-defined union types are not supported in Visual Basic.

Chapter 10

IDL Attributes

This chapter provides a reference for most of the IDL attributes. The information for each attribute is divided into several sections. The *Description* and *Notes* fields immediately following the attribute provide a general description of the attribute along with any notable features.

The IDL section includes several fields. The *Present in TLB* and *Present in Oicf* fields denote whether information about the attribute is present in standard type information and Oicf type information, respectively. The *Notes* field provides further information about using the attribute in IDL. The *Syntax* field shows the outline syntax for using the attribute in IDL. Where the IDL language supports multiple syntaxes, each syntax is shown in a separate *Syntax* field. The *Applies to* field lists the IDL keywords and constructs to which the attribute can be applied. Keywords are listed first, followed by constructs such as parameter, method, or structure field. Examples of using the attribute in IDL are also provided. Where more than one example is provided, each one is numbered separately.

The C++ and Visual Basic sections provide notes about the mapping of the attribute into the programming language. Finally, examples are provided in each language where appropriate. Where multiple numbered examples are provided in the IDL section, the C++ and Visual Basic examples are numbered accordingly. For example, a Visual Basic example labeled "Example 2" corresponds to the IDL example labeled "Example 2."

■ appobject

Description: Indicates that the methods and properties of the interfaces listed on the coclass are globally available without having to instantiate the coclass explicitly.

■ IDL

Present in TLB: Yes

Present in Oicf: No

SYNTAX
```
appobject
```

Applies to: coclass

Example

```
[
  uuid(8C8B24D2-58CD-4D27-A01A-6F863C3C95DF),
  appobject
]
coclass SomeApp
{
  interface ISomeApp;
}
```

■ C++

Notes: The [appobject] attribute has no effect in C++.

■ Visual Basic

Notes: The [appobject] attribute allows methods and properties of the interfaces listed on the coclass to be used directly in Visual Basic without creating an instance of the coclass explicitly.

Example

```
Dim x As String
x = SomeApp.SomeMethod ( "Hello" )
```

■ async_uuid

Description: Denotes the uuid that identifies the asynchronous version of the interface.

■ IDL

Present in TLB: Special

Present in Oicf: Yes

Notes: Although the asynchronous version of an interface appears in any type library that references that interface, type library marshaling cannot be used.

Consequently, interfaces marked with [async_uuid] should not be marked with the oleautomation or dual attribute.

SYNTAX
```
async_uuid(<uuid>)
```

Applies to: interface

Example
```
[
  uuid(74241B75-264B-4f60-8420-33AE876BB619),
  async_uuid(7BE7E5B7-774A-45dd-9583-6B3F8811B297),
  object,
  pointer_default(unique)
]
interface IMath : IUnknown
{
  HRESULT CalculatePrimes ( [in] long nMaxNumber,
    [out] long* pnPrimes,
    [out,size_is(,*pnPrimes)] long** ppResults );
};
```

▨ C++

Notes: An interface annotated with the [async_uuid] attribute produces two C++ abstract base classes: one for the synchronous version of the interface and another for the asynchronous version.

Example
```
MIDL_INTERFACE("7BE7E5B7-774A-45dd-9583-6B3F8811B297")
AsyncIMath : public IUnknown
{
public:
  virtual HRESULT STDMETHODCALLTYPE
  Begin_CalculatePrimes ( long nMaxNumber) = 0;
  virtual HRESULT STDMETHODCALLTYPE
  Finish_CalculatePrimes ( long *pnPrimes, long **ppResults) = 0;
};
```

▨ Visual Basic

Notes: Any asynchronous interface that is referenced in a library block is a valid interface type in Visual Basic. However, Visual Basic is unable to call ICallFactory::CreateCall directly.

■ call_as

Description: Denotes the remote method of a pair of methods, the other of which is the local version and is annotated with the `[local]` attribute, q.v. This technique is known as method aliasing.

■ IDL

Present in TLB: Special

Present in Oicf: Special

Notes: Using the `[call_as]` attribute requires the interface designer to provide two functions, one client side and one server side, to map the local method call to the remote version. By default, the remote version of the method pair appears in any containing type library. See Chapter 5 for a workaround for this bug. Oicf strings are generated for the remote method only.

SYNTAX
```
call_as(<local method name>)
```

Applies to: method

Example
```
[local]
HRESULT Next ( [in] ULONG celt,
  [out] IUnknown **rgelt,
  [out] ULONG *pceltFetched);
[call_as(Next)]
HRESULT RemoteNext ( [in] ULONG celt,
  [out, size_is(celt), length_is(*pceltFetched)] IUnknown
**rgelt,
  [out] ULONG *pceltFetched);
```

■ C++

Notes: The generated abstract base class contains the local version of the interface. Function prototypes are also generated for the two mapping functions that must be compiled into the proxy-stub DLL.

Example
```
HRESULT STDMETHODCALLTYPE
IEnum_Next_Proxy ( IEnum * This,
  ULONG celt,
```

```
   IUnknown **rgelt,
   ULONG *pceltFetched);
 HRESULT STDMETHODCALLTYPE
 IEnum_Next_Stub ( IEnum * This,
   ULONG celt,
   IUnknown **rgelt,
   ULONG *pceltFetched);
```

▨ Visual Basic

Notes: If the workaround described in Chapter 5 is used, Visual Basic can call aliased methods, provided that the interface definition is provided in a type library.

■ custom

Description: Attaches a custom attribute to the IDL construct that it annotates.

Notes: Custom attributes can be retrieved through the `ITypeLib2` and `ITypeInfo2` interfaces. This is typically done at deployment time or runtime by some infrastructure component such as the Component Services administration tool.

▨ IDL

Present in TLB: Yes

Present in Oicf: No

Notes: The value of a custom attribute must be of a type that is compatible with the VARIANT data type. It may also be zero, which effectively attaches only the uuid of the custom attribute to the annotated IDL construct.

SYNTAX
```
custom ( <uuid>, <value>)
```

Applies to:

typedef	interface	parameter
coclass	dispinterface	field
library	method	

Example

```
[
  uuid(8BCD07A5-9F6C-4F37-8CC1-4A746A01C69E),
  custom(17093CC5-9BD2-11cf-AA4F-304BF89C0001,0)
]
coclass SomeTxClass
{
  interface IUnknown;
  interface SomeTxInterface;
}
```

■ C++

Notes: The [custom] attribute has no effect on the C++ mapping.

■ Visual Basic

Notes: The [custom] attribute has no effect on the Visual Basic mapping.

■ default

Description: Denotes the interface that provides the default functionality of the object. This typically corresponds to the set of methods that are available through IDispatch.

■ IDL

Present in TLB: Yes

Present in Oicf: No

Notes: The [default] attribute may appear at most twice—once on an incoming interface and once on an outgoing, source interface. If the [default] attribute is not present on any of the interfaces in the coclass statement, the first interface that is not annotated with the [restricted] attribute is used.

> **SYNTAX**
> ```
> default
> ```

Applies to: Interface in coclass

Example

```
[
  object,
  oleautomation,
  uuid(5E6A672D-0E62-46E9-94D3-6971C344480E)
]
```

```
interface IDataInput : IUnknown
{
  HRESULT AddValue ( [in] short s );
  HRESULT GetResult ( [out,retval] long* pl );
  [propput] HRESULT Threshold ( [in] long lThreshold );
  [propget] HRESULT Threshold ( [out,retval] long* plThreshold );
}
[
  object,
  oleautomation,
  uuid(E7F4CCCD-E05E-46AC-A717-EEFA613C7FE8)
]
interface IDataEvents : IUnknown
{
  HRESULT OverThreshold();
}
[
  uuid(88F4C5C9-83F4-41B8-B88C-4D140F4CC513)
]
coclass DataBinder
{
  [default] interface IDataInput;
  [default,source] interface IDataEvents;
}
```

▐ C++

Notes: The [default] attribute has no effect on the C++ mapping.

▐ Visual Basic

Notes: Visual Basic hides the default interface, although it is still accessible.
The name of the coclass may be used in place of the default interface. Where
a coclass is annotated with a default source interface, the WithEvents
keyword can be used to hook up event handlers.

Examples

EXAMPLE 1
```
Dim obj As New DataBinder
obj.AddValue 10
obj.Threshold = 100
```

EXAMPLE 2
```
Dim WithEvents binder As New DataBinder
' Event handler
Public Sub binder_OverThreshold()
End Sub
```

■ defaultvalue

Description: Provides a default value for a method parameter enabling the caller of the method to omit the parameter.

Notes: Implies the [optional] attribute.

■ IDL

Present in TLB: Yes

Present in Oicf: No

Notes: For BSTR data types, the only possible default value is 0, the null string, because putting string literals in the IDL does not produce the correct results. Parameters marked with the [defaultvalue] attribute must appear after parameters not so marked. The value may be an enumerated type. The [optional] and [defaultvalue] attributes may not appear together.

SYNTAX
```
defaultvalue(<value>)
```

Applies to: parameter

Examples

EXAMPLE 1
```
HRESULT M1 ( [in, defaultvalue(10)] long l );
```

EXAMPLE 2
```
enum SIZE
{
  SMALL,
  MEDIUM,
  LARGE,
}
HRESULT CreateShirt ( [in, defaultvalue(MEDIUM)] enum SIZE
size );
```

■ C++

Notes: The [defaultvalue] attribute has no effect on the C++ mapping.

Examples

EXAMPLE 1
```
pObj->M1 ( 10 ); // Still have to pass a value
```

EXAMPLE 2
```
pObj->CreateShirt ( SMALL ); // Other values can be passed
```

■ Visual Basic

Notes: In Visual Basic, if a parameter annotated with the [defaultvalue] attribute is omitted from a call, the value specified by the [defaultvalue] attribute will be used.

Examples

EXAMPLE 1
```
obj.M1 ' The value 10 will be passed to the method
```

EXAMPLE 2
```
obj.CreateShirt SMALL ' defaultvalue overridden by explicit
parameter
```

■ dllname

Description: Provides the name of the DLL to which a module statement applies.

■ IDL

Present in TLB: Yes

Present in Oicf: No

Notes: The [dllname] attribute is mandatory for module statements containing function declarations.

SYNTAX
```
dllname ( "<dll name>" )
```

Applies to: module

Example
```
[
  dllname("pca.dll"),
  uuid(75FB8FA8-B87C-44A1-BCAA-2F2CE415F540)
]
module pca
{
  [entry(1)] HRESULT _stdcall
  CoCreateChannelProxy ( [in] BSTR progid,
      [in] BSTR transportProgId,
      [out,retval] IUnknown**ppUnk );
}
```

■ C++

Notes: The [dllname] attribute has no effect on the C++ mapping.

■ **Visual Basic**

Notes: The [dllname] attribute has no effect on the Visual Basic mapping.

■ dual

Description: Denotes an interface that can be called through a v-table and through IDispatch.

Notes: This attribute is merely a hint to development tools and runtime environments as to what the v-table looks like.

■ **IDL**

Present in TLB: Yes

Present in Oicf: No

Notes: Interfaces annotated with the [dual] attribute must derive from IDispatch or an interface that has IDispatch in its interface hierarchy, although the MIDL compiler does not enforce this restriction. The [dual] attribute implies the [oleautomation] attribute, q.v. The MIDL compiler will generate [id] attributes, q.v., for any methods of a dual interface not annotated with an explicit [id] attribute.

SYNTAX
```
dual
```

Applies to: interface

Example
```
[
  uuid(C82C0DA8-E62E-4F93-8CE2-923A93BAD54A),
  dual,
  object
]
interface IAsteroid : IDispatch
{
  HRESULT Collide ( [in] IAsteroid* pOther );
}
```

■ **C++**

Notes: The [dual] attribute has no effect on the C++ mapping.

■ **Visual Basic**

Notes: The [dual] attribute has no effect on the Visual Basic mapping.

■ entry

Description: Defines the name or ordinal by which a given function is exported from a DLL.

Notes: If an exported function is marked with _dllexport in the C/C++ source file, the name specified by the [entry] attribute should be the same as the function name. If the function is exported by name in a module definition file, the name specified by the [entry] attribute should match the name in the module definition file. If the function is exported by ordinal value in a module definition file, the value specifed by the [entry] attribute should match the value in the module definition file. Note that the MIDL compiler does not check names and ordinal numbers in [entry] attributes against the C/C++ source or the module definition file.

■ IDL

Present in TLB: Yes

Present in Oicf: No

Notes: Applications can retrieve the name or ordinal of a function within a module in order to bind dynamically to the function at runtime.

SYNTAX 1
```
entry ( <ordinal> ) <function declaration>
```

SYNTAX 2
```
entry ( "<name>" ) <function declaration>
```

Applies to: Function in module

Examples

EXAMPLE 1
```
[
  uuid(22F5FD5A-AA11-40F4-98B2-322974272062),
  dllname("pca.dll")
]
module PcaModule
{
  [entry(1)] HRESULT _stdcall CoCreateChannelProxy ( [in] BSTR
progid, [out] IUnknown**ppUnk );
}
```

```
[
  uuid(CC9714E8-E321-420C-8B80-75A4CBDCB759),
  dllname("atom.dll")
]
module PcaModule
{
  [entry("CreateMatter")] HRESULT _stdcall CreateMatter (
[out] IUnknown**ppUnk );
}
```

■ C++

Notes: The [entry] statement has no effect on the C++ mapping.

■ Visual Basic

Notes: The [entry] statement has no effect on the Visual Basic mapping.

■ first_is

Description: Defines the index of the first array element to be transmitted, enabling partial transmission of fixed and conformant arrays. See also [last_is] and [length_is].

Notes: Because the size of the transmission buffer for the array is smaller than the actual array size, an extra memory copy into a correctly sized buffer is incurred on the receiving side. For arrays annotated with the [in] attribute, the receiver is the server. For arrays annotated with the [out] attribute, the receiver is the client.

■ IDL

Present in TLB: Special

Present in Oicf: Yes

Notes: The [first_is] attribute does not appear in the type library, so type library marshaling cannot be used. Furthermore, structures containing fields annotated with the [first_is] attribute cannot appear in a type library; error MIDL2106 is generated if such a structure is referenced in the library block. The presence of the [first_is] parameter in a method declaration confuses the type library generation code in the MIDL compiler, resulting in an incorrect definition appearing in the type library. The workaround described in Chapter 5 for the local/call_as problem is also applicable here, as shown in Example 1. The [first_is] attribute along with [length_is] and [last_is] are used to define varying arrays. When used in conjunction with `[size_is]` or `[max_is]`, the array is called an open array. Both varying and open arrays are inefficient as both `[in]` and `[out]` parameters and should be avoided.

SYNTAX
```
first_is(<expression>)
```

Applies to:

parameter

field

Examples

EXAMPLE 1
```
#ifdef BUILDINGPS
HRESULT TakeSomeData ( [in] short nFirst, [in,
first_is(nFirst)] short nData[20] );
#else
HRESULT TakeSomeData ( [in] short nFirst, [in] short nData[20] );
#endif
```

EXAMPLE 2
```
struct SomeData
{
  short nFirst;
  [first_is(nFirst)] short nData[100];
}
```

■ C++

Examples

EXAMPLE 1
```
short rgPrimes[] = { 1, 2, 3, 5, 7, 11, 13, 17, 19,
    23, 29, 31, 37, 41, 43, 47, 53, 59, 61, 67 };
// Transmit primes 11-20
pObj->TakeSomeData ( 10, rgPrimes );
```

■ Visual Basic

Notes: Methods that use the `[first_is]` attribute may be called but not implemented by Visual Basic.

Examples

EXAMPLE 1
```
' Array of primes defined elsewhere
Sub CallMethod ( rgPrimes() As Integer )
pObj.TakeSomeData 10, rgPrimes
End Sub
```

■ helpcontext

Description: Defines an identifier in a help file that refers to the annotated item.

Notes: The `helpcontext` can be retrieved through `ITypeLib::Get Documentation` or `ITypeInfo::GetDocumentation`.

▨ IDL

Present in TLB: Yes

Present in Oicf: No

Notes: The `[helpcontext]` attribute is typically used with the `[helpfile]` attribute, q.v.

SYNTAX
```
helpcontext ( <integer;> )
```

Applies to:

typedef	coclass	module
interface	library	method
dispinterface		

Example

```
[
  uuid(270EAB6E-0F3F-4B2A-92F7-8D8D7BC143DC),
  version(1.0),
  helpcontext(10)
]
library AtomLib
{
  [
    uuid(5B4A6CF9-B34C-4581-9EA2-EB7B61FC4170),
    oleautomation,
    object,
    helpcontext(0x20)
  ]
  interface IAtomSmasher : IUnknown
  {
    [helpcontext(30)] HRESULT SmashAtom();
  }
}
```

■ C++

Notes: The [helpcontext] attribute has no effect on the C++ mapping.

■ Visual Basic

Notes: The [helpcontext] attribute has no effect on the Visual Basic mapping.

■ helpfile

Description: Specifies the name of the help file for the type library.

Notes: The help file can be retrieved through ITypeLib::GetDocumentation. All helpcontext attributes defined in the type library block are assumed to be present in the help file.

■ IDL

Present in TLB: Yes

Present in Oicf: No

SYNTAX
```
helpfile ( "<filename>" )
```

Applies to: library

Examples
```
[
   uuid(270EAB6E-0F3F-4B2A-92F7-8D8D7BC143DC),
   version(1.0),
   helpfile("atom.hlp"),
   helpcontext(10)
]
library AtomLib
{
}
```

■ C++

Notes: The [helpfile] attribute has no effect on the C++ mapping.

■ Visual Basic

Notes: The [helpfile] attribute has no effect on the Visual Basic mapping

■ helpstring

Description: Attaches a human-readable string to a construct in the type library.

■ IDL

Present in TLB: Yes

Present in Oicf: No

Notes: While type libraries can contain help strings containing up to 2^{32} characters, the MIDL compiler can handle strings up to only 260 characters in length. Strings of more than 260 characters are truncated without warning.

SYNTAX
```
helpstring("<string>")
```

Applies to:

typedef	coclass	module
interface	library	method
dispinterface		

Examples

```
[
  uuid(270EAB6E-0F3F-4B2A-92F7-8D8D7BC143DC),
  version(1.0),
  helpstring("The ATOM Type Library")
]
library AtomLib
{
  [
    uuid(5B4A6CF9-B34C-4581-9EA2-EB7B61FC4170),
    oleautomation,
    object,
    helpstring("Interface for smashing atoms to pieces")
  ]
  interface IAtomSmasher : IUnknown
  {
    [helpstring("Smash an atom to pieces")] HRESULT SmashAtom();
  }
}
```

■ C++

Notes: The [helpstring] attribute has no effect on the C++ mapping.

■ Visual Basic

Notes: The [helpstring] attribute has no effect on the Visual Basic mapping.

■ hidden

Description: Instructs a type library browser to hide the IDL construct from the user.

■ IDL

Present in TLB: Yes

Present in Oicf: No

Notes: The [hidden] attribute is only a hint to a type library viewer or development environment and may not be enforced.

Applies to:

interface	library	method
dispinterface	coclass	property

SYNTAX

```
hidden
```

Examples

EXAMPLE 1

```
[
  uuid(B1D2AEE9-2D78-456C-ADC9-4A082AEB24C2),
  version(1.0)
  hidden
]
library hiddenLib
{
  ...
}
```

EXAMPLE 2

```
[
  uuid(3498A156-96D5-4978-8890-0B0D0DBAFFD1),
  oleautomation,
  object,
  hidden
]
interface IAtom : IUnknown
{
  ...
}
```

EXAMPLE 3

```
[
  uuid(6290D1F4-F683-46FF-B89F-5803820CBE56),
  oleautomation,
  object
]
interface IParticle : IUnknown
{
  [propget] HRESULT Energy ( [out,retval] long* plJoules );
  [propput,hidden] HRESULT Energy ( [in] long lJoules );
}
```

■ C++

Notes: The [hidden] attribute has no effect on the C++ mapping.

■ Visual Basic

Notes: Visual Basic will not list type libraries marked with the [hidden] attribute in the "Project References" dialog box. However, such libraries can be loaded manually. Other IDL constructs marked with the [hidden] attribute will not appear in the object browser, although this can be overridden by using the "Show Hidden Members" option.

■ id

Description: Attaches a 32-bit integer to a method. This integer is known as the dispatch ID and is the number returned by IDispatch::GetIdsOfNames.

■ IDL

Present in TLB: Yes

Present in Oicf: No

Notes: All methods related to the same property, [propget], [propput], and [propputref], must be annotated with the same id value. Negative id values are prohibited and will be replaced with positive numbers generated by the MIDL compiler. The MIDL compiler automatically generates [id] attributes for methods and properties of dual interfaces that do not have an explicit id.

Applies to:

method

property

SYNTAX

```
id(<integer>)
```

Examples

EXAMPLE 1
```
[id(1)] HRESULT Add ( [in] short s );
```

EXAMPLE 2
```
[id(0x000DEAD0)] HRESULT Subtract ( [in] short s );
```

EXAMPLE 3
```
[id(0x1000),propput] HRESULT Size ( [in] short nSize );
[id(0x1000),propget] HRESULT Size ( [out,retval] short* pnSize );
```

▩ C++

Notes: The id value can be used by C++ clients in calls to `IDispatch::Invoke`. The id value can be retrieved through `IDispatch::GetIdsOfNames`.

▩ Visual Basic

Notes: The `[id]` attribute has no effect on the Visual Basic mapping. The Visual Basic runtime environment will use `IDispatch::GetIdsOfNames` and `IDispatch::Invoke` when calling methods through an object reference on type `Object`.

ignore

Description: Tells the interception layer not to marshal the attributed pointer.
Notes: This marshaling optimization loses information during the marshal. On the remote side of the call, the information provided by the field marked with the `[ignore]` attribute is unavailable.

▩ IDL

Present in TLB: No
Present in Oicf: Yes
Notes: The `[ignore]` attribute can be applied only to pointer fields in structures or unions. The MIDL compiler is unable to generate a type library containing a reference to a structure containing a field annotated with the `[ignore]` attribute.

SYNTAX
```
ignore
```

Applies to: field

Example

```
struct Node
{
  BSTR bstr;
  struct Node*pNext;
  [ignore] struct Node*pPrev;
};
```

■ C++

Notes: The [ignore] attribute has no effect on the C++ mapping.

Example

```
struct Node
{
  BSTR bstr;
  struct Node*pNext;
  struct Node*pPrev;
};
```

■ Visual Basic

Notes: The [ignore] attribute is not relevant to Visual Basic because Visual Basic is unable to deal with structures containing embedded pointers.

■ iid_is

Description: Allows object references to be typed at runtime rather than at IDL compile time.

Notes: The interception layer marshals an object reference of the type specified.

■ IDL

Present in TLB: No

Present in Oicf: Yes

Notes: The [iid_is] attribute can be applied only to object references or void pointers.

SYNTAX

```
iid_is(<parametername>)
```

Applies to:

parameter

field

Examples

```
HRESULT PersistObject ( [in] REFIID riid, [in,iid_is(riid)]
IUnknown*pUnk ) ;
```

```
HRESULT QueryInterface ( [in] REFIID riid, [out,iid_is(riid)]
void**ppv) ;
```

```
struct Info
{
  BSTR bstrDesc;
  long lId;
  IID iid;
  [iid_is(iid)] IUnknown* pUnk;
};
```

■ C++

Notes: The [iid_is] attribute is most useful when combined with the Visual C++ __uuidof operator.

Examples

```
IPersistXML* p;
// Initialize p
pObj->PersistObject ( __uuidof ( p ), p );
```

■ Visual Basic

Notes: Visual Basic can call but not implement interfaces whose methods contain [iid_is] attributes.

Examples

```
Dim p as IPersistXML
' Initialize p
pObj.PersistObject guid, p
```

■ in

Description: Denotes a parameter that is used for input and is present in the method request.

Notes: Parameters annotated with the [in] attribute may also be annotated with the [out] attribute, q.v. Directionality semantics cannot be enforced in cases where there is no interception layer between the caller and the callee.

■ IDL

Present in TLB: Yes

Present in Oicf: Yes

Notes: Parameters that are not annotated with either the [in] or the [out] attribute are implicitly marked [in]; however, not providing a directionality attribute is considered bad style.

SYNTAX

```
in
```

Applies to: parameter

Examples

EXAMPLE 1

```
HRESULT TakeAShort ( [in] short s );
```

EXAMPLE 2

```
HRESULT TakeAShortRef ( [in] short* ps );
```

EXAMPLE 3

```
HRESULT TakeAndReturnAShort ( [in,out] short* ps );
```

■ C++

Examples

EXAMPLE 1

```
pObj->TakeAShort ( 10 );
```

EXAMPLE 2

```
short s = 30;
pObj->TakeAShortRef ( &s );
```

EXAMPLE 3

```
short s = 20;
pObj->TakeAndReturnAShort ( &s );
```

■ Visual Basic

Notes: Parameters annotated with the [in] attribute that are not pointers are marked ByVal in Visual Basic.

Examples

EXAMPLE 1

```
pObj.TakeAShort 10
```

EXAMPLE 2
```
pObj.TakeAShortRef 30
```
EXAMPLE 3
```
Dim s As Integer
pObj.TakeAndReturnAShort s
```
EXAMPLE 4
```
Private Sub ITakeShorts_TakeAShort(ByVal s As Integer)
End Sub
Private Sub ITakeShorts_TakeAndReturnAShort(ps As Integer)
End Sub
Private Sub ITakeShorts_TakeAShortRef(ps As Integer)
End Sub
```

■ last_is

Description: Defines the index of the last array element to be transmitted, enabling partial transmission of fixed and conformant arrays. See also [first_is] and [length_is].

Notes: Because the size of the transmission buffer for the array is smaller than the size of the actual array, an extra memory copy into a correctly sized buffer is incurred on the receiving side. For arrays annotated with the [in] attribute, the receiver is the server. For arrays annotated with the [out] attribute, the receiver is the client.

■ IDL

Present in TLB: No

Present in Oicf: Yes

Notes: The [last_is] attribute does not appear in the type library, so type library marshaling cannot be used. Furthermore, structures containing fields annotated with the [last_is] attribute cannot appear in a type library; error MIDL2106 is generated if such a structure is referenced in the library block. The presence of the [last_is] parameter in a method declaration confuses the type library generation code in the MIDL compiler, resulting in an incorrect definition appearing in the type library. The workaround described in Chapter 5 for the local/call_as problem is also applicable here, as shown in Example 1. The [last_is] attribute, along with [first_is], is used to define varying arrays. When used in conjunction with [size_is] or [max_is], the array is called an open array. Both varying and open arrays are inefficient as both

[in] and [out] parameters and should be avoided. The [last_is] and [length_is] attributes are mutually exclusive.

SYNTAX
```
last_is(<expression>)
```

Applies to:

parameter

field

Examples

EXAMPLE 1
```
#ifdef BUILDINGPS
HRESULT TakeSomeData ( [in] short nLast, [in,
last_is(nLast)] short nData[20] );
#else
HRESULT TakeSomeData ( [in] short nLast, [in] short nData[20] );
#endif
```

EXAMPLE 2
```
struct SomeData
{
  short nLast;
  [last_is(nLast)] short nData[100];
}
```

■ C++

Example
```
short rgPrimes[] = { 1, 2, 3, 5, 7, 11, 13, 17, 19,
    23, 29, 31, 37, 41, 43, 47, 53, 59, 61, 67 };
// Transmit primes 1-10
pObj->TakeSomeData ( 9, rgPrimes );
```

■ Visual Basic

Notes: Methods that use the [last_is] attribute may be called but not implemented by Visual Basic.

Example
```
' Array of primes defined elsewhere
Sub CallMethod ( rgPrimes() As Integer )
pObj.TakeSomeData 9, rgPrimes
End Sub
```

■ lcid

Description: When applied to a library using syntax 1 below, identifies the locale for the generated type library and enables international character processing inside the library block. When applied to a method parameter, denotes that the annotated parameter is a locale ID.

Notes: To enable international character processing outside the library block, use the `/lcid` command line switch.

■ IDL

Present in TLB: Yes

Present in Oicf: No

Notes: A parameter annotated with the `[lcid]` attribute must be of type long or unsigned long, must be the only parameter so annotated, and must be the last parameter to the method unless the method has an `[out,retval]` parameter.

SYNTAX 1
```
lcid(<localeid>)
```

SYNTAX 2
```
lcid
```

Applies to:

library

parameter

Examples

EXAMPLE 1
```
[
  uuid(BDFD69E7-0EF2-4736-A0FA-2F2BF4B4643D),
  version(2.0),
  lcid(0x0809) // UK-English
]
library FooLib
{
  ...
}
```

EXAMPLE 2
```
HRESULT GetLocalizedString ( [in] long nId, [in,lcid] long lcid,
[out,retval] BSTR bstr );
```

■ C++

Notes: The `[lcid]` attribute has no effect on the C++ mapping.

■ Visual Basic

Notes: The [lcid] attribute has no effect on the Visual Basic mapping

■ length_is

Description: Allows runtime specification of the number of array elements to be transmitted, allowing partial transmission of fixed arrays, conformant arrays, and conformant pointers.

Notes: Because the size of the transmission buffer for the array is smaller than the size of the actual array, an extra memory copy into a correctly sized buffer is incurred on the receiving side. For arrays annotated with the [in] attribute, the receiver is the server. For arrays annotated with the [out] attribute, the receiver is the client.

■ IDL

Present in TLB: No

Present in Oicf: Yes

Notes: The [length_is] attribute does not appear in the type library, so type library marshaling cannot be used. Furthermore, structures containing fields annotated with the [length_is] attribute cannot appear in a type library; error MIDL2106 is generated if such a structure is referenced in the library block. The presence of the [length_is] parameter in a method declaration confuses the type library generation code in the MIDL compiler, resulting in an incorrect definition appearing in the type library. The workaround described in Chapter 5 for the local/call_as problem is also applicable here, as shown in Example 1. The [length_is] attribute, along with [first_is], is used to define varying arrays. When used in conjunction with [size_is] or [max_is], the array is called an open array. Both varying and open arrays are inefficient as both [in] and [out] parameters and should be avoided. The [length_is] and [last_is] attributes are mutually exclusive.

SYNTAX
```
length_is(<expression>)
```

Applies to:

parameter

field

Examples

EXAMPLE 1

```
#ifdef BUILDINGPS
HRESULT TakeSomeData ( [in] short nLength, [in,
length_is(nLength)] short nData[20] );
#else
HRESULT TakeSomeData ( [in] short nLength, [in] short
nData[20] );
#endif
```

EXAMPLE 2

```
struct SomeData
{
  short nLength;
  [last_is(nLength)] short nData[100];
}
```

■ C++

Examples

EXAMPLE 1

```
short rgPrimes[] = { 1, 2, 3, 5, 7, 11, 13, 17, 19,
    23, 29, 31, 37, 41, 43, 47, 53, 59, 61, 67 };
// Transmit primes 1-10
pObj->TakeSomeData ( 10, rgPrimes );
```

■ Visual Basic

Notes: Methods that use the [length_is] attribute may be called but not implemented by Visual Basic.

Examples

EXAMPLE 1

```
' Array of primes defined elsewhere
Sub CallMethod ( rgPrimes() As Integer )
  pObj.TakeSomeData 10, rgPrimes
End Sub
```

■ local

Description: Specifies that an interface or method is not remoteable.

Notes: When applied to a method, denotes the local method of a pair of methods, the other of which is the remote version and is annotated with the [call_as] attribute, q.v. This technique is known as method aliasing. If the [call_as] method is missing from the interface definition, then the v-table slot for the method is empty, resulting in an access violation if a call is attempted.

■ IDL

Present in TLB: Special

Present in Oicf: Special

Notes: The [local] attribute does not make it into the type library and is effectively ignored on interfaces that use type library marshaling. Putting an interface definition inside the library block and not applying either the [oleautomation] or the [dual] attribute is equivalent to marking the interface with the [local] attribute. Oicf type information is not generated for interfaces annotated with the [local] attribute. The method aliasing technique requires the interface designer to provide two functions, one client side and one server side, to map the local method call to the remote version. By default, the remote version of the method pair appears in any containing type library. See Chapter 5 for a workaround for this bug. Oicf strings are generated for the remote method only.

SYNTAX
```
local
```

Applies to:

interface

method

Examples

EXAMPLE 1
```
[
  uuid(BB87953B-169F-4E6B-9E2C-9E381E83B2E7),
  object,
  local
]
interface ILocalItf : IUnknown
{
  . . .
}
```

EXAMPLE 2
```
[local]
HRESULT Next ( [in] ULONG celt,
  [out] IUnknown **rgelt,
  [out] ULONG *pceltFetched);
```

```
[call_as(Next)]
HRESULT RemoteNext ( [in] ULONG celt,
   [out, size_is(celt), length_is(*pceltFetched)] IUnknown
**rgelt,
   [out] ULONG *pceltFetched);
```

■ C++

Notes: The abstract base class for a local interface looks just like the abstract base class for a standard remoteable interface. For method aliasing, the generated abstract base class contains the local version of the interface. Function prototypes are also generated for the two mapping functions that must be compiled into the proxy-stub DLL.

Example
```
HRESULT STDMETHODCALLTYPE
IEnum_Next_Proxy ( IEnum * This,
   ULONG celt,
   IUnknown **rgelt,
   ULONG *pceltFetched);
HRESULT STDMETHODCALLTYPE
IEnum_Next_Stub ( IEnum * This,
   ULONG celt,
   IUnknown **rgelt,
   ULONG *pceltFetched);
```

■ Visual Basic

Notes: Visual Basic can call local interfaces provided that the interface definition is provided in a type library. If the workaround described in Chapter 5 is used, Visual Basic can call aliased methods provided that the interface definition is provided in a type library.

■ max_is

Description: Specifies the maximum valid index of a conformant array or pointer.

Notes: The [max_is] and [size_is] attributes are very similar. For a given call, size_is = max_is + 1.

■ IDL

Present in TLB: No
Present in Oicf: Yes

Notes: The [max_is] attribute does not appear in the type library, so type library marshaling cannot be used. The [max_is] and [size_is] attributes are mutually exclusive.

SYNTAX
```
max_is ( <expression> )
```

Applies to:

parameter

field

Examples

EXAMPLE 1
```
HRESULT TakeSomeData ( [in] short nMax, [in, max_is(nMax)]
short nData[20] );
```

EXAMPLE 2
```
HRESULT TakeSomeMoreData ( [in] short nMax, [in,
max_is(nMax)] short* pData );
```

EXAMPLE 3
```
struct SomeData
{
  short nMax;
  [max_is(nMax)] short nData[100];
}
```

■ C++

Example
```
short rgPrimes[] = { 1, 2, 3, 5, 7, 11, 13, 17, 19,
    23, 29, 31, 37, 41, 43, 47, 53, 59, 61, 67 };
// Transmit primes 1-11
pObj->TakeSomeData ( 10, rgPrimes );
```

■ Visual Basic

Notes: Methods that use the [max_is] attribute may be called but not implemented by Visual Basic.

Example
```
' Array of primes defined elsewhere
Sub CallMethod ( rgPrimes() As Integer )
  pObj.TakeSomeData 10, rgPrimes
End Sub
```

◼ nonextensible

Description: Denotes that when the annotated interface is exposed through
`IDispatch`, the properties and methods exposed must exactly match those
listed in the interface definition. Extra methods and properties are not allowed.

◼ IDL

Present in TLB: Yes

Present in Oicf: No

SYNTAX

```
nonextensible
```

Applies to:

dispinterface

interface

Examples

EXAMPLE 1

```
[
  object,
  uuid(2AAE03D6-F865-48AE-9309-F9B0BE096F1D),
  dual,
  nonextensible
]
interface IMolecule : IDispatch
{
  [propget] HRESULT AtomicWeight ( [out,retval] long* plWeight );
}
```

EXAMPLE 2

```
[
  object,
  uuid(5B3B2439-7367-4B61-B723-70A86D087335),
  oleautomation,
  nonextensible
]
interface ISplitMolecule : IUnknown
{
  HRESULT Split ( [in] IMolecule* pInput, [out] IMolecule**
pp1, [out] IMolecule** pp2 );
}
```

■ C++

Notes: The [nonextensible] attribute has no effect on the C++ mapping.

■ Visual Basic

Notes: The [nonextensible] attribute has no effect on the Visual Basic mapping.

■ object

Description: Denotes that an interface is a COM interface, as opposed to an RPC interface.

Notes: Because the MIDL compiler infers that an interface is a COM interface from the presence of a base interface, the [object] attribute is not strictly necessary. However, it should still be specified in order to avoid accidental definition of an RPC interface. The MIDL compiler generates dynamically bound proxy and stub code for COM interfaces, as opposed to the statically bound client and server stubs it generates for RPC interfaces.

■ IDL

Present in TLB: Yes

Present in Oicf: Yes

SYNTAX
```
object
```

Applies to: interface

Example
```
[
  uuid(4F08CF13-A9CC-40A4-AB21-FE2596C30323),
  object
]
interface IAtom : IUnknown
{
  [propget] HRESULT Protons ( [out,retval] short* pnProtons );
  [propget] HRESULT Neutrons ( [out,retval] short*
pnNeutrons );
  [propget] HRESULT Electrons ( [out,retval] short*
pnElectrons );
}
```

■ C++

Notes: The [object] attribute (or the presence of a base interface) causes the MIDL compiler to emit a C++ abstract base class for the interface.

Example
```
MIDL_INTERFACE("4F08CF13-A9CC-40A4-AB21-FE2596C30323")
IAtom : public IUnknown
{
public:
  virtual HRESULT STDMETHODCALLTYPE get_Protons ( short
*pnProtons) = 0;
  virtual HRESULT STDMETHODCALLTYPE get_Neutrons ( short
*pnNeutrons) = 0;
  virtual HRESULT STDMETHODCALLTYPE get_Electrons ( short
__RPC_FAR *pnElectrons) = 0;
};
```

■ Visual Basic

Notes: COM interface definitions present in a type library may be called and/or implemented by Visual Basic, provided that the types used are compatible with Visual Basic.

■ oleautomation

Description: Denotes that interception code for an interface should be produced by the universal marshaler from standard type information contained in a type library.

Notes: The [dual] attribute implies the [oleautomation] attribute.

■ IDL

Present in TLB: Yes

Present in Oicf: No

Notes: Oicf type information will be generated for an interface defined outside of a library block whether the [oleautomation] attribute is present or not. However, any such interface that is referenced inside a library block will use the universal marshaler unless the proxy-stub DLL for the interface is registered after the type library containing the reference. Because this is difficult to enforce, interfaces marked [oleautomation] ideally should appear only inside a library block.

```
oleautomation
```

Applies to: interface

Example

```
[
  object,
  uuid(DBDFC954-985E-46D4-8142-C995F2A7894B),
  oleautomation
]
interface IAtomCracker : IUnknown
{
  ...
}
```

■ C++

Notes: The [oleautomation] attribute has no effect on the C++ mapping.

■ Visual Basic

Notes: The [oleautomation] attribute has no effect on the Visual Basic mapping.

■ optional

Description: Specifies that the annotated parameter may be omitted when calling the method.

■ IDL

Present in TLB: Yes

Present in Oicf: No

Notes: Parameters marked [optional] must appear after parameters not so marked. The [optional] and [defaultvalue] attributes may not be used together.

```
optional
```

Applies to: parameter

Example

```
HRESULT MaybeTakeTwoStrings ( [in] BSTR bstr1, [in,optional]
BSTR bstr2 );
```

■ C++

Notes: The [optional] attribute has no effect on the C++ caller mapping. C++ method implementations will receive zero or null values if an optional parameter is omitted by a Visual Basic caller.

■ Visual Basic

Notes: The [optional] attribute allows Visual Basic code to omit the parameter when calling the method.

■ out

Description: Denotes a parameter that is used for output and is present in the method response.

Notes: Parameters annotated with the [out] attribute must be reference types. They may also be annotated with the [in] attribute, q.v. Directionality semantics cannot be enforced in cases where there is no interception layer between the caller and the callee.

■ IDL

Present in TLB: Yes

Present in Oicf: Yes

Notes: Parameters that are not annotated with either the [in] or the [out] attribute are implicitly marked [in]; however, not providing a directionality attribute is considered bad style.

SYNTAX
```
out
```

Applies to: parameter

Examples

EXAMPLE 1
```
HRESULT ReturnAShort ( [out] short* ps );
```

EXAMPLE 2
```
HRESULT TakeAndReturnAShort ( [in,out] short* ps );
```

■ C++

Examples

EXAMPLE 1
```
short s = 0;
pObj->ReturnAShort ( &s );
```

EXAMPLE 2
```
short s = 20;
pObj->TakeAndReturnAShort ( &s );
```

■ Visual Basic

Notes: Parameters annotated with the [out] attribute are marked ByRef in Visual Basic. Visual Basic cannot implement interface methods that have [out] only parameters.

Examples

EXAMPLE 1
```
Dim s As Integer
pObj.ReturnAShort s
```

EXAMPLE 2
```
Dim s As Integer
s = 20
pObj.TakeAndReturnAShort s
```

EXAMPLE 3
```
Private Sub ITakeShorts_TakeAndReturnAShort(ps As Integer)
End Sub
```

■ pointer_default

Description: Specifies the pointer behavior in terms of [ref], [unique], or [ptr], q.v., of embedded pointers that are not explicitly annotated with [ref], [unique], or [ptr].

Notes: The [pointer_default] attribute modifies the processing performed by the interception layer for embedded pointers.

■ IDL

Present in TLB: No
Present in Oicf: Yes

SYNTAX
```
pointer_default ( <ref|unique|ptr> )
```

Applies to: interface

Example
```
[
  uuid(ff7bdab7-5df8-462e-a18e-864a65e21de0),
```

```
   object
   pointer_default(ptr)
]
interface IHaveEmbeddedPointers : IUnknown {
  HRESULT ReturnAString ( [out] LPOLESTR* ppwsz );
}
```

■ C++

Notes: The [pointer_default] attribute has no effect on the C++ mapping.

■ Visual Basic

Notes: The [pointer_default] attribute has no effect on the Visual Basic mapping.

■ propget

Description: Specifies that a given method can get treated as a Property Get by environments such as Visual Basic.

Notes: The last parameter to the method must be marked [out, retval].

■ IDL

Present in TLB: Yes

Present in Oicf: No

SYNTAX
```
propget
```

Applies to: method

Examples

EXAMPLE 1
```
[propget] HRESULT Sum ( [out,retval] long* pSum );
```

EXAMPLE 2
```
[propget] HRESULT ValueAtIndex ( [in] short nIndex, [out,retval]
long* pValue );
```

■ C++

Notes: The [propget] attribute prefixes the C++ method signature with get_.

Examples

EXAMPLE 1
```
long lSum = 0;
pObj->get_Sum ( &lSum );
```

EXAMPLE 2
```
long lVal = 0;
pObj->get_ValueAtIndex ( 1, &lVal );
```

■ Visual Basic

Notes: The [propget] attribute allows the method call to appear on the right-hand side of the assignment operator.

Examples

EXAMPLE 1
```
Dim lSum As Long
lSum = pObj.Sum
```

EXAMPLE 2
```
Dim lVal As Long
lVal = pObj.ValueAtIndex ( 1 )
```

■ propput

Description: Specifies that a given method can get treated as a Property Let by environments such as Visual Basic.

■ IDL

Present in TLB: Yes
Present in Oicf: No

SYNTAX
```
propput
```

Applies to: method

Examples

EXAMPLE 1
```
[propput] HRESULT Sum ( [in] long Sum );
```

EXAMPLE 2
```
[propget] HRESULT ValueAtIndex ( [in] short nIndex, [in] long
Value );
```

■ C++

Notes: The [propput] attribute prefixes the C++ method signature with put_.

Examples

EXAMPLE 1
```
long lSum = 10;
pObj->put_Sum ( lSum );
```

EXAMPLE 2
```
long lVal = 20;
pObj->put_ValueAtIndex ( 1, lVal );
```

◼ Visual Basic

Notes: The [propput] attribute allows the method call to appear on the left-hand side of the assignment operator.

Examples

EXAMPLE 1
```
Dim lSum As Long
lSum = 10
pObj.Sum = lSum
```

EXAMPLE 2
```
Dim lVal As Long
lVal = 20
pObj.ValueAtIndex ( 1 ) = lVal
```

◼ propputref

Description: Specifies that a given method can get treated as a Property Set by environments such as Visual Basic.

Notes: Applies only to methods with object references as the parameter type.

◼ IDL

Present in TLB: Yes
Present in Oicf: No

SYNTAX
```
propputref
```

Applies to: method

Examples

EXAMPLE 1
```
[propputref] HRESULT Atom ( [in] IAtom* pAtom );
```

EXAMPLE 2
```
[propputref] HRESULT AtomAtIndex ( [in] short nIndex, [in]
IAtom* pAtom );
```

■ C++

Notes: The [propputref] attribute prefixes the C++ method signature with
[putref_].

Examples

EXAMPLE 1
```
IAtom* pAtom;
// Intialize IAtom here
pObj->putref_Atom ( pAtom );
```

EXAMPLE 2
```
long lVal = 20;
pObj->put_AtomAtIndex ( 1, lVal );
```

■ Visual Basic

Notes: The [propputref] attribute allows the method call to appear on the
left-hand side of the assignment operator when the Set keyword is used.

Examples

EXAMPLE 1
```
Dim pAtom As IAtom
' Initialize pAtom here
Set pObj.Atom = pAtom
```

EXAMPLE 2
```
Dim pAtom As IAtom
' Initialize pAtom here
Set pObj.AtomAtIndex ( 1 ) = pAtom
```

■ ptr

Description: Specifies that full pointer semantics are required for a reference
type, causing the interception layer to detect null pointers and duplicate pointer
values.

Notes: Provides the same pointer semantics as C++.

■ IDL

Present in TLB: No
Present in Oicf: Yes

Notes: The [ptr] attribute carries more overhead than [unique] and [ref],
q.v. Consequently, it should be used only if the parameters to the method may
contain duplicate pointers.

SYNTAX
```
ptr
```
Applies to:

typedef

parameter

field

Examples

EXAMPLE 1
```
HRESULT TakeTwoPointers ( [in,ptr] long* p, [in,ptr] long* q );
```

EXAMPLE 2
```
struct Node {
  long x,y;
  [ptr] struct Node* pNext;
  [ptr] struct Node* pPrev;
}
```

▨ C++

Notes: The [ptr] attribute has no effect on the C++ mapping.

▧ Visual Basic

Notes: The [ptr] attribute has no effect on the Visual Basic mapping.

▨ public

Description: Specifies that typedefs for a given construct—a structure, for
example—should be entered into the type library.

Notes: The [uuid] attribute implies the [public] attribute when used on a
typedef.

▨ IDL

Present in TLB: Yes

Present in Oicf: No

Notes: If a [public] typedef for a structure appears outside the library block
and is referenced inside the library block, the name of the resulting typedef in
the type library will have been prefixed with tag.

public

Applies to: typedef

Examples

EXAMPLE 1
```
[ public ] typedef long* PLONG;
```

EXAMPLE 2
```
[ public ] typedef struct Point {
  long x,y;
} Point;
```

■ C++

Notes: The [public] attribute has no effect on the C++ mapping

■ Visual Basic

Notes: With the exception of the tag prefix, as noted above, the [public] attribute has no effect on the Visual Basic mapping.

■ range

Description: Specifies a range of values that a method parameter or structure field can take. At runtime, the interception layer will ensure that values fall within the specified range.

Notes: Only contiguous ranges can be specified. The IDL file must be compiled with the /robust switch.

■ IDL

Present in TLB: No

Present in Oicf: Yes

Notes: Can be applied only to [in] parameters.

SYNTAX
range

Applies to:

parameter

field

Examples

EXAMPLE 1
```
HRESULT TakeARangedValue ( [in,range(1000,10000)] short s );
```

EXAMPLE 2

```
struct RangedPoint
{
  [range(1,25000)] short x;
  [range(1,25000)] short x;
}
```

■ C++

Notes: The [range] attribute has no effect on the C++ mapping.

■ Visual Basic

Notes: The [range] attribute has no effect on the Visual Basic mapping.

■ ref

Description: Specifies that reference pointer semantics are required for a reference type, requiring that a valid value always be passed; null values are not allowed. The interception layer does not detect null pointers or duplicate pointer values.

Notes: Provides the same semantics as a C++ reference.

■ IDL

Present in TLB: No

Present in Oicf: Yes

Notes: The [ref] attribute carries the least overhead of the three pointer attributes. Top-level [out] parameters must be reference pointers. In the absence of [ref], [unique], or [ptr], top-level pointers default to [ref]. Embedded pointers default to the [pointer_default] for the interface.

SYNTAX

```
ref
```

Applies to:

typedef

parameter

field

Examples

EXAMPLE 1

```
HRESULT TakeTwoPointers ( [in,ref] long* p, [in,ref] long* q );
```

```
struct Line {
  [ref] struct Point* porigin;
  [ref] struct Point* pend;
}
```

■ C++

Notes: The [ref] attribute has no effect on the C++ mapping apart from disallowing null values.

■ Visual Basic

Notes: The [ref] attribute has no effect on the Visual Basic mapping apart from disallowing null values.

■ retval

Description: Specifies that an output parameter should be treated as a return value.

■ IDL

Present in TLB: Yes

Present in Oicf: No

Notes: Can be applied only to the last [out] parameter in a method signature.

SYNTAX
```
retval
```

Applies to: parameter

Example
```
HRESULT Sum ( [in] short x, [in] short y, [out,retval] long*
pSum );
```

■ C++

Notes: The [retval] attribute has no effect on the C++ mapping.

■ Visual Basic

Notes: The [retval] attribute allows the Visual Basic runtime to treat the output parameter as a return value.

Example
```
Dim sum As Long
sum = pObj.Sum ( 10, 20 )
```

■ size_is

Description: Specifies the number of elements in a conformant array or the number of elements referenced by a conformant pointer.

Notes: The [max_is] and [size_is] attributes are very similar. For a given call, size_is = max_is + 1.

■ IDL

Present in TLB: No

Present in Oicf: Yes

Notes: The [size_is] attribute does not appear in the type library, so the universal marshaler cannot be used. The [max_is] and [size_is] attributes are mutually exclusive.

SYNTAX
```
size_is ( <expression> )
```

Applies to:

parameter

field

Examples

EXAMPLE 1
```
HRESULT TakeSomeData ( [in] short nElems, [in,
size_is(nElems)] short nData[20] );
```

EXAMPLE 2
```
HRESULT TakeSomeMoreData ( [in] short nElems, [in,
size_is(nElems)] short* pData );
```

EXAMPLE 3
```
struct SomeData
{
  short nElems;
  [size_is(nElems)] short nData[100];
}
```

EXAMPLE 4
```
HRESULT ReturnSomeData ( [out] short *pnElems, [out,
size_is(,*pnElems)] short**ppData );
```

■ **C++**

Examples

EXAMPLE 1
```
short rgPrimes[] = { 1, 2, 3, 5, 7, 11, 13, 17, 19,
    23, 29, 31, 37, 41, 43, 47, 53, 59, 61, 67 };
// Transmit primes 1-11
pObj->TakeSomeData ( 11, rgPrimes );
```

■ **Visual Basic**

Notes: Methods that use the [size_is] attribute may be called but not implemented by Visual Basic.

Examples

EXAMPLE 1
```
' Array of primes defined elsewhere
Sub CallMethod ( rgPrimes() As Integer )
  pObj.TakeSomeData 11, rgPrimes
End Sub
```

■ source

Description: Denotes that an interface is an outgoing interface, also known as an event interface.

■ **IDL**

Present in TLB: Yes

Present in Oicf: No

Notes: At most, one [source] interface may also be annotated with the [default] attribute.

SYNTAX
```
source
```

Applies to: Interface in coclass

Example
```
[
  object,
  oleautomation,
  uuid(5E6A672D-0E62-46E9-94D3-6971C344480E)
]
interface IDataInput : IUnknown
{
  HRESULT AddValue ( [in] short s );
```

```
  HRESULT GetResult ( [out,retval] long* pl );
  [propput] HRESULT Threshold ( [in] long lThreshold );
  [propget] HRESULT Threshold ( [out,retval] long* plThreshold );
}
[
  object,
  oleautomation,
  uuid(E7F4CCCD-E05E-46AC-A717-EEFA613C7FE8)
]
interface IDataEvents : IUnknown
{
  HRESULT OverThreshold();
}
[
  uuid(88F4C5C9-83F4-41B8-B88C-4D140F4CC513)
]
coclass DataBinder
{
  [default] interface IDataInput;
  [default,source] interface IDataEvents;
}
```

■ C++

Notes: The [source] attribute has no effect on the C++ mapping.

■ Visual Basic

Notes: The [source] attribute allows the WithEvents keyword to be used to hook up event handlers.

Example

```
Dim WithEvents binder As New DataBinder
' Event handler
Public Sub binder_OverThreshold()
End Sub
```

■ string

Description: Specifies that the length of a given char/wchar_t/byte array or pointer will be determined by a language-specific function. In C++, this means that the parameter or field is null-terminated.

■ IDL

Present in TLB: No
Present in Oicf: Yes

`string`

Applies to:

typedef

parameter

field

Examples

EXAMPLE 1

`HRESULT TakeAString ( [in,string] wchar_t* pwsz );`

EXAMPLE 2

`HRESULT ReturnAString ( [out,string] wchar_t**ppwsz );`

■ C++

Notes: The [`string`] attribute has no effect on the C++ mapping.

■ Visual Basic

Notes: The [`string`] attribute has no effect on the Visual Basic mapping. Futhermore, Visual Basic cannot call or implement methods that take `char` or `wchar_t` arrays as parameters.

■ switch_is

Description: Specifies the method parameter or structure field that is the discriminant for a nonencapsulated union.

Notes: The type of the parameter or field must match the type specified by the [`switch_type`] attribute, q.v., on the union definition.

■ IDL

Present in TLB: No

Present in Oicf: Yes

SYNTAX

`switch_is ( <token> )`

Applies to:

parameter

field

Example

`[switch_type ( short )] union Salary {`

```
    [case(1)] short ;
    [case(2)] long l;
    [case(3)] double lf;
};
[
  uuid(ac93fa4f-938f-48b8-9859-f21052d89bf1),
  object
]
interface IReallyDoUnions : IUnknown {
  HRESULT ProcessSalary ( [in] short nField,
    [in,switch_is(nField)] union Salary sal );
}
```

■ C++

Notes: The [switch_is] attribute has no effect on the C++ mapping.

■ Visual Basic

Notes: User-defined union types are not supported in Visual Basic.

■ switch_type

Description: Specifies the IDL type of the discriminant for a nonencapsulated union.

Notes: The type of the parameter or field specified by the [switch_is] attribute, q.v., must match the type specified by the [switch_type] attribute.

■ IDL

Present in TLB: No
Present in Oicf: Yes

SYNTAX
```
switch_type ( <integral type> )
```

Applies to: union

Example
```
[switch_type ( short )] union Salary {
  [case(1)] short ;
  [case(2)] long l;
  [case(3)] double lf;
};
[
  uuid(ac93fa4f-938f-48b8-9859-f21052d89bf1),
  object
]
```

```
interface IReallyDoUnions : IUnknown {
  HRESULT ProcessSalary ( [in] short nField,
    [in,switch_is(nField)] union Salary sal );
}
```

■ C++

Notes: The [switch_type] attribute has no effect on the C++ mapping.

■ Visual Basic

Notes: User-defined union types are not supported in Visual Basic.

■ transmit_as

Description: Specifies an alias between a transmission type and a presentation type.

Notes: See Chapter 5 for a full treatment of this attribute, including examples.

■ IDL

Present in TLB: No

Present in Oicf: Special

Notes: Type information about both types appears in the Oicf strings. However, the interface designer also has to provide functions that map between the two types. The transmission type must not contain any reference types.

SYNTAX
```
transmit_as ( <transmission type> )
```

Applies to: typedef

Example
```
typedef struct Node
{
  short s;
  struct Node*pNext;
} Node;
typedef struct NodeXmit
{
  unsigned long cElems;
  [size_is(cElems)] short rgs[];
} NodeXmit;
typedef [transmit_as(NodeXmit)] Node* PNODE;
```

■ C++

Notes: The [transmit_as] attribute has no effect on the C++ mapping.

■ **Visual Basic**

Notes: The [transmit_as] attribute has no effect on the Visual Basic mapping.

■ unique

Description: Specifies that unique pointer semantics are required for a reference type, causing the interception layer to detect null pointers but not duplicate pointer values.

■ IDL

Present in TLB: No

Present in Oicf: Yes

Notes: The [unique] attribute carries more overhead than [ref] but less than [ptr], q.v. It should be used only if the parameters to the method do not contain duplicate pointers but may contain null values.

SYNTAX
```
unique
```

Applies to:

typedef

parameter

field

Examples

EXAMPLE 1
```
HRESULT TakeTwoPointers ( [in,unique] long* p, [in,unique] long*
q );
```

EXAMPLE 2
```
struct ListNode {
  long x,y;
  [unique] struct Node* pNext;
}
```

■ C++

Notes: The [unique] attribute has no effect on the C++ mapping.

■ **Visual Basic**

Notes: The [unique] attribute has no effect on the Visual Basic mapping.

■ uuid

Description: Attaches a UUID to an IDL construct.

■ IDL

Present in TLB: Yes

Present in Oicf: Yes

SYNTAX 1
```
uuid (       -  -  -  -          )
```

SYNTAX 2
```
uuid ( "     -  -  -  -       ")
```

Applies to:

coclass	library	typedef
dispinterface	struct	union
interface		

Examples

EXAMPLE 1
```
[
  object,
  uuid(A2CD4002-A3FA-4388-8CF1-9B0F73D74CD5)
]
interface IAmUnique : IUnknown
{
}
```

EXAMPLE 2
```
[
  uuid(44507F36-5B47-4904-B8E7-7B0B3FFA3D18)
]
struct Line
{
  long startx, starty;
  long endx, endy;
}
```

■ C++

Notes: The UUIDs for library, coclass, dispinterface, and interface definitions will be available as a constants in the MIDL-generated identifier file. UUIDs will also be attached to the underlying C++ construct through __DECLSPEC_UUID and hence can be retrieved through __uuidof.

Examples

EXAMPLE 1

```
MIDL_INTERFACE("A2CD4002-A3FA-4388-8CF1-9B0F73D74CD5")
IAmUnique : public IUnknown
{
public:
};
```

EXAMPLE 2

```
struct
DECLSPEC_UUID("44507F36-5B47-4904-B8E7-7B0B3FFA3D18")
Line
{
  long startx;
  long starty;
  long endx;
  long endy;
};
```

■ Visual Basic

Notes: The [uuid] attribute has no effect on the Visual Basic mapping.

■ v1_enum

Description: Specifies that an enumerated type should be transmitted as 32 bits on the wire. By default, enumerations are represented by 32 bits in memory and 16 bits on the wire. This can lead to loss of information at transmission time.

■ IDL

Present in TLB: No

Present in Oicf: Yes

Notes: The universal marshaler always transmits enumerated types as 32 bits.

SYNTAX

```
v1_enum
```

Applies to: enum

Example

```
[v1_enum] enum GEAR
{
  PARK,
```

```
        DRIVE,
        REVERSE,
        SECOND,
        FIRST
    };
```

■ C++

Notes: The [v1_enum] attribute has no effect on the C++ mapping.

■ Visual Basic

Notes: The [v1_enum] attribute has no effect on the Visual Basic mapping.

■ vararg

Description: Specifies that a method takes a variable number of arguments

Notes: The method must take a parameter of type SAFEARRAY(VARIANT). This parameter must appear after all other parameters except those annotated with the [lcid] or [retval] attribute.

■ IDL

Present in TLB: Yes

Present in Oicf: No

SYNTAX
```
vararg
```

Applies to: method

Example
```
[
  uuid(D58DB975-3FA7-4D94-B226-746F76E9F43F),
  object,
  pointer_default(unique)
]
interface IDoVarArg : IUnknown
{
  [vararg] HRESULT TakeSomeParams ( [in] short s, [in] long
l, [in] SAFEARRAY(VARIANT)*ppsaVarArgs );
}
```

■ C++

Notes: The [vararg] attribute has no effect on the C++ mapping.

■ Visual Basic

Notes: The [vararg] attribute denotes that the SAFEARRAY(VARIANT) parameter is marked with the ParamArray keyword. This allows Visual Basic to call the method by passing an arbitrary number of parameters where the SAFEARRAY(VARIANT) parameter occurs.

Examples

EXAMPLE 1
```
Sub CallMethod ( pObj As IDoVarArg )
  pObj.TakeSomeParams 10, 20, "Hello", "World"
End Sub
```

EXAMPLE 2
```
Private Sub IDoVarArg_TakeSomeParams ( s As Integer, l As
Long, ParamArray ppsaVarArgs() As Variant )
End Sub
```

■ version

Description: Attaches a version number to an IDL construct, typically a library block.

■ IDL

Present in TLB: Yes

Present in Oicf: No

Notes: The [version] attribute has an effect only when applied to a library statement, where it modifies the behavior of LoadRegTypeLib. While version information about dispinterfaces, interfaces, and coclasses is stored in the type library, the information is not used by COM.

SYNTAX
```
version ( <majorversionnumber.minorversionnumber> )
```

Applies to:

coclass

dispinterface

interface

library

Example
```
[
    uuid(83B497C4-47E5-44E4-90D9-8ADA65FCD95F),
    version(2.4)
```

```
]
library SomeLib
{
}
```

■ C++

Notes: The [version] attribute has no effect on the C++ mapping.

■ Visual Basic

Notes: The [version] attribute has no effect on the Visual Basic mapping.

■ wire_marshal

Description: Specifies an alias between a transmission type and a presentation type.

Notes: See Chapter 5 for a full treatment of this attribute, including examples.

■ IDL

Present in TLB: No

Present in Oicf: Special

Notes: Type information about both types appears in the Oicf strings. However, the interface designer also has to provide functions that map between the two types. The transmission type must be of a fixed size; it may not contain a conformant array.

SYNTAX
```
wire_marshal ( <transmission type> )
```

Applies to: typedef

Example
```
typedef struct Node
{
  short s;
  struct Node*pNext;
} Node;
typedef struct NodeMarshal
{
  unsigned long cElems;
  [size_is(cElems)] short* prgs;
} NodeMarshal;
typedef [wire_marshal(NodeMarshal)] Node* PNODE;
```

■ **C++**

Notes: The `[wire_marshal]` attribute has no effect on the C++ mapping.

■ **Visual Basic**

Notes: The `[wire_marshal]` attribute has no effect on the Visual Basic mapping.

Index

as structure members, 162–163
in structures, 161–162
const and, 111–112
declaration of, 107
full, 114
language mappings and, 130–133
null, 127
object references and, 133–134
reference, 118, 127, 134
semantics of, 112–118, 126–130
"this" or "me," 7–9
top-level vs. embedded, 118–130
memory management and, 120–126
semantic issues, 126–130
unique, 115–118
inside user-defined types, 110–111
in Visual Basic, 107, 112, 131–133
Polymorphism, 99
pragma keyword, 275–276
Presentation type, mapping between transmission
type and, 191–199
Properties, 94–98
in C/C++, 94–95
method annotation to describe, 94–97
in Visual Basic, 95–98
[propget] attribute, 94, 95–96, 321–322
[propput] attribute, 94, 95–97, 322–323
[propputref] attribute, 94, 97–98, 323–324
Proxy, 4–6
ProxyStubClsid32 key, 20, 28, 30
Proxy-stub DLL, building, 27–31
[ptr] attribute, 114, 324–325
[public] attribute, 91, 92, 325–326

Q

QueryInterface method, 33, 58–59, 61,
100–101
[iid_is] attribute and, 63–64

R

[range] attribute, 53, 54, 326–327
Range checking, 53, 54
in Visual Basic, 56
"Reader-makes-right" technique, 4

[ref] attribute, 134, 327–328
Reference parameters, 13, 14
Reference pointers, 118, 127, 134
Reference types. See Pointers
RegisterTypeLib, 19
Registry, 17
Request packet, 4, 5
Response packet, 5, 10
Return address, 7, 8–9
[retval] attribute, 12–13, 328–329
/robust compiler switch, 53
RPC memory management, 122–124
Runtime, 6

S

SafeArrayAllocDescriptorEx API, 172
SafeArrayDestroy API, 177
SafeArrayDestroyData API, 177
SafeArrayGetDim API, 178
SafeArrayGetLBound API, 178
SafeArrayGetUBound API, 178
SafeArrayGetVartype API, 178
SAFEARRAYs, 69, 163–180, 242–243
allocation of descriptor, 172, 174–175
C/C++ mapping for, 167, 171
column-major ordering of multidimensional,
173–174
destroying after use, 176–177
element size specification, 172–175
fFEATURES field, 165
IDL syntax for describing, 165–171
in-memory representation of, 164–165
retrieving data type information, 178
of structures, 175–177
typed, 168–169
untyped, 169–170
Visual Basic mapping for, 168
SAFEARRAY (VARIANT), 170
Scripting clients, 101
Self-referential structures, 111
Semantics
of interface, 6
of pointers, 112–118, 126–130
Set keyword (Visual Basic), 98